# Woolf Studies Annual

Volume 6, 2000

PACE UNIVERSITY PRESS • New York

Copyright © 2000 by
Pace University Press
One Pace Plaza
New York, NY 10038


All rights reserved
Printed in the United States of America


ISSN 1080-9317
ISBN 0-944473-50-4(pbk: alk.ppr.)


Member

Council of Editors of Learned Journals


♾ ™ paper used in this publication meets the minimum requirements of American National Standard for information Sciences—Permanence of Paper for Printed Library Materials,
ANSI Z39.48—1984

## Editor

Mark Hussey — *Pace University*

## Editorial Board

| | |
|---|---|
| Tuzyline Jita Allan | *Baruch College, CUNY* |
| Eileen Barrett (*Book Review Editor*) | *California State University, Hayward* |
| Kathryn N. Benzel | *University of Nebraska-Kearney* |
| Pamela L. Caughie | *Loyola University Chicago* |
| Wayne K. Chapman | *Clemson University* |
| Patricia Cramer | *University of Connecticut, Stamford* |
| Beth Rigel Daugherty | *Otterbein College* |
| Anne Fernald | *Purdue University* |
| Val Gough | *University of Liverpool* |
| Sally Greene | *University of North Carolina Chapel Hill* |
| Leslie Kathleen Hankins | *Cornell College* |
| Karen Kaivola | *Stetson University* |
| Jane Lilienfeld | *Lincoln University* |
| Toni A. H. McNaron | *University of Minnesota* |
| Patricia Moran | *University of California, Davis* |
| Vara Neverow | *Southern Connecticut State University* |
| Annette Oxindine | *Wright State University* |
| Beth Carole Rosenberg | *University of Nevada, Las Vegas* |
| Bonnie Kime Scott | *University of Delaware* |

## Consulting Editors

| | |
|---|---|
| Nancy Topping Bazin | *Old Dominion University* |
| Morris Beja | *Ohio State University* |
| Louise DeSalvo | *Hunter College, CUNY* |
| Carolyn G. Heilbrun | *Avalon Foundation Professor in the Humanities Emerita, Columbia University* |
| Jane Marcus | *Distinguished Professor, CCNY and CUNY Graduate Center* |
| Lucio Ruotolo | *Stanford University* |
| Brenda R. Silver | *Dartmouth College* |
| Susan Squier | *Pennsylvania State University* |
| Peter Stansky | *Stanford University* |
| J.J. Wilson | *Sonoma State University* |
| Alex Zwerdling | *University of California, Berkeley* |

*Woolf Studies Annual* is indexed in the American Humanities Index, *ABELL*, and the *MLA Bibliography*

Lagora
River Bank
W. Molesey
Surrey
5th Dec

Dear Madam,
 I have just finished reading "Three Guineas" & felt that I must express to you a little of my satisfaction at finding aspiring woman's case stated so clearly & logically, without irritation or animosity. I hope and believe that your book will have far-reaching influence, not only on the position of women, but in increasing the liberty

of the individual – man and woman alike.

I do hope you will not consider this letter tiresome, but as a woman (I need hardly add semi-educated), as a wage-earner (of course paid less than my husband for similar work) and as the mother of a daughter, still too young to realize the disabilities of her sex, I am profoundly grateful to you for the thought & labour you have put into your book.

Yours sincerely
Phyllis Preen.

The Society of Authors has been appointed to act for the Virginia Woolf Estate. Inquiries concerning permissions should be addressed to:

Mr. Jeremy Crow
The Society of Authors
84 Drayton Gardens
London SW10 9SB

Fax: 0171-373-5768
Tel: 0171-373-6642

# Contents

**W**oolf
**S**tudies
**A**nnual

Volume 6, 2000

|  |  |  |
|---|---|---|
|  | ix | Abbreviations |
| Anna Snaith | 1 | Wide Circles: The *Three Guineas* Letters |
|  | 13 | Index of *Three Guineas* Letters |
|  | 17 | *Three Guineas* Letters |

## GUIDE

|  | 169 | Guide to Library Special Collections |
|---|---|---|

## REVIEWS

| Patricia Cramer | 181 | *Reading Alcoholisms:Theorizing Character and Narrative in Selected Novels of Thomas Hardy, James Joyce, and Virginia Woolf* by Jane Lilienfeld |
|---|---|---|
| Susan Hudson Fox | 184 | *Women in the Milieu of Leonard and Virginia Woolf: Peace, Politics and Education* Ed. Wayne K. Chapman and Janet Manson |
| Diane F. Gillespie | 188 | *Virginia Woolf and the Great War* by Karen L. Levenback |
| Elizabeth Lambert | 194 | *Solid Objects* by Douglas Mao |
| Karen L. Levenback | 198 | *The Hours: A Novel* by Michael Cunningham *Mr. Dalloway: A Novella* by Robin Lippincott |

|  |  |  |
|---|---|---|
|  |  | *Mitz: The Marmoset of Bloomsbury* by Sigrid Nunez |
|  |  | *Virginia Woolf's "Jacob's Room": The Holograph Draft* Transcribed and edited by Edward L. Bishop |
|  |  | *Virginia Woolf "The Hours": The British Museum Manuscript of* Mrs. Dalloway Transcribed and edited by Helen M. Wussow |
| Madeline Moore | **207** | *Virginia Woolf: Feminism, Creativity, and the Unconscious* by John R. Maze |
| Merry Pawlowski | **210** | *The Nightmare of History: The Fictions of Virginia Woolf and D. H. Lawrence* by Helen Wussow |
| Theresa Thompson | **213** | *Mappings: Feminism and the Cultural Geographies of Encounter* by Susan Stanford Friedman |
| **Note on Contributor** | **218** |  |
| **Policy** | **219** |  |

# Abbreviations

| | |
|---|---|
| *AHH* | *A Haunted House* |
| *AROO* | *A Room of One's Own* |
| *BP* | *Books and Portraits* |
| *BTA* | *Between the Acts* |
| *CDB* | *The Captain's Death Bed and Other Essays* |
| *CE* | *Collected Essays* (4 vols.) |
| *CR 1* | *The Common Reader* |
| *CR 2* | *The Common Reader, Second Series* |
| *CSF* | *The Complete Shorter Fiction* |
| *D* | *The Diary of Virginia Woolf* (5 vols.) |
| *DM* | *The Death of the Moth and Other Essays* |
| *E* | *The Essays of Virginia Woolf* (6 vols.) |
| *F* | *Flush* |
| *FR* | *Freshwater* |
| *GR* | *Granite & Rainbow: Essays* |
| *JR* | *Jacob's Room* |
| *L* | *The Letters of Virginia Woolf* (6 vols.) |
| *M* | *The Moment and Other Essays* |
| *MEL* | *Melymbrosia* |
| *MOB* | *Moments of Being* |
| *MT* | *Monday or Tuesday* |
| *MD* | *Mrs. Dalloway* |
| *ND* | *Night and Day* |
| *O* | *Orlando* |
| *PA* | *A Passionate Apprentice* |
| *RF* | *Roger Fry: A Biography* |
| *TG* | *Three Guineas* |
| *TTL* | *To the Lighthouse* |
| *TW* | *The Waves* |
| *TY* | *The Years* |
| *VO* | *The Voyage Out* |

# Wide Circles: The *Three Guineas* Letters
## *Anna Snaith*

"Let us consider letters" (*JR* 125). They occupy a crucial space in Virginia Woolf's thinking about the contingency of language. Letters highlight the importance of the moment of composition, as well as the time of reading—witness Jacob Flanders' post-coital reading of his mother's letter (*JR* 124). Letter-writing is about writing the self, a piece of self which on arrival becomes "alien" (*JR* 125). "To see one's own envelope on another's table" is to see oneself severed, out of context (*JR* 125). Woolf knew this all too well, being a prolific letter writer, sometimes writing three letters a day. Letter-writing was part of her daily routine. In her writing—fiction and non-fiction alike—letters are politicized and theorized. In her novels, she takes the letter beyond its traditional role as plot device (the intercepted letter) or narrative vehicle (the transcribed love letter), and invests the genre itself with political significance. Letters appear as part of larger attempts at dialogue, conversation, connection: they "carry the voices that try to penetrate" (*JR* 126). Sometimes, as in Betty Flanders' case, the voices don't make it. The letters in this edition carry voices which have penetrated.

Letters are of paramount importance for Woolf's feminist politics: they both empower and limit women in her writing. Betty Flanders, while her son is writing "long letters about art, morality and politics to young men" (*JR* 127), is scribbling in "pale, profuse" ink over the fire: not able to "write" herself, she writes instead of friends and neighbors (122). In *The Years*, Eleanor writes a letter to her brother, Edward, but has to ask Morris to venture out into the dark London streets to post it for her (43). Without a man's assistance, her access to language and communication is contained within the private home. Letters play a symbolic role in women's move from private to public. Lady Bruton in *Mrs Dalloway*, for all her political involvement, has to get Hugh Whitbread to write her letters to *The Times*. Her private voice has to be translated, encoded in the public language of journalism from which she feels excluded. Letter-writing makes Lady Bruton feel the "futility of her own womanhood as she felt it on no other occasion" (142). Hugh Whitbread, on the other hand, is "able to put things as editors liked them put," and she marvels at the way in which he transforms her "tangles to sense" (143).

On those occasions when Woolf uses letters in her writing as a rhetorical strategy, however, they invariably signify communicative possibility. Her politics of genre include the letter. "Memories of a Working Women's Guild" (1931), an introduction to a collection of working women's autobiographical writings, denies its own prefatory capabilities. Woolf is in no place to speak for the women from whom she feels "irretrievably cut off" (Davies xxi). Instead, the anti-introduction is a letter to Margaret Llewelyn Davies, therefore the instigation (or continuation) of a dialogue. The letter blurs public and private boundaries in that it is a published document which is addressed "not to the public" but to Davies (xvii). It is not prescriptive or by way of a summary; rather its subjectivity (an autobiographical account of Woolf's attendance at a Women's Guild Conference in Newcastle in 1913) makes it an addition to the accounts rather than a pronouncement on them.

*Three Guineas* itself, of course, is structured as a series of letters. Provisional titles for the text included "Answers to Correspondents" and "Letters to an Englishman." The barrister's letter to the narrator asking how war might be prevented has lain unanswered for several years. This gap, representing the hope that it will not require an answer, must now be closed, given the imminence of war in the late 1930s. Writing the reply is fraught with difficulties: the many ellipses in the text represent gaps in communication which are due to the difference in experience and opportunity between addresser and the addressee. This means that one letter is not enough: letters proliferate. The barrister's letter produces not only the text, but the letters (and the guineas) to the treasurer of the women's college and the society supporting women's employment in the professions.[1] His letter has triggered support and discussion, but he is silenced—his image symbolically constructed by the narrator—to allow space for women's voices: the narrator's, the treasurers' and the many quotations from women.

Women's voices also fill the space that surrounds *Three Guineas*. Critics often speculate about the constitution of Woolf's reading public. As Melba Cuddy-Keane argues, "our knowledge is limited primarily to the response in high-brow literary circles." Here, for the first time, are published 82 letters which were sent to Woolf in response to *Three Guineas*, now held in the Monk's House Papers at the University of Sussex. *Three Guineas* was published by the Hogarth Press on 2 June 1938, so these letters range in date from May 1938 to January 1940. They offer us substantial new insight into Woolf's readership. Many aspects of *Three Guineas* ironically foreshadow the letters: the first provisional title, "Answers to Correspondents," since Woolf replied to so many of the letters; the difference in experience between addresser and addressee, since many of the correspondents were not of her class or back ground; and the proliferation of letters, since these correspondents felt a need to continue the discussion, to add another letter to the debate. The collection

---

[1] Woolf refers here to the Newnham College Appeal and the London and National Society for Women's Service.

represents a diversity of readers and points of view, contributing further to the revision of prevalent images of Woolf as apolitical and elitist. The letters contribute to and augment work on Woolf's political involvement in the 1930s, both in terms of their content and her reactions to them. As Brenda Silver has argued, "the publication of *Three Guineas* was not the end of her critical dialogue with the wider culture" (270).

In the Monk's House Papers, these 82 letters are filed as follows: 58 letters from "unknown" readers form one file, and letters from Woolf's friends and relatives are filed in separate author-named files. Anne Olivier Bell has informed me that it was she, not Woolf, who separated the letters into those from friends as against unknown readers; therefore this distinction has not been preserved in publication (Bell). This separation led to certain anomalies, such as Agnes Smith's letters—a working class weaver from Yorkshire who corresponded with Woolf from 1938 until Woolf's death—which are filed in a separate file because she developed a friendship with Woolf, even though she wrote her first letter in response to *Three Guineas* as an "unknown" reader.

Woolf may not, of course, have kept all the letters she received. We do know, however, that she either kept or received many more letters about *Three Guineas* than any of her other texts. The numbers of letters from "unknown" readers at Sussex are: *Three Guineas*: 58, *The Waves*: 23, *A Room of One's Own*: 14, *Orlando*: 10, *To the Lighthouse*: 6. Either *Three Guineas* demanded more urgent responses from its readers than the other texts (highly likely given the subject matter and the threat of war), or Woolf decided to keep more responses to *Three Guineas*, again because of the immediacy of the subject and the importance to her of public opinions on feminism and pacifism. She writes to Ethel Smyth: "I'm getting the oddest letters, which I shall collect as a valuable contribution to psychology" (*L6* 247); she clearly sees them as part of the "evidence" of the text. She also calls them, at one point, "my own, now numerous, semi-official 3 Gs letters," again suggesting that the text has extended beyond its boundaries (*D5* 173).

The 82 letters come from a range of countries (Britain, France, America and Canada) and their 65 authors, 50 of whom are women, represent diversity in class, education and occupation. The letters immediately disprove Q. D. Leavis' attack on *Three Guineas* as "a conversation between her [Woolf] and her friends" (203). Three of the respondents identify themselves as working class (Letters 64, 70, 72) and three further respondents situate themselves as different from Woolf in terms of class and/or education (7, 68, 80). Most correspondents, of course, do not provide information on their class or education. The letters from working class women are particularly interesting, in that Woolf deliberately did not represent working class experience in *Three Guineas*. She stayed within the sphere of which she had first hand knowledge. Agnes Smith writes initially that she is disturbed by Woolf's omission of working class women's experience, but later acknowledges the politics of Woolf's decision not to speak for all women (Letters 64 & 66). The *Times Literary*

*Supplement* reviewer also admits that, "Mrs Woolf cannot solve the whole problem if she only states it for educated women of a civilized *bourgeoisie*. Nevertheless, she limits her scrutiny with her eyes open" (379). The letters from working class women, in part, fill in the silences left by Woolf's consciously limited perspective.[2] Agnes Smith writes: "the real answer to your book would be for me to write a similar one from the working woman's point of view," but cites her limited financial and educational resources as obstacles (Letter 64). The remainder of the letter, and the letters from her which follow, become that account. In later correspondence, Woolf urged Smith to publish her autobiography with the Hogarth Press, but Smith eventually wrote *A Worker's View of the Wool Textile Industry*, published in 1944 by Hillcroft Studies. In her first letter to Woolf (Letter 64), Smith doubts whether Woolf will read her long letter, but of course Woolf does and an extensive correspondence develops, though unfortunately only one side of it has survived. The conversation was worth continuing: the gap not too wide to talk across. As Woolf writes in *Jacob's Room*, letters constitute a large part of "the unpublished works of women" (123). Betty Flanders' letters would be fascinating, the narrator writes, "could one read them year in, year out" (123).

While several people close to Woolf disliked *Three Guineas* (Vita Sackville-West, Leonard Woolf and E. M. Forster amongst them) the response from her public cheered her: "the reception of 3 gs. has been interesting, unexpected. . . .Not one of my friends has mentioned it. My wide circle has widened" (*D*5 193). *Three Guineas* elicited many responses from Quakers, for example, who identified particularly with her pacifism and her notion of the Society of Outsiders. Another woman correspondent outlines her contribution to the Outsiders: her topless sunbathing campaign (Letter 36). Woolf was undoubtedly intrigued by the variety of interpretation of her ideas. Her diary entries from the period are full of references to the letters, often to specific, individual letters, all of which I have referenced and included in the notes to the letters themselves. Very few of Woolf's replies to the "unknown" readers have survived, but of the eight "unknown" correspondents who sent a second letter, seven of them received replies from Woolf, which they acknowledge in their second letter (Letters 18, 19, 56, 64, 70, 72, 79). There are, therefore, a possible seven Woolf letters still to uncover, and potentially many more which didn't elicit a second letter from the correspondent. Gladys Rossiter thanks Woolf for her "prompt and kind reply," proof of the seriousness and interest with which Woolf read her fan mail. "I devote the time I usually read or talk to dealing with them," she writes to Ethel Smyth (*L*6 253). In one diary entry, she mentions the "letters from schoolmasters" adding "Oh & I must answer one of them" (*D*5 161). She was pleased by the variety and intensity of response, but

---

[2] For a discussion of class and reactions to *Three Guineas* see Chapter Five of my *Virginia Woolf: Public and Private Negotiations* (Macmillan, 2000).

her interest was surely tested by Ernest Huxley, a bus conductor from Birkenhead, who writes her two extremely long and offensive letters. Woolf did reply; indeed, Huxley opens his second letter with a quote from her reply to his first: "And should like to talk on equal terms with the conductors," again evidence of her open-mindedness (Letter 73). She is careful not to overlook his sexism, however, providing what he calls "a well deserved and swift rebuke" (Letter 73). His letter both demands her response, as well as substantiating her arguments in *Three Guineas*. Huxley's image of her letter to him, which he values, he says, not for its own sake, but for the time she has taken in becoming his correspondent, symbolizes the wide circle. The extended text encompasses not only *The Years* and the twelve notebooks which she filled with research and evidence, but the discussion and correspondence which *Three Guineas* instigated.[3]

Woolf's interest in the letters she received shows her ideas about the common reader put into practice. As she writes in "How Should One Read a Book?," the reader's independence is of primary importance (*CR2* 258). She wanted her readers to engage with the text in dialogue, pleased at the "splash in the inkpots": that the letters got readers writing (*D5* 156). The *Times Literary Supplement* reviewer writes: "all should read it, not only for their enjoyment of its admirable style and wit, but that they may define in their own minds their answer to her arguments" (379). It is no surprise that Woolf was interested and inspired by the letters that kept arriving, when they enacted her democratic ideas about the reading process: a "dangerous & exciting game, which it takes two to play at" (Daugherty 146). This includes not only engagement with, but also access to the text. Literature should be accessible to all: "Literature is no one's private ground: literature is common ground," she writes in "The Leaning Tower," a paper she gave to the Workers' Educational Association in 1940 (*M* 125). The *Three Guineas* letters demonstrate Woolf's role as a public intellectual, but one with whom her public readership felt they could debate, discuss and correspond. Many of the correspondents raise the issue of the price, availability of the text and the need to increase the reading public even further (Letters 2, 5, 9, 18, 24, 27, 32, 33, 34, 46, 70, 73, 79, 80).[4] Two correspondents in particular ask for the publication of a cheaper edition (Letters 32 & 46). Constance Cheke writes that she could not have afforded *Three Guineas* had Smith's not reduced it to 2/- (Letter 70). The first edition of *Three Guineas* cost 7s 6d. The second British edition, published in 1977, cost 80p. Ironically, in 1938, the second edition of the *Common Reader, Second Series*, was printed

---

[3] See Silver for further discussion of the relationship between *Three Guineas* and the twelve reading notebooks.

[4] For a more extensive discussion of issues surrounding the reading public in the 58 letters see my article: "Virginia Woolf and Reading Communities: Respondents to *Three Guineas*."

costing 6d, but Woolf foresaw the fate of *Three Guineas*, writing to Ethel Smyth: "Alas, there won't be a 2nd edition in my lifetime. L. printed 15 thousand" (*L6* 235).

Woolf's interest in public libraries is crucial here. She would surely have been fascinated by John McAdam's letter about the virtues of public libraries (Letter 24). Unfortunately, she doesn't seem to have taken up his offer that she write a piece for "Book News," which, reprinted in the local press, could give her a circulation of 40 — 50,000 he argues. In 1938 she was supporting Philippa Strachey's fundraising campaign for the Marsham Street library of the London and National Society for Women's Service, later to be called the Fawcett Library. Woolf's dislike of societies and organizations was often superseded by the importance of the cause itself, as in her joining the London and National Society for Women's Service in 1932. Her support of the library campaign itself revolved around letter-writing. She signed letters asking for donations of money and books for the library, as well as donating books herself. *Three Guineas* made money for this campaign: Margaret Rhondda wrote that she had donated twice what she would have had she not read *Three Guineas* (Letter 4). In her replies to those friends who supported the campaign one can read her awkwardness about asking for donations (placing her in the position of the *Three Guineas* barrister), as well as her profound belief in the importance of public libraries. To Rhondda she writes: "books have always been so prolific in my life that I can't help being shocked to think that there are those who go without" (*L6* 236). She has the deepest empathy for women without access to books, libraries being synonymous with education for her: "I ought to apologise for adding another letter to the daily heap. I owe all the education I ever had to my father's library, and so perhaps endow libraries with more divinity than I should" (*L6* 234). Referring to *Three Guineas*, Woolf writes to Ethel Smyth: "I think its [Marsham Street Library] almost the only satisfactory deposit for stray guineas, because half the readers are bookless at home, working all day, eager to know anything and everything" (*L6* 232). The Marsham Street library also provides a space in which to read: "a very nice room, with a fire even, and a chair or two, is provided" (*L6* 232). The material comfort, the space and quiet parallel the mental space required for reading. In "How Should One Read a Book?," a talk given at Hayes Court School for girls in 1926, Woolf writes: "to admit authorities. . .into our libraries and let them tell us how to read, what to read, what value to place upon what we read, is to destroy the spirit of freedom which is the breath of those sanctuaries" (258). The *Three Guineas* letters are proof that working women were getting hold of her books, many of them likely from public libraries. Melba Cuddy-Keane has elucidated Woolf's comment: "I was glad to see the C. R. [Common Reader] all spotted with readers at the Free Library" (*D5* 329). The literal spots and stains of food on the book are proof of its common readership. Woolf was delighted to see this evidence of "the book as a possession of the people, there to be handled and used." As Cuddy-Keane writes, there is "no better sign for her work as a public intellectual, working for the integration of literature into our daily lives." Agnes Smith, too, writes to Woolf that if she had money to spare she would use it to build a new library at the Working Women's College in Surbiton, south west London (Letter 64).

Anticipating the reviews and letters which *Three Guineas* will produce, Woolf meditates on the possibility of writing a further pamphlet on its reception, and that if her "facts are challenged" she will "get 29 M[arsham]. S[treet]. to reply" (*D5* 146). The library is important not only in terms of access, but also as a repository and archive of women's history. *Three Guineas* is such a repository, as are the 82 surviving letters written in response (and of course there may have been more which have not survived). So many of the letters offer corroboration, further evidence of Woolf's arguments.

That corroboration often emerges, in the letters, as a result of the correspondent's political involvement. Aside from Woolf's friends, almost all of whom are involved politically, many of the "unknown" correspondents have similar experience: in suffrage, the W. S. P. U., women's journalism, the League of Nations Union, as well as socialist and pacifist groups (Letters 20, 41, 42, 44, 62, 76). Woolf's own political involvement in the late 1930s revolves around *Three Guineas*. After writing in early 1939 to May Sarton about her "repulsion from societies," she did indeed send Sarton the manuscript of *Three Guineas* to sell, proceeds to go to the Refugees Society (*L6* 314). In 1940, she was working for Storm Jameson at the International PEN club, assisting Austrian Jewish refugees Mela and Robert Spira. Robert had been interned, and was eventually freed in September 1940 (*D5* 305 & 326).[5] She donated a signed copy to a League of Nations sale (Letters 52 & 59), and she allowed and paid for extracts to be published by the Married Women's Association (Letter 57). Shena Simon writes of a Fabian Society meeting in Manchester devoted to discussing *Three Guineas*: "what effect Three Guineas has had even in the few months since it appeared" (Letter 65). Again, despite her revulsion from societies, just after the publication of *Three Guineas*, she advised Ethel Smyth to write to the National Council for Civil Liberties about the exclusion of women instrumentalists from the Bournemouth Municipal Orchestra. The council, she writes, receives her "occasional guinea" (*L6* 234). Her use of the central motif from *Three Guineas* underlines the link between pacifism and feminism.

Woolf supported a number of anti-fascist organizations during the 1930s, including the International Association of Writers in Defence of Culture, For Intellectual Liberty (based on the French Vigilance), the Artists' International Association, and she signed a petition in support of the Spanish government in 1936 (Lee 686). She was present at the initial meetings of FIL in December

---

[5] For Woolf's letters to the Spiras see the *Virginia Woolf Bulletin* of the Virginia Woolf Society of Great Britain, 2 (1999): **4-12.**

1935 and February 1936, held in Adrian Stephen's flat, but "at one level Woolf's book was prompted by her vexatious involvement with both the IAWDC and, in particular, FIL" (Bradshaw 58). She developed her own anti-fascist arguments, centering much more on issues of gender. In 1935 she had agreed to support Elizabeth Bibesco's Anti-Fascist Exhibition, but withdrew her support after finding out that the "woman question" was not to be represented (Lee 685). Feminism, for Woolf, was integral to anti-fascism. The third section of *Three Guineas* resounds with the phrase "to protect culture and intellectual liberty," a version of the key phrase in the FIL's manifesto (Bradshaw). For Woolf, however, the phrase had to be placed in a rather different context: women cannot protect that which they themselves do not have.

The *Three Guineas* letters extend Woolf's argument about cultural and intellectual freedom. She found some of the letters "heartbreaking," confirmation that *Three Guineas* had to be written (*L6* 253). On one hand the letters are full of testimonies of women's cultural and intellectual oppression, but the letters themselves signify intellectual freedom, women defining and expressing intellectual opinions, women engaging with issues of culture and politics. For many, writing and sending the letter must have been difficult. Many of the female correspondents begin or end their letter with expressions of inadequacy: "I have never before written to an author or celebrity" (Letter 13); "Forgive me for troubling you for I am a very ordinary member of the public" (Letter 20); "Why I bother you with this I don't know [....] From an inarticulate & very grateful 'outsider'" (Letter 54), but then go on to situate themselves very clearly and definitely in relation to Woolf. The letters are by no means all in agreement with *Three Guineas*. The letters, "infinitely brave, forlorn" come in from Woolf's wide circle (*JR* 125).

In 1940, in the aftermath of the publication of *Roger Fry*, Woolf answered an attack from Ben Nicolson on the elitism and insularity of the Bloomsbury Group. Anxious to assert her individuality, Woolf carefully drafted a reply to Nicolson, part of which reads as follows:

> I never went to school or college. My father spent perhaps £100 on my education. When I was a young woman I tried to share the fruits of that very imperfect education with the working classes by teaching literature at Morley College; by holding a Womens Cooperative Guild meeting weekly; and, politically, by working for the vote....I did my best to make them [her books] reach a far wider circle than a little private circle of exquisite and cultivated people. And to some extent I succeeded. (*L6* 419-20)

I have no doubt that Woolf's confidence in her wider circle is based, to a large extent, on the *Three Guineas* letters, proof of that success.

On one of my detective hunts during the work on these letters—chasing up references, tracking down relatives of correspondents—I came across another important piece of evidence. In her letter, Geraldine Ostle mentions that she has edited *The Notebooks of a Woman Alone* (1935) (Letter 2). This is a fascinating text. Ostle compiled the text from eight notebooks written by a woman called Evelyn Wilson. The notebooks are full of comments and quotations from Wilson's reading. Wilson lived, unmarried, in London, worked as a stenographer, and died at age 48 due to ill health, unemployment and her family's refusal to support her. Denied an education, Wilson lived for reading, and the quotations are from "all sorts of material; from newspapers, letters, novels, conversations, magazines" on a wide range of subjects (x). The author of the introduction, Geraldine Waife, writes: "I did not know that there were women, poorly educated, unable to spell without the help of a dictionary, knowing only their own language, untravelled, and yet with a passion for art and literature; who read and re-read books from free libraries, and who went without meals to buy a few more" (vii-viii). I like to think that perhaps, after receiving Ostle's letter, which she notes in her diary (*D*5 145), Woolf consulted *Notebooks*, where she would have found confirmation of so many of her ideas about the importance of access to books and libraries for working women. Ostle's desire to publish Wilson's notebooks sprang from *A Room of One's Own*, and Woolf would also have found echoes of *A Room of One's Own* all through Wilson's jottings: "my home is any room across the door of which I can draw the bolt" (26). Then, on page 210, she would have found a quotation taken straight from "How Should One Read a Book?," again proof that her work was being read by ordinary women. Her imperfect education was offering inspiration and support to women like Evelyn Wilson, not privileged enough to have even an imperfect education, let alone financial security.

In that same essay from which Wilson quotes, Woolf writes of the importance of discarded literature, "its record of vanished moments and forgotten lives" (*CR*2 263). Ostle rescued Wilson's discarded notebooks and with them a forgotten life. In my hunt for copyright holders, I wrote to all of the return addresses on the letters. Gradually letters began to come back to me, from people, many of whom had no idea that their mother or grandfather had written to Virginia Woolf. A further proliferation of letters ensued, often letters filled with biographical details, outlining the fascinating, hidden lives of the women and men who had written to Woolf in the late 1930s. The *Three Guineas* letters have been overlooked in Woolf studies. They were by no means discarded texts for Woolf: "it may be one letter—but what a vision it gives!" (*CR*2 263)

## Works Cited

Bell, Anne Olivier. Letter to Anna Snaith. 21 February 1998.
Bradshaw, David. "British Writers and Anti-Fascism in the 1930s, Part II: Under the Hawk's Wings." *Woolf Studies Annual* 4 (1998): 41-66.
Cuddy-Keane, Melba. "Pedagogical Woolf: Between the Academic Devil and the Mass-Culture Sea." A talk presented at the 1997 MLA Convention.
Daugherty, Beth Rigel. "Virginia Woolf's 'How Should One Read a Book?'" *Woolf Studies Annual* 4 (1998): 123-185.

Leavis, Q. D. "Caterpillars of the Commonwealth Unite!" *Scrutiny* 7.2 (1938): 203-14.

Lee, Hermione. *Virginia Woolf.* London: Chatto and Windus, 1996.

Davies, Margaret Llewelyn, ed. *Life as We Have Known It.* London: Virago, 1977.

Ostle, M. Geraldine, ed. *The Notebooks of a Woman Alone.* London: J. M. Dent, 1935.

Silver, Brenda R. "*Three Guineas* Before and After: Further Answers to Correspondents." *Virginia Woolf: A Feminist Slant.* Ed. Jane Marcus. Lincoln: U of Nebraska P, 1983: 254-276.

Snaith, Anna. "Virginia Woolf and Reading Communities: Respondents to *Three Guineas*." *Virginia Woolf and Communities: Selected Papers from the Eighth Annual Conference on Virginia Woolf.* Ed. Jeanette McVicker and Laura Davis. NY: Pace U P, 1998: 219-226.

———. *Virginia Woolf: Public and Private Negotiations.* Basingstoke: Macmillan, 2000.

"Women In A World of War: A 'Society of Outsiders': Mrs Virginia Woolf's Searching Pamphlet." *Times Literary Supplement*, 4 June 1938: 379.

Woolf, Virginia. *The Common Reader, Second Series.* London: Hogarth P, 1974.

———. *The Diary of Virginia Woolf.* Vol. 5. Ed. Anne Olivier Bell. London: Hogarth P, 1984.

———. *Jacob's Room.* Ed. Kate Flint. London: Oxford U P, 1992.

———. *The Letters of Virginia Woolf.* Vol. 6. Ed. Nigel Nicolson. London: Hogarth P, 1980.

———. *The Moment.* London: Hogarth P, 1947.

———. *Mrs Dalloway.* Ed. Claire Tomalin. London: Oxford U P, 1992.

———. *The Years.* Ed. Hermione Lee. London: Oxford U P, 1992.

**Transcription of the letters**

I have transcribed the letters exactly as they are, letting stand all errors. The letterheads appear in italics, and I have noted whether letters are typed or handwritten and where enclosures are mentioned in the letter but have not survived. References are provided for two letters from Vita Sackville-West which have already been published.

Originally, the letters from "unknown" readers were numbered 1 to 58, but I have incorporated the letters from "known" readers (found at the MHP in separate author files) and numbered all 82 letters chronologically, placing those without a date at the end of the collection. This numbering system corresponds to that used in my book (*Virginia Woolf: Public and Private Negotiations*) but not to the numbering in my article on the letters, which deals with the 58 and so uses the original numbering system.

All reasonable attempts have been made to trace and contact copyright holders prior to publication. In some cases, however, this has proved impossible. I will be pleased to rectify any omissions at the earliest opportunity.

The editorial markings I have used are as follows:

[    ] = illegible
[example?] = uncertain reading
<example> = insertion by author
~~example~~ = cancellation by author
{example} = in square brackets by author

**Acknowledgments**

I would like to express my deepest gratitude to Adrian Peasgood, the Librarian at the University of Sussex, for permission to publish these letters, and to Bet Inglis, Assistant Librarian in the Manuscripts Section, University of Sussex, for all her help during my visits to the Monk's House Papers. On many occasions she has gone out of her way to answer my queries and requests. Thanks also to Mark Hussey for first suggesting *Woolf Studies Annual* as an appropriate space for publication and for being such a meticulous and caring editor. Pierre-Eric Villeneuve translated Letter 30 from the French: thanks to him for his time and dedication.

Many people assisted me in my searches for permission to publish these letters: Cecil Woolf, Hermione Lee, David Sutton of Reading University, David Doughan and Anna Greening of the Fawcett Library, and Jo Hodder of the Society of Authors. Thanks to Anne Olivier Bell for providing information about how the letters were filed. Anglia Polytechnic University provided funding for the project and gave me the use of a laptop during the transcription process. I am grateful for conversations and emails I have exchanged with other Woolf scholars working on these and other letters to Woolf: Brenda Silver, Melba Cuddy-Keane, and Alice Staveley.

Most importantly, my heartfelt thanks go to the relatives of Woolf's correspondents, who took the time to answer my letters, write to me about their relative and give their permission for the letter(s) to be published. Thanks especially to Hilary Bishop-Preen, who allowed her mother's letter to be reproduced for the frontispiece (Letter 67).

# Index of *Three Guineas* Letters

1. Margaret Rhondda - May 23, 1938
2. M. Geraldine Ostle - May 27, 1938
3. Philippa Strachey - May 30, 1938
4. Margaret Rhondda - June 2, 1938
5. Ray Strachey - June 4, 1938
6. Judith Stephen - June 6, 1938
7. Diana S. Boyes - June 6, 1938
8. A. Ruth Fry - June 11, 1938
9. M. A. R. Tuker - June 11, 1938
10. Violet Dickinson - June 12, 1938
11. Shena D. Simon - June 12, 1938
12. H. M. Swanwick - June 13, 1938
13. Gladys Rossiter - June 14, 1938
14. Alfred G. Sayers - June 14, 1938
15. Eleanor Cecil - June 15, 1938
16. Vita Sackville-West - June 15, 1938
17. E. E. Leake - June 16, 1938
18. Alfred G. Sayers - June 17, 1938
19. Gladys Rossiter - June 21, 1938
20. Lilian Mitehill - June 21, 1938
21. Toby Henderson - June 21, 1938
22. Naomi Mitchison - June 21, 1938
23. Margaret Llewelyn Davies - June 23, 1938
24. John McAdam - June 24, 1938
25. Margery Snowdon - June 25, 1938
26. Alfred G. Sayers - July 2, 1938
27. Margaret Paul - July 4, 1938
28. Naomi Mitchison - July 4, 1938
29. Shena D. Simon - July 5, 1938
30. Andrée Ito- July 7, 1938
31. David Freeman - July 12, 1938
32. R. A. Harman - July 12, 1938
33. Margaret Amiss - July 14, 1938
34. C. E. Brumwell - July 14, 1938
35. Jean Aitken - July 15, 1938
36. R. Ranken - July 17, 1938

37. G. H. Bosworth - July 18, 1938
38. Vita Sackville-West - July 23, 1938
39. Shena D. Simon - July 25, 1938
40. Emmeline Pethick-Lawrence - July 30, 1938
41. William Platt - August 1, 1938
42. Ellen Crockren - August 14, 1938
43. Unsigned - August 17, 1938
44. Annie Colles - August 18, 1938
45. Dorothy Soden - August 18, 1938
46. Jane Walker - August 31, 1938
47. E. Elizabeth Thornton - September 4, 1938
48. B. M. Bryson - September 4, 1938
49. William Drummond - September 10, 1938
50. William Drummond - September 11, 1938
51. Alan D. Cuthbert - September 12, 1938
52. Herbert Fisher - September 14, 1938
53. Isabel S. Johnson - September 14, 1938
54. Dorothy Mather - September 14, 1938
55. Fanny Mounsey - September 14, 1938
56. Fanny Mounsey - September 22, 1938
57. Granita Frances - September 24, 1938
58. Amelia Forbes Emerson - September 29, 1938
59. Nowell Smith - October 2, 1938
60. Leonard J. Holson - October 11, 1938
61. Elizabeth Nielsen - October 16, 1938
62. William J. Piggott - October 17, 1938
63. Agnes K. Potter - November 2, 1938
64. M. Agnes Smith - November 7, 1938
65. Shena D. Simon - November 17, 1938
66. M. Agnes Smith - November 28, 1938
67. Phyllis Preen - December 5, 1938
68. Frances Barnes - January 20, 1939
69. J. E. Callister - February 5, 1939
70. Constance Cheke - May 12, 1939
71. Constance Cheke - May 1939
72. Ernest Huxley - June 1939

# INDEX OF *THREE GUINEAS* LETTERS

73. Ernest Huxley - June 1939
74. Philippa Tristain - July 5, 1939
75. Philippa Woolf - September 18, 1939
76. Ronald Heffer - December 12, 1939
77. I. G. Bartholomew - December 13, 1939
78. Shena D. Simon - January 8, 1940
79. Belinda Jeliffe - date unknown
80. Belinda Jeliffe - date unknown
81. Belinda Jeliffe - date unknown
82. Amy Le Blanc-Smith - date unknown

**1
Handwritten
May 23, 1938**

Hampstead 3445.

*1B Bay Tree Lodge
Frognal
London, N.W.3*

23-5-38
Dear Mrs Woolf

  I can't prevent myself from writing to you about "Three Guineas" - I haven't read it all yet, for we have, so far, only one copy in the house & Theodora[1] has first claim on that as she is reviewing it. (Also I am laid up with an exasperating form of dermatitis & not allowed to use my eyes very much.) But she spent yesterday reading long passages to me, & I don't know how to tell you how exciting I found it or how profoundly it moved me.

  Such a book coming from you (you are the one right person in all the world to have written it) at such a time may have I think (if only Europe doesn't too quickly break into flames) a profound effect. I know too how much courage it takes to break the silence you speak of - most of us in one way or another fail in that courage. I told you all I thought about your courage in a dream yesterday, in which you & I were in a traffic jam in a rather dilapidated motor - & an errand boy shouted to us to look behind us, for there was the new moon. I took off my spectacles so as not to look at it through glass, & we looked round into a soft blue afternoon sky, it was very difficult to distinguish a scrap of a silver moon in it - & that minute the parlourmaid woke me up saying an aunt had come to tea -
Please forgive this long rambling letter from a very grateful Outsider
      Margaret Rhondda

*Margaret Haig Thomas, Viscountess Rhondda (1883-1958) founded* Time and Tide *in 1920 and was editor from 1926. For reply see L6 229 (3387): Woolf writes that Rhondda's letter has given her "great pleasure all day" and that she is very glad Rhondda calls herself "an outsider." Also see D5 141-2 where Woolf notes that Rhondda's response is a "good omen" and that* Three Guineas *"will make more splash among the ink pots" than she thought.*

[1] Theodora Bosanquet reviewed *Three Guineas* in *Time and Tide* on June 4 1938.

2
**Typed**
**May 27, 1938**

Mountview 1690

27, Holly Lodge Mansions,
Highgate,
London. N.6.

I apologise for this bad typing.
But there is no need to read it!

27th May 1938

Miss Virginia Woolf

Dear Madam:

  In October 1929 I wrote to you from the Froebel Society to thank you for your book A ROOM OF ONE'S OWN  I was then Registrar and Secretary of this woman's educational society.[1] Now I am alone and reading for pleasure as well as help in my work as I had to do then.
  And a reviewer has lent me your book THREE GUINEAS. I have been enthralled by it. A ROOM OF ONE'S OWN is on my 'best' book shelf. I shall now put THREE GUINEAS next to it.
  If only the unconverted would read and could understand all you express so delicately and yet with such force.
I shall not see it in my life time…I am 57…..but I think your two books will be the best help women have ever had towards their fight for justice,
  At the time of my work at the Froebel Society I had to come by train every day from Eltham Park to Charing Cross. For a long time I had, of course, the usual third class season. A generous Chairman gave me a first|class season. How well I remember taking my seat in comfort on Monday 2nd January; and how well I remember the glares I got from all the men in the carriage. Being blissfully ignorant that they were|angry, I went on my way. Before the first week was up one of the men mmm beckoned to a ticket inspector at Blackheath and|indicated my unwanted society. This inspector not only inspected my ticket but asked for the date and|then slammed the door without even making a show of looking at the men's. Later I found two other women who travlled in comfort. One was married and the other a buyer for a huge dress firm. They both agreed that they had had the same experience. The married woman said that men did not mind so much about her for she had a ring|on the proper finger but the other owned that men hated the fact that she was able to buy her self the usual comforts that 'belonged' to men. I have no quarrel

# THREE GUINEAS LETTERS                           Snaith        19

with men, they have often been kinder to me than my women relatives. But the fact still remains that we must do the hard work without the comforts unless the men can provide them. If you earn enough to have an occasional cocktail or a first class season...they hate it.

Is it because|it means that marriage does not now mean of necessity more comforts for the married woman?

I asked a season ticket holder the other day if the same thing happened. She said there was no doubt about it.

So once more let me|offer you my sincere thanks for your work for us.

Its a grand book and I am buying it as soon as it is out.

No one has expressed our difficulties in making a living better than you.

Why|men should mind...except for the marriage problem....I cannot think.

And some women are|just as queer. My married sister thinks it awful if I produce a bottle of sherry in my one-room flat andcalls me extrvagant because I know what food to get and how to furnish my room. Yet she will mmmmmmmmmm talk of my brother....income £3,000...as 'quite poor'

Oh for some more women with your brain.

Yours gratefully,

M Geraldine Ostle

I edited THE NOTEBOOKS OF A WOMAN ALONE in which I tried to express some of the difficulties women labour under.[2] Your first book started it.

---

[1] Mary Geraldine Ostle was Secretary and Librarian of the Froebel Society, an agency for teachers and governesses founded in 1874 and located in Bloomsbury Square, London. Miss Ostle's letter to Woolf about *A Room of One's Own* is in the Monk's House Papers and expresses her thanks for that text. See *D5* 145 for Woolf's comment: "Miss Osler or some such name writes to thank & praise - my grand work &c &c."

[2] *The Notebooks of A Woman Alone*, by Evelyn Wilson and edited by Ostle, was published in 1935 by J. M. Dent & Sons. It consists of the reading notebooks and writings of Wilson, a single working woman, and was published posthumously by Ostle and another colleague of Wilson's.

3
**Handwritten**
**May 30, 1938**

---

*London & National Society for Women's Service*
*(Formerly London Society For Women's Suffrage. Dating from 1866)*
*Non Party. Affiliated to the National Council of Women*
*President - The Rt. Hon. Viscount Cecil of Chelwood K.C.*
*Hon. Treasurer - The Hon. Mrs. Spencer Graves*
*Chairman of Executive - Miss Ethel Watts*
*Secretary - Miss Philippa Strachey*

*29 Marsham Street,*
*Westminster, S.W.1.*
*Telephone:*
*30th May 38*

My dear Virginia

I have read it with rapture - It is what we have panted for for years & years - Something that the gentlemen of our acquaintance will be forced to take up on account of its author & will be unable to put down on account of its amusingness until they have reached the bitter end.

I think you have worked out the argument with marvellous skill. It goes on piling itself up & the last letter is a sledge hammer. It really is a monumental piece of work - the notes are worthy of Beyle[1] & more effective by being collected together at the end instead of creeping in & out round the margins. (One note, by the bye, seemed to be missing - 41 or 42 to part 3 I think, but I've passed on the book to Ray and may be altogether mistaken about it as it only struck me in passing.)[2]

Your pen has often before provided me with intense pleasure but this time the pleasure is swollen by all sorts of extraneous currents including the joys of a vent to evil feelings. You don't display these yourself but the exposition of the case for them is extraordinarily comforting to the restrained furies.

One of the pleasures is making lists of the people who are to receive my presentation copies - mostly enemies but a few selected friends headed by Gide[3] who is to have the first.

I don't know what you'll make of the blessings from females that will descend upon your head. Such a weight that I hardly like to add those (unmitigated by knees and stockings) of

Yours P.S. [Philippa Strachey]

P.S. £5 recd this morning from Shena Simon. No accompanying letter, so easily dealt with by a polite message of gratitude.[4]

*The Stracheys were neighbors of the young Virginia Stephen when she lived in Gordon Square, Bloomsbury. Philippa Strachey (1872-1968), sister to Lytton, was active in the suffrage movement and it was for the London National Society for Women's Service that Woolf gave the speech on January 21 1931, "Professions for Women," that became* The Pargiters. *See* D5 *147 for Woolf's comment: "this is the last load off my mind - which weighed it rather heavy, for I felt if I had written all that & it was not to her liking I should have to brace myself pretty severely in my own private esteem." Woolf was most anxious about Philippa and Ray Strachey's (Philippa's sister-in-law) responses (see* D5 *149).*

[1] Henri Marie Beyle (1783-1842) was a French novelist who published under the pseudonym Stendahl. His novels include *Le Rouge et le Noir* (1830) and *La Chartreuse de Parme* (1839). He also wrote books on art and music.

[2] References 40 and 41 to Part 3, both quotations from Stephen Gwynn's *The Life of Mary Kingsley*, are included in the same note.

[3] André Paul Guillaume Gide (1869-1951) was a French novelist and diarist.

[4] Woolf offered to help Philippa raise money for the Marsham Street Library (later the Fawcett Library). Philippa's letter to Woolf of May 17 1938 (Monk's House Papers) describes how Woolf can help by writing to women writers and requesting donations of books and money. Woolf herself also donated books to the library. See *L6* 231, 232 and 236 for acknowledgements of donations from Vita Sackville-West, Ethel Smyth and Lady Rhondda (see Letter 4). See also *D5* 144.

**4**
**Handwritten**
**June 2, 1938**

*Churt Halewell,*
*Shere...Surrey.*
*Shere 248....Clandon Stn.*

2-6-38

Dear Mrs Woolf

I am interested in what you say about the subject being a risky one. That is quite true. And I don't think that two years ago anyone could have written such a book as yours. But a change has been taking place. I have felt it (though I can't explain it) all this winter & spring, & now such a book is possible - from you. It seems to me to have come at exactly the right moment. I do hope it may be true that there is really an inherent difference between men & women on that matter of combativeness. If there really is, & if we could get the power we might really help. But in my own heart I find it, seems to me, such echoes of all the pride, vanity & combativeness I ever see in men that I don't need to have it explained, I <u>know</u>. Still it is true that we don't do the actual killing - & don't want to  - so perhaps.....if there may only be time.

But there were a terrible lot of rooks in the elms round the house I was brought up in.....and its so extraordinarily difficult to hate dictatorship without being insensibly drawn into hating dictators - and those who follow dictators. Though when one thinks of it in cold blood its ridiculous to hate people for having gone mad under provocation - but one's blood will not stay as cold as it should.

I've sent my donation with great good wishes to the Millicent Fawcett Library - small, but twice what it would have been if I hadn't just read Three Guineas through twice running, straight on end -[1]

      Yours sincerely
      Margaret Rhondda

Yes, I do believe that something - perhaps a great deal - could be done with that outsiders idea. I can't see clearly at the moment. I feel as if a flood had poured over me & was still eddying about.

No woman who tried to run a Weekly Review could remain unaware of how much she was an Outsider.

Its not only that to run that kind of paper one <u>must</u> know something of the inside gossip that is going on & almost all the Official Gossip Centres are closed to women. (Its like trying to make something without the tools). It is also that the presumption amongst the average general public is that that kind of paper can't be run by women & all advertisers belong to the general public. Also the general public is convinced that what women have to say on public affairs cannot have any real weight, so that if one uses many women's names ones circulation & - again - ones advertising are affected. I go through the paper every week taking out women's names & references to matters especially concerning women because if I left them in it would soon kill the paper. But its maddening.

---

*See L6 236 (3397) for reply.*

[1] See Letter 3, Note 4.

**5**
**Handwritten**
**June 4, 1938**

> The Mud House,
> Friday's Hill,
> Haslemere.
> Fernhurst 18
>
> June 4. 38

Dear Virginia

Your book has given me so much joy that I don't quite know how to express it. Its simply <u>perfect</u>, & if the imbeciles in high places are not now pulverized it will only be because they are so densely stupid.

I have told Lady Astor[1] that she must send a copy to all the male devils she knows. As there are some thousands of these your sales should leap up if she obeys me! I'd like to see Winston's face while he reads it.

Yours Ray  [Ray Strachey]

---

*Ray Strachey, née Costelloe, (1887-1940) was parliamentary secretary to the London Society of Women's Suffrage and editor of the suffrage journal* Women's Leader. *She is the author of works including* The Cause *(1928), a history of suffrage, and a biography of Millicent Fawcett (1931). She met Woolf in 1909 at a party in Gordon Square and in 1911 she married Oliver Strachey, Lytton's brother. She was also published by the Hogarth Press.*

[1] American born Lady Nancy Witcher Astor (née Langhorne 1879-1964) became Conservative Member of Parliament for Plymouth in 1919 making her Britain's first woman MP. She would have known Sir Winston Churchill (1874-1965) through her involvement in politics. In the mid 1930s Churchill, who became Prime Minister in 1940, criticized the government for its complacency regarding the rising Nazi threat and the possibility of war.

**6
Handwritten
June 6, 1938**

Monday	Sidgwick Hall,
	Newnham College,
	<u>Cambridge</u>.

My dear Virginia -
    Thank you very much for your letter & the copy of "Three Guineas" - which I have just finished reading. I enjoyed it very much ; but find it difficult to summarise the main argument at the end, which is partly due to my having read it mainly at night, but also I think to its being rather diffuse. One doesn't generally try to summarise a book of yours but in this case I feel one ought to be able to, because what you say at any given point depends so much on what has gone before. However, I am going to read it again. The pictures are lovely, especially the General, who has completely won the hearts of all to whom I have showed him! Professor Moore in particular was delighted. By the way, did you know that Tom was being presented with an Honorary Degree here on Thursday?[1] I am going to try to sneak my way in & see him & Anthony Eden[2] receiving the purple or whatever one does receive.

    I've just finished taking my Part I exam & am entitled to be just as lazy as I please until next October. I am going to read Anthropology for the next 2 years - it is apparently a cross between sociology & [ ] on colonial administration & is read mainly by clergymen & potential Outposts of Empire like Leonard. But I think it might be fun to see how little we are removed from the savages.

    Look, Toby Henderson[3] says she would very much like to have a copy of "Three Guineas" & so would Margaret,[4] who has become Mrs Paul & lives at 16, Clarendon Road, Cambridge, in a combined welter of philosophy & domesticity. When you aren't disporting yourself with Skye terriers in the frozen north, will it be possible to come & see you this summer? Because I know Leonard won't ~~tell~~ let you ask ~~you~~ me, but I would like to come. And if it is possible, I would like to bring one of the "heavenly people" - if you can stand two of us at once! Anyway when next in town I will timidly press your bell & hope to be admitted.

                  Yours ever
                    Judith [Judith Stephen]

---

*Judith Stephen(1918-1972) was the daughter of Woolf's brother Adrian.*

[1] T. S. Eliot was given an honorary degree in Cambridge on June 9 1938 (see *D*5 150). The degree was conferred by Lord Baldwin, former Prime Minister and the Chancellor of Cambridge University, who appears in the third photo in *Three Guineas*.

[2] Sir (Robert) Anthony Eden (1897-1977) succeeded Churchill as Prime Minister in 1955. In 1935 he was Foreign Secretary, resigning in 1938 due to differences with Neville Chamberlain over policy regarding Fascist Italy. In 1940 Eden became Churchill's Secretary of State for War.

[3] Joan Cedar (Toby) Henderson (1916- ) was the daughter of Faith and Hubert Henderson, editor of the *Nation and Athenaeum*. See Letter 21.

[4] Margaret Paul went on to become an economist and Emeritus Fellow of Lady Margaret Hall, Oxford University. See Letter 27.

**7**
**Handwritten**
**June 6, 1938**

3a, Orford Gardens,
Strawberry Hill
11.6.38.

Dear Mrs. Woolf,

I understand, from a review of your latest book, that the thought of working in an office from nine to six makes you shudder.

After 2 years in an office I am quite numb, devoid of all sensibility. It is an effort to read, to think, to feel - simple pleasures - impossible. It kills for you all in life that is genuinely lovely, it turns you into one those horrid creatures that wear hats with bows under their chins, and shoes with heels 3 inches high.

It makes me wonder whether "emancipation" has after all given the majority of women, freedom, and not driven us to an even more soul killing existence. Imagine, typing all day from 9 till 5 - its an unhappy existence. Oh for a war to relieve the monotony. This isn't self pity its just despair.

I believe you to be the finest contemporary writer, your books will live.

Sincerely
Diana S. Boyes

**8**
**Handwritten**
**June 11, 1938**

*Telegrams*                      11.VI.38            *Thorpeness,*
*& Telephones,*                                     *Suffolk.*
*Aldeburgh 163.*

Dear Virginia.

    I can't resist telling you that my dear Lady Gibb is reading aloud to me "Three Guineas", & we are chortling with delight & entertainment, on top of deep satisfaction at your effective telling! So thank you very much for writing it. (And I do want you to meet Lady Gibb[1] - she is a niece of Dame Millicent Fawcett[2] & Mrs Garrett Anderson,[3] as well as being herself.)

    We think you may be entertained by the enclosed, sent to me by the writer, Mr H.S. Alexander, editor of the Public Ledger, a brilliant, pathetic little man, a friend of ours.

    No need to return or acknowledge.

                Yours  A. Ruth Fry

*Enclosure missing.*

*Published courtesy of Ms. Betty Taber, Ruth Fry's great niece.*
*Anna Ruth Fry (1876-1962) was Roger Fry's youngest sister. She was a pacifist, a Quaker and she served as General Secretary to the Friends' War Victims Relief Committee 1914-1923. She is the author of* A Quaker Adventure *(1926) about Friends' Relief work during and after WWI,* Quaker Ways *(1933),* Three Visits to Russia *(1942) about her work in Russia 1922-1925, and numerous privately printed pamphlets on pacifism and Quakerism.*

  [1] Lady Norah Gibb was the wife of Sir Alexander Gibb the civil engineer. Fry lived with her in Thorpeness for many years.

  [2] Dame Millicent Fawcett (née Garrett, 1847-1929) was an educational reformer and active suffragist, being President of the National Union of Women's Suffrage Societies from 1897 to 1919. She was one of the founders of Newnham College, Cambridge.

  [3] Elizabeth Garrett Anderson (1836-1917), the older sister of Millicent Fawcett, was the first English woman doctor. In 1866 she opened the first dispensary for women in London and in 1908 she became Mayor of Aldeburgh, making her the first woman mayor in England.

**9**
**Handwritten**
**June 11, 1938**

---

*Grosvenor 2262.*                                     *17 Stratton Street, W.1.*
                                                      *June 11 1938*

Dear Mrs Virginia Woolf

    I have bought and read your book - you will remember (?) I wrote to you (last Nov.) about my book - Past & Future of Ethics, Oxford University Press - wh. did not appear till the end of January this year. When I wrote it was especi<u>ally</u> <u>your</u> interest - I so much hoped to enlist for the subject of my book - & now yours has appeared!

I am immensely interested in it - Viola Meynell[1] came round to tell me about it. You get at them at every point; the book will be a thunder-clap on the right side; it will make 'their' hair sit up - every page is telling. And, as it was in the vote battle, so it is now, for there is <u>no</u> <u>answer</u> to it.

The prestige of your name secures you reviews - but how those reviewers wish you had never written the book!

When I troubled you with my letter it was to tell you I feared nasty attacks - what has happened I had not thought of - <u>no</u> attack - The Times Lit. Suppl. Reviewed it without mentioning the 1/3rd of the book dealing with your subject.[2] It was preferable to forgo the pleasure of slanging the woman writer than to call attention to it & enable people to read the book for themselves.

<u>I beg you now to read it</u>. The Times Book Club & even Boots (both of wh. refused for weeks to take it for the lending dept) have it & have "a waiting list". Do read the chapter <u>Biological Sources of Ethics</u> & <u>Woman & Woman</u>, & what is said of war, of <u>Force</u> as the male method of morals, & of <u>Money</u>. I wrote an article for the "Nineteenth Century" (republished as a pamphlet) about clerical roles for women - & "Cambridge" (publ. A & C Black, 1907) contained the first account of the rise of Newnham & Girton, & an appreciation of Anne J. Clough.[3] I knew her and Bodichon.[4]

    One of the things we have in common is french blood (& things are possible to those with a racial mixture wh. are not possible to those without it!)

                    Yours sincerely
                    M.A.R. Tuker

a frivolous detail - for I saw you had once written about Beau Brummel.[5] When I was 15 I was lunching with a then well-known Home-Ruler M.P., & we were shown in the drawing room a magnificant set of Sèvres plates, each with the portrait of a Queen of France - my host said they had no history of it whatever. I told him it must be the set wh. was sold at Brummell's sale in Calais - & so it was proved to be.

---

[1] Viola Meynell (1886-1956) was a poet, novelist and short story writer. Her publications in the 1930s include *The Frozen Ocean and Other Poems* (1931) and *Follow Thy Fair Sun* (1935). She published a memoir of her mother, the poet Alice Meynell, in 1929.

[2] Miss M. A. R. Tuker's book, *Past and Future of Ethics* (Oxford UP, 1938), was reviewed anonymously in the *Times Literary Supplement* April 2 1938: 228. The reviewer called it "a work marked by vigour of thought and expression and by wide knowledge of the literature of the writer's subject."

[3] Anne Jemima Clough (1820-1892) became the Secretary to the North of England Council for Promoting the Higher Education of Women in 1867 and then the first Principal of Newnham College, Cambridge in 1879.

[4] Barbara Bodichon (1827-1891) helped to found *The Englishwoman's Journal* in 1858 and the college for women that became Girton College, Cambridge.

[5] Beau (George Bryan) Brummel (1778-1840) was a society dandy famous for his wit and his impeccable dress. At one time friends with the Prince Regent, George Prince of Wales, he died penniless in an asylum due to gambling losses. In Woolf's essay "Four Figures," one section is devoted to Brummel (*CE3* 187-93).

**10**
**Handwritten**
**June 12, 1938**

---

*Burnham Wood,*
*Welwyn.*

June 12 1938
My Sp:[1]

    Are you bubbling over amid letters glittering with brilliance? I <u>am</u> enjoying t.Guineas tho' we paid our Board of Control ladies twenty years ago about £1500 a year or so.[2]
The actor comic Weymouth[3] (Katie's[4] nephew) a year or two ago had a Bookcase in his [ ] & one shelf filled by you - & one of War books.
"The only books I collect."
I wondered if he'd read one of them [ ]. but didn't dare ask! I've spent my remaining [Chink?] on your Guineas. I'm known as "The Tragedy" now as I can't waddle - or haven't done so for a year.
    Love to Leonard
& to you - if acceptable?
        yrs Violet [Violet Dickinson]
How do you feel? any headaches? I wish I could have them for you.

*Violet Dickinson (1865-1948) was an old friend of Woolf's known for her philanthropic work. Woolf's "Friendship's Gallery" (1908) is a mock biography of Dickinson, written in violet ink and bound in violet leather. See L6 237 (3398) for reply.*

[1] Short for Sparroy, Dickinson's nickname for Woolf.
[2] Dickinson's brother Oswald, with whom she lived throughout her life, was Secretary to the Board of Control (of Lunacy and Mental Deficiency).
[3] Weymouth was the eldest son of the Marquess of Bath and himself became the Marquess in 1946.
[4] Katherine Cromer (née Thynne).

---

**11**
**Handwritten**
**June 12, 1938**

*Broomcroft*
*Ford Lane*
*Didsbury, Manchester 20*
*Telephone: Didsbury 3368*

My dear Virginia.

I read "Three Guineas" , a week ago as I was being driven from Cambridge - when I found Pernel[1] enchanted with it - to the Quantocks.[2] It was a perfect day, so that I was able to enjoy, simultaneously the scenery & your writing. I had to break off to read the Times. There was a notice to the effect that the Literary Supplement of that date contained a review of, & a leading article on, - "Three Guineas", so that when I turned to the first leader "Doctrine, Deaconesses & Diocesans", I thought at first the the part about women preaching was a quotation from your book, & I looked for the quotation marks - But, apparently, the writer had not read it & was perfectly serious in what he said about Deaconesses.[3]

I am now reading it for the second time & find that I had missed many subtleties in my eagerness to get to the end. I never imagined that you could write a second "Room of One's Own" which would equal if not surpass (I haven't quite decided yet) the original, & the footnotes raise the whole level of references to a height that no other writer can ever hope to reach. I only hope that they won't be missed by some readers who don't like to turn to the end of a book.

Quite apart from my general feeling of joy that you have said what so many of us have felt, so much better than anyone else could have said it, I am personally grateful to you. As a girl I was much too concerned with other people's opinions, & with the fear of hurting their feelings. The suffragette agitation - although I took an infinitesimal part in it, turned me into a rebel, & ever since I have been perhaps too little concerned with other people's opinions of me & my actions. When I was Lady Mayoress I refused to give away Christmas presents at the leading hospital here for women because it refused to have women doctors on the staff - & the storm that simple action caused was an eye-opener to me - & I wrote a Ministry report when my men colleagues evidently felt that it wasn't quite playing the game - even those who agreed with my point of view -, & I make a great nuisance of myself on the Consultative Committee[4] - when the other women behave in a way that commends them to the men. I have sometimes wondered whether I ought to adopt a different attitude, but as I am completely independent, in the sense that I don't want "honours" or appointments or anything from the powers that be, I have always decided that, unlike many other women, I can afford to be unpopular. Now, after reading Three Guineas, I am more confirmed in my belief, & shall probably become more & more of an "Outsider".

There are many other points that I long to discuss with you but I won't add to this already lengthy [ ], as I hope that you are now in the wilds of Scotland, - they will keep until we next meet. But I could not wait until then to thank you -

Yours Shena D. Simon

Of course you won't answer this. SDS
June 12

---

*Published courtesy of Professor Brian Simon, Baron of Wythenshawe, son of Shena Simon.*

*Lady Shena Simon (née Potter, 1883-1972) was an educationalist and public figure. In 1907 she accepted a degree from an Irish university because her degree from Newnham College, Cambridge was, at that time, an unrecognized qualification. She became known as a 'statutory woman' due to her many appointments to local and national committees on education and social welfare. In 1938 she published* A Hundred Years of City Government: Manchester 1838-1938.

*She first met Woolf in 1933 at Tavistock Square and wrote to Leonard Woolf in 1941 that Virginia was one of the few people "who really counts in my life." Leonard asked her to give a memorial lecture after Woolf's death. For reply see L6 239 (3401) in which Woolf reassures Simon: "of course you're an outsider." Simon's letters to Woolf can also be found in Joan Simon's (Shena Simon's daughter-in-law) biographical study, "Shena Simon, Feminist and Educationist" (1986). Chapter Five of this study is entitled "Conversations with Virginia Woolf 1933-1941: Updating Feminism." The study was privately produced and copies are held in the Fawcett Library, Manchester Library and Newnham College Library.*

[1] Pernel Strachey (1876-1951) was Principal of Newnham College 1923-1941. She was the fourth of Lytton's five sisters.
[2] The Quantock Hills in Somerset.
[3] The article was published in *The Times*, June 4 1938. See Letter 39.
[4] Simon served on the Consultative Committee of the Board of Education from 1933 to 1938.

**12**
**Handwritten**
**June 13, 1938**

13-VI-1938

Dear Mrs Woolf,

I have been reading your '<u>Three Guineas</u>' with much pleasure. It says so many things that need saying.

As the book will certainly go through many editions, I venture to draw your attention to an error in Note 5 Part 2 (p.286) which could easily be corrected in a subsequent edition. You quote from my book, '<u>I have been Young</u>'[1] (p.189), that 'the W.S.P.U. had an income from gifts in the 'year 1912 of £42,000.' If you will refer to '<u>I have been young</u>' you will see that what I wrote was 'I would claim for <u>Mrs Fawcett's great Union</u>' (which, as you know, was the National Union of Women's Suffrage Societies & not the Women's Social & Political Union) 'not only her 'devoted record of over half a century's persistent toil, but its fruits in a 'national membership far exceeding in numbers that of the militant societies '& an income, from gifts, in the year 1912, of £42,000.'

In a little book published in 1913 by Messrs. Bell, under the title '<u>The Future of the Women's Movement,</u>' I stated that the National Union had, in twelve months, raised £42,000; that I assumed the W.S.P.U. to have done as much (they did not publish accounts) & that the thirty - odd other Suffrage Societies (Women's Freedom League, Church League, Conservative & Unionist W.S.S., & so forth) must have brought that year's contributions to at least £100,000. I see now that £150,000 would have been well within the mark & that without taking into account the considerable sums spent by volunteers in travelling etc.

I also think that it gives a wrong impression to say that in 1912 the Women's Freedom League & the Women's Social & Political Union were 'opposed.' Their object was one; only their methods of approach were opposed.

With kind rememberance, very truly yours
<u>H.M. Swanwick</u>

*Helena Swanwick (1864-1939) was a member of the North of England Suffrage Society and editor of the suffrage newspaper* The Common Cause *between 1909 and 1914. In 1915 she became Chairperson of the Women's International League for Peace. Swanwick's book* The Roots of Peace *(1938) was reviewed on 4 June 1938 on the same page of the* Times Literary Supplement *as* Three Guineas.

[1] Published 1935.

13
Typed
**June 14, 1938**

*15, Prince Edward Mansions,*
*Pembridge Square, W.2.*
*Bayswater 0436.*

Miss Virginia Woolf,                        14th June 1938.
C/O. The Hogarth Press.

Madam,
    I have never before written to an author or celebrity, and after the probable and possibly merited rebuff of being ignored - or worse - by you, I very likely never shall again. On reading your "Three Guineas" however, which is giving me a great measure of delight, two questions keep revolving in my mind, and in spite of inner warnings from my instinct and intelligence, I seem unable to follow the course of reticence and prudence, and to my horror observe myself addressing a perfect stranger. I will at least attempt to be brief:
-

(1).    Have you forgotten that a prodigious number of undergraduates recently voted that under no circumstances would they ever fight for King and Country and, in ignoring this fact, are you being quite fair to the other sex and to the Universities which, after all, may be producing a generation of pacifists?

(2).    Much as one loathes and abhors the very thought of War, is one smilingly to turn the other cheek when Germany - enormously strong through her forcible annexation of Czechoslavakia, the Tyrol, Memel, etc. turns her greedy eyes to these islands? Is one meekly to allow oneself to be bombed, annexed, and are we and our Empire to submit without resistance to becoming a minor German State?

> Yours faithfully,
>
> (<u>Mrs</u>) Gladys Rossiter

P.S. I have not yet read every word of your book, but I presume that had you been going to deal with either of these questions, you would by now have mentioned them.

---

*See Letter 19 for evidence that Woolf replied to Rossiter. The reply has not survived.*

**14
Handwritten
June 14, 1938**

A.A. \*\*\* R.A.C.
*Telephone,
315 Cirencester.*

14 June 1938

Dear Madam,

*Wellesley House Hotel.
Cirencester.
Glos.*

as from
Parkwern
Pembroke Rd
Sevenoaks

I agree with <u>Time & Tide</u> (I think it was) in hailing <u>Three Guineas</u> as the book of the year: not to be superseded! To bring in the actual LCJ and the actual Head of the Church, & dear old Baldwin - not caricatured, but at their best - is a real triumph![1] I only hope and pray that women will not succumb to the robing, wigging, macing business! - here and there they have done so! - your book may arrest them.
I confess that in my own propaganda I have thought of the Robes Wigs Maces business as quite distinct from the Professional, Commercial fight for opulence: though of course it is the lure of titles that promotes the struggle.
  Doubtless it might have overweighted your brilliant book, to show that the Law is administered primarily for the Lawyers - that the city is really infamous for the administrations of the vast funds of the City Companies. A

client of mine who was warden of one (not the wealthiest) took me once to quite a commonplace dinner in their hall. The luxury & extravagance were merely disgusting. He told me afterward that the Company's income was £100,000 a year! - & that they kept certain poor scholars at one of the Universities! Reverting for a moment to the Law (the High Court) - is it not inevitable that when presently the Courts rise for Long Vacation - they will be leaving a mass of Causes unheard, while the Judges go fishing & travelling & golfing for 10 weeks! The other Vacations run into weeks!

The above is a mere <u>Extension</u> of your own theme: examples within your own thesis are superfluous - but I will give one: - my friend Dorothy S S (M A Oxford) has been called to the bar; but the mean dodges of the man barristers in her Chambers, have so prevented briefs reaching her, that she has taken to some of the very hard, poorly paid work on the confines of the profession.

I hope it will not bore you too much to have read this note - which in essence is one immense vote of thanks for your book.

I venture on one criticism. You almost seem to have been at pains to avoid referring to the Pethick- Lawrences[2] in your references to the WSPU. Perhaps you did not approve of their share in the movement. Emmeline PL has been my particular friend for many years. Perhaps there are facts referred to in 'My part in 'a changing world' which spoil your sympathies to-her-ward!

With much appreciation,<br><u>Alfred G. Sayers</u>

---

*Published courtesy of D. M. Sayers, grandson of A. G. Sayers.*

*A. G. Sayers was a chartered accountant who set up his own company (as A. G. Sayers, Seaton and Butterworth) in the West End of London. The firm still operates today as Sayers Butterworth. The later years of his life were spent in Sevenoaks, Kent. Sayers was an active liberal, supporting the Social Credit movement and thereby meeting and socializing with the Pethick-Lawrences. He suffered a nervous breakdown due to self-inflicted pressure of work and died during the Second World War. For Woolf's reply see L6 238-9 (3400) in which she writes: "your letter about my book Three Guineas has given me great pleasure."*

[1] Sayers is referring to the photos in *Three Guineas* of Gordon Hewart (1870-1943) who became Lord Chief Justice in 1922, William Cosmo Gordon Lang (1864-1945) who became Archbishop of Canterbury in 1928 and Stanley Baldwin (1867-1947), former British Prime Minister.

[2] Emmeline Pethick-Lawrence (1867-1954) joined the Women's Social and Political Union in 1906 and became its honorary treasurer. With her husband, Frederick William Pethick-Lawrence (1871-1961), she edited the weekly newspaper *Votes for Women* between 1907 and 1914. In 1912 she left the WSPU and subsequently became President

of the Women's Freedom League. She also formed the non-militant Votes for Women Fellowship. Her autobiography, *My Part in A Changing World*, was published in 1938. See Letter 40.

**15**
**Handwritten**
**June 15, 1938**

*Sloane 7011*                        *16, South Eaton Place, S.W.1.*
                                                June 15, 38

My dear Virginia
      Violet[1] gave me your book for my birthday & I have enjoyed it enormously & maliciously. The best of it is when <u>you</u> write something it won't be out of date like a pamphlet but will be there for use whenever the occasion comes - this "strong pepper & curry mustard for leading gentlemens" as Mrs Nansen wrote to me about some speech lately, & I hope the leading gentlemens get it stuffed down their throats again & again - and the backward gentlewomens too - that is the sad part of the story - if we stuck together as men do —- wouldn't we have got everything worth having long ago?
You have always had an absolute genius for quotation - your exhibits are too amusing & deadly - & your comments - to quote Mrs Nansen again "full of visedom & spirit & truth" - I am glad you believe in the Bible - one of the prophets is my favourite political economist - I could write to you for ever about the queer questions you raise - if I were'nt too empty headed to do it - luckily for you - so goodbye & bless you for your works
                         ever yr affec te
                             EC [Eleanor Cecil]
(not a pacifist yet!)

*Published courtesy of the Marquess of Salisbury and Ann Lambton.*

*Lady Eleanor Cecil, wife of Lord Robert Cecil, was often referred to by Woolf as "Nellie." She and Woolf shared a column in the* Cornhill Magazine *in 1908. For Woolf's reply see L6 242 (3404).*

[1] Violet Dickinson, a close friend of Eleanor Cecil.

**16**
**15 June 1938**

From Vita Sackville-West
Published in *The Letters of Vita Sackville-West to Virginia Woolf*, ed. Louise DeSalvo and Mitchell A. Leaska (London: Hutchinson, 1984: 440) (NY: William Morrow and Company, 1985: 412-13).

*Vita writes: "you [...] exasperate one with your misleading arguments." For Woolf's reply see L6 242-3 (3405).*

**17**
**Typed**
**June 16, 1938**

June 16, 1938.

Dear Madam,
    In "Three Guineas" it is suggested that the daughters of educated men should not subscribe to papers that encourage intellectual slavery. But how can they know which encourage slavery and which do not? Is there any publication which tells them, "This paper encourages intellectual slavery. This one does not"? Will editors and proprietors tell them? They can form their own private opinion, of course, but opinion is not knowledge.
    The whole question of accurate knowledge is a very important and a very difficult one for the ordinary man. He is expected to form judgments and to vote on the scantiest material. He has no friends in high places or behind the scenes to give him "inside information." When even Parliament is not always in possession of all the facts how can he be expected to come to sane decisions? "Lips are sealed" and so often "it is not in the public interest to discuss these matters." Then again, he is so often asked to choose between hypothetical cases ("If we take this course, this will happen," says one. "On the contrary, this will happen," says another). Where there is so much opinion it seems profitless to talk of truth. It seems that the ordinary man will have to go on comparing the news in at least three different publications and thereby, presumably, subscribing to papers which encourage intellectual slavery. But whether it seems profitless or not, search for truth and knowledge we must.
                  Yours, etc.,
                  (Miss) E.E. Leake.

**18**
**Handwritten**
**June 17, 1938**

*Telegrams,*                        *Devonshire Club,*
*"Luxive, Piccy, London"*            *St. James's, S.W.1.*
*Telephone, Regent 1714 (6 Lines)*

say Parkwern, Sevenoaks, 17.6.38

Dear Madam,

         I should never think of <u>exaggeration</u> in connection with your pungent book.[1] It is as you say an 'outline' - & therefore, as a complete exposition, oversimplified. But all the better for that. If you expanded the book to comprehend distinctions, & exceptions; & relate the thesis up to a wider society, you would make a valuable <u>tome</u>; but that would curtail your public: As it is, my own forecast is that everybody will have to read you among the public that makes opinions - & the monthlies & quarterlies will hail your art & expose your 'fallacies' in articles of ineptitude.

     I have for long had on the stocks a series of essays, comprehended in the term 'Reform', dealing with your theses - whose fate is what might be expected respecting one exercising a profession for 5 days per week in London; & at the week-end adjudicating the precious hours between reading & writing - <u>ie</u> - endless revision, & never completion! Your book now puts my draft out of date again:

     It won't be of much interest to you that I enclose a copy of a few pars I did in the train this morning for our local paper.

     Many thanks for your remarks re the Pethick-Lawrences. I thought your 'play-boy' stroke might have been aimed at such as the Member for E Edinburgh. If I understand that point aright, it is one that I think very arguable!

     But that is another story.

Yours very sincerely

         A.G. Sayers

Mrs Virginia Woolf

*Enclosure missing.*

*Published courtesy of D. M. Sayers.*

*No reply to this letter has survived but Letter 26 indicates that Woolf did write to Sayers again.*

[1] In reply to Sayers' letter of June 14 1938 Woolf wrote: "I am glad that you do not think me guilty of exaggeration!" (*L6* 238).

**19**
**Typed**
**June 21, 1938**

*15, Prince Edward Mansions,*
*Pembridge Square, W.2.*
*Bayswater 0436.*

21st June 1938.

Madam,
    I thank you for your prompt and kind reply to my letter which I greatly appreciated. I have now finished "Three Guineas", and am much moved by its magnificent idealism, and I marvel that you had enough faith to write such a stirring document whilst millions of tiny children (in Dictatorship countries) are being taught to Hate as their foremost creed.
    I am only sorry that some of the reviewers - mostly males - so deliberately ignored the real meaning and message of your very beautiful work.

        Yours faithfully,

        Gladys Rossiter

**20**
**Handwritten**
**June 21, 1938**

11 Western Place
Edinburgh 12.

21st June 1938

Dear Madam,
    Forgive me for troubling you for I am a very ordinary member of the public but I do want to say how grateful I am for your "Three Guineas", more

especially for the last part.

I was in the W.S.P.U. Movement from the age of 23 to 28 when the war broke out, (have been in prison five times) since then I have worked in other movements, trusting that equality of opportunity was coming along all right. But, the Church has always given me the old "Votes for Women" feeling & now since reading your book it - the feeling - is upon me very strongly.

I am a member of the Scottish Episcopal Church, - very backwards on the position of women, & the Ch. of Scotland is nearly as bad, though there is an effort being made in it, feebly, to establish equality. I have spoken to some of the members & they say it will come gradually from within. My conviction is that the Movement will have to come from without, a non-sectarian movement of Christians.

If you should hear of any thing of the sort being made, I should be so glad to know of it. Yours very gratefully
    (Miss) Lilian Mitehill

**21**
**Handwritten**
**June 21, 1938**

---

        5 South Parks Rd.
        Oxford
        <u>21st June</u>

Dear Virginia,

Many, many thanks for Three Guineas: it was angelic of you to send it to me. I read Ann's[1] copy of it during the last glorious week of term when all the exams were over & we were completely free to do anything we liked. Judith[2] & I took a boat up the river one after-noon & had a superb after-noon lazing in the sun reading Three Guineas & discussing it together & with other people as they passed by. I did enjoy it immensely; but to remember all your points I shall have to read it again, & will do so at the earliest opportunity; but, for the time being, various members of the family have appropriated the book. Why on earth don't all writers on whatever subject they choose write in a style which will give enjoyment to the reader? was what I wanted to ask at the end. If only all our text books were written in such a style we'd learn so much more than we do now purely because of the pleasure we'd be getting. And we'd also become accustomed to grasping the points presented in a literary fashion more easily than those put forward in a straight text-book.

I'm afraid I've been ages writing to thank you, but we were pretty busy last week preparing for an Oxford-Cambridge party. It was a great pity Judith wasn't able to come, as she'd probably have enjoyed it. Several of the people had been at your party last Christmas. One person forgot to bring any clothes at all, & another forgot his trousers & another got his £10 car stuck in a ditch in the Parks where it had to remain till morning. But it was all very enjoyable. I wish Angelica had turned up, she said she would & never did, the wretch, so do scold her if you see her.

        Yours,
        Toby [Toby Henderson]

---

*Joan Cedar (Toby) Henderson (1916- ) was the daughter of Faith and Hubert Henderson, the former editor of the* Nation and Athenaeum.

[1] Ann Stephen, Adrian Stephen's daughter.

[2] Judith Stephen, Adrian Stephen's daughter. See Letter 6. Toby Henderson and Ann Stephen were studying for degrees in 1938 and Judith Stephen was about to start the second year of a degree in anthropology at Cambridge in September 1938. Ann Stephen married Richard Llewelyn Davies in 1938.

**22**
**Typed**
**June 21, 1938**

---

*Telephone, Riverside 2287*        *River Court,*
*Station, Ravenscourt Park 3 1/2 Minutes*    *Hammersmith Mall,*
                     *London. W.6.*

21st
Dear Virginia Woolf
   I meantx to write to you a long time ago, after reading The Years. I didn't, I suppose, because I wasn't quite clear what I wanted to say. It seemed to me that it was, like all the few great books which I have read, in some ways an answer to a question. But it seemed silly to say that when I could not begin to formulate either the question or what your answer had been. Only it gave me a sense of peace, in reading, such as comes from having a question answered. I found that my eldest boy, who was reading it too, found the same thing. Apart from that, of course, I enjoyed it, as, I think, I don't enjoy any books except your's. By the way - I think it might amuse you - they set a "gobbet" out of that in a Winchester English Literature prize paper, to guess the author.
   Now, about Three Guineas. I am sure I must write now, because I am one the 250 "daughters" who are in such an economic position that they can answer your appeal. Actually, I make between 300£ and 400£ a year, so, if I hadn't a husband who could "support" me, I couldn't keep more than, say, two of my five children, and couldn't give any of them a fancy education. Actually, I try not to be kept myself, and in a way this is silly, because Dick has always wanted me to have a definite settlement from him (we were married during the

war, without one) and is always wanting to give me things. Only I feel I mustn't live that way, so I ration myself on clothes and that sort of thing to about £50 a year; I spend rather more on books partly because they are the tools of my trade and partly because they are read byx all the family and borrowed widely. I am only telling you this to make my position plain. I don't need any more than I make (or, theoretically, even that: I have a quite small unearned income, enough to dress on, but not enough for the many good causes which seem to be what most of one's income goes on), though I like making more, just because of all those good causes. Equally, of course, Dick could deal with the good causes, but - there it is, I want to do it myself! A good deal of the earned income is from B.B.C? stuff, an articles, not all of which I want to write. But I always feel two things about them: they take very little time to do, can be written in tains and things, and it is usually possible to get something into them which will reach an audience which otherwise one caouldn't possibly reach (and I have evidence that this does actually happen - people writing to me). I always refuse them f they are definitely going to be all bilge! Equally I worked for the B.B.C. education dept, not doing quite what I wanted, but compromising and finding it intere ting, until such a time as I completely disagreed with themon history. All this is compromise.

I hope and suppose I should refuse all "honours" (I got a thing from the French - the palms of the Academy - when I was quite young, and was awfully pleased with it!) but they are unlikely to come my way. I haven't got a degree, and am not likely to be offered an honorary one.

But about doing things or writing things without motives, as you hopefully suggest we should on page 175. I think one can get rid of the power and advertisement motives and vanity motive, very largely, at any rate, and of the <u>direct</u> economic motive. But I can't see anyone but a saint getting rid of all motives, being as utterly disintere ted, as you would have us be. We have been conditioned in one class outlook (as you admit on p.193, when you say we mustn't mix with other classes; here I think there is much in your criticism, but I don't entirely accept it); we are certain to have some persons we are fond of and want to protect or be biassed about. Especually if we are going to have an adequate amount of knowledge of public affairs, say, to write about them disinterestedly, we shall almost certain, in the course of finding out, have been enveigled into action and bias. I think you demand an impossible abilty to be and remain audessus de la melee, which only very long-term-minded people of either sex can achieve. If you are a short-termer, you getx involved, as, indeed, I have done myself.

Thus I am questionning the whole policy of "indifference". I think it postulates a very ununusual kind of person, one who is not bound to the wheel of affection in any way. How can I, for instance, be indifferent to whether or not my sons get involved in the next war? (My brother, on the other hand, would himself be indifferent to any indifference of mine!) Even if I pretended to be indifferent, they would know I wasn't.

You avoided the discussion of revolutionary action, or at least it didn't arise. But here again, I don't see how I could stand out, even if I knew for certain, as all sensible people must, that any revolution brings after it, not what it's makers hope for and dream of, but only, with luck, something in that direction. Revolutions only seem to arise in intolerbale situations, and then I should be bound to share the intolerable situation with the rest of my fellow-beings.

And I can't help wondering whether a writer does not lose something if he or she is remote from action, only a looker-on, dispassionate as a god? That may be romanticism, of course, but I can't help thinking that one must have contacts with ordinary life, and once one has them, one can't help doing things in connection with them.

I wonder what you think of all this. You ee, in writing this book, you must have wanted people to listen to you - you must have wanted to influence them, to have, in a way, power over them, So you must exepct to be written to!

I wonder, also, whether others of the 250 women to whom you specially wrote, have answered! Anyhow, forgive me for bothering you. Your book seemed like part of an eternal argument that is bound to go on in one's mind, on and off, the whole time.

Yours sin<br>Naomi Mitchison

---

*Naomi Mitchison (1897-1999) was a novelist and was active in the women's movement. Her most controversial novel,* We Have Been Warned *(1935), was censored because of sexual explicitness. In 1937 she moved to Scotland and became involved in Scottish politics. The Hogarth Press published* Socrates *(1937) by Mitchison and R. H. S. Crossman as part of their World Makers and World Shakers children's series.*

---

**23**
**Handwritten**
**June 23, 1938**

---

Sandells, Reigate Road
Dorking, Surrey
June 23d

I have been wanting to write to you, very dear Virginia, ever since I had your letter which was so good to get. And now there are so many things to communicate about, & I am not in v. good trim for writing. But just a few words. You will have felt another of your friends' deaths & tho' Ka[1] was not a personal friend of <u>mine</u>, she was of my friends (she & Willy & Mark had all been to see Janet,[2] who thought greatly of her) - & I knew her mother in law, Mary

Maskelyne & her terribly unattractive husband came to see us in Blandford Square - & recall how you & Leonard stayed at the Eagle's Nest, & also how you & I drove back past it, seeing poor old Mrs Westlake walking there, supported by sticks & people.

Lilian[3] & I had to decamp from Hillspur a fortnight ago, on acct of Mrs Redhouse's holiday, & the failure of an engaged "temporary" - (we return in a week) & here we are in the midst of ancients who are deaf & blind and hop & go-one & mentally ill & shant we be glad to back in our lovely garden, ie (Himalaya popies, too many peaches on Leonard's tree to count & anchursa in the sun - utterly exquisite etc etc) - but not very happily suited with a Swiss maid who spoke no English

As to your last book - to read the first sentence was like a Himalaya poppy - or the murmur of innumerable bees in immemorial elms - or beauty born of murmuring sound, or the satisfaction given of a musical phrase & other things, - the style was so delicious. Of course the book would appeal to me no end - for on acct of peace & anti-humbug & justice. I shd like you to see some of my pictures in a scrap-book - & have you got the delightful monogram on Mary Kingsley[4] whom I saw at a party - quaintest looking with enormous teeth & a tiny knob at the back of her plain-lying & parted hair. I always thought she ought to be a Govenor of a colony. Mrs J R Green gave it me as I admired it. It is in the S. African (Geographical?) Magazine. And I have a little book, I cd also lend you, "Eighteen Maxims of Neatness & Order, to which is prefixed An Introduction by Theresa Tidy" (then a quotation from "Poor Richard") Hatchard 1818. I have not read "The Third" "Three" yet - (I can read so little) & Lilian is sadly dependent on Braille)

I hardly like to say I feel the book might be still better, rather shortened - but I disapprove of some parts I have read of some of G.M.Young's review[5] & of Mrs Stocks (tho' approving of agreeing with his appreciative points). because your books are not to be treated pedantically (they are not blue books, thank heaven), or sort-of-mistakes-of-exaggeration -or -minimisation-to be criticised - the case is just to be presented with your own kind of fantasy & tellingness & beauty...... I am not quite sure I might have chosen some different women. And now it is just the 12.30 dinner time of the Antiquities & strange mentalities <One who is 80 used to smoke 100 cigs in a day. As soon as her mother died, she took to smoking & dancing at about 50. "Suppression", and there is another younger very odd case I shd say of suppression possibly> (you will feel sympathy, but not till my age) - when Lilian is sadly starved. <but I am having mine in a large balcony overlooking a garden with Indian [Ponds?] Lilian alone in the lounge>

Did you see enclosed? (I am so glad you wrote that letter for us about another Congress) - I am sadly afraid Leonard wont like it - nor things we have written.

    So much love to you both. Margaret [Llewelyn Davies]

Lilian's niece, Mary Chance, had a stall at a great GFS[6] Festival in Dorking -

& we actually looked in for a little while at the Sale part - & the opening by GFS Ladies - Oh dear -

---

*Enclosure missing*

*Margaret Llewelyn Davies (1861-1944) was General Secretary of the Women's Co-operative Guild. For reply see L6 250 (3412).*

[1] Katherine Arnold-Forster (née Cox) died on May 22 1938. She was married to Will Arnold-Forster and had a son, Mark. See *D5* 142-3.

[2] Janet Case died on July 15 1937.

[3] Lilian Harris (1866-1949) was friend and companion to Llewelyn Davies. She was Assistant Secretary of the Women's Co-operative Guild.

[4] Mary Kingsley (1862-1900) was an anthropologist and travel writer, author of *Travels in West Africa* (1897) and *West African Studies* (1899).

[5] G. M. Young's review of *Three Guineas* appeared in *The Sunday Times*, June 19 1938.

[6] The Girls' Friendly Society.

24
Typed
June 24, 1938

*County Borough of Warrington*
*Municipal Library*

*John McAdam, F.L.A.,*          *Museum Street,*
*Chief Librarian*                *24th June 1938*
*Telephone No. 873*

Dear Madam,
    I have just read your recent book "Three Guineas" with enjoyment and interest. My interest was not unnaturally aroused by your repeated references to the fact that biographies and other books referred to by you can be obtained in public libraries and the statement on p.161 that "as paid for education is still raw and young, and as the number of those allowed to enjoy it at Oxford and Cambridge is still strictly limited, culture for the great majority of educated men's daughters must still be that which is acquired outside the sacred gates, in public libraries or in private libraries, whose doors by some unaccountable oversight have been left unlocked." These statements will give all who read them a much better opinion of public libraries than a statement of

Mr. H.G. Wells, who, in a talk published in "The Listener" on December 22nd, 1937 said "There are public libraries, of course, where you can wait for books for quite a long time".

Now it happens that members of the Warrington Municipal Library do not have to wait a long time for books. They can obtain almost any book they require in a very short time and it is my desire that more and more people should take advantage of the service offered to them. I also endeavour to stimulate interest in the new books added to the library in a variety of ways. One of the most useful of these methods is the regular production of a list of new books entitled "Book News" a copy of which I enclose.

Now as you have expressed your opinion that culture can be acquired in public libraries I should exteem it a very great favour if you would kindly express this opinion at greater length in a future issue of "Book News". Five thousand copies of each number are distributed freely at our issue counter, but I feel sure that if you would contribute an introduction, one, two or three pages in length to our next issue early in September, it would be reprinted by the local press and reach a much wider public. Probably 40,000 -50,000 people would read your words in this locality.

You would, of course, be given complete liberty to draw attention to any book or books you might deem worthy of special notice and I should include in the number a list of your own works.

May I hope, Madam, that you will consider my request favourably, and that I may expect a reply in the enclosed envelope in the near future.[1]

                Yours faithfully,
                John McAdam
                Chief Librarian.

Mrs. Virginia Woolf,
    52, Tavistock Square,
        LONDON. W.C.1.

---

*Enclosure missing*

*Published courtesy of Jean Brocklehurst, daughter of John McAdam.*

*John McAdam served in the First World War, rising to the rank of Major, but suffering severe heart and lung damage from gas exposure. After the war, when his health improved, he resumed his post at the Warrington Library. His work there included fifteen years as Deputy Librarian and twenty-seven years as Chief Librarian and clerk to the committee.*

[1] There is no evidence that Woolf ever wrote such an introduction.

**25**
**Handwritten**
**June 25, 1938**

---

*Cranford,*
*Christ Church Road,*
*Cheltenham.*
*June 25th 1938*

My dear Virginia,

    I am going to be in town next week at the Condray Club, 20 Cavendish Square. It would be a great pleasure to see you - If you are free, would you come to tea on Thursday? - and would you think 4.15 too early?-

    I am reading "Three Guineas" & am full of admiration - It is very fine, and if I may say so, - so sincere. All those who care, must feel grateful to you for writing it, - certainly I do.

                  Yours affect.
                  Margery Snowdon

---

*Margery Snowdon (1878-1966) was a friend whom Vanessa met during life drawing classes at the Royal Academy of Art.*

**26**
**Handwritten**
**July 2, 1938**

---

*Telephone 567.*                                                                    *Parkwern,*
                                                                              *Pembroke Road,*
                                                                                *Sevenoaks.*

                                                                                        2.vii.38.

Dear Mrs. Woolf

    My proper feeling, not to bother you with another letter, would have been proof against anything but the delightful irony of my 'more important work'! - not irony in the writer, but the sense of it in the recipient! I was lunching with Emmeline Pethick-Lawrence on Thursday: she had now read *Three Guineas*, & has written you! We had a little uprorious text slinging - choice bits from the book: I leading with the Judge's remarks.

    I can picture the 'bristling' - & of course plenty of the tedious complainants, like Renée Haynes (I think that's the name) in todays <u>Time and Tide</u>.[1]

Then there's G M Young in the <u>Sunday Times</u>! ( I do wonder if you will hear from Baldwin - it will tickle him to death I'm sure)
  Of course its a tremendously shrewd thrust, & you will be prepared for the bludgeon & the rapier in the retorts.
  With much admiration & respect.
    Yours sincerely
     A G Sayers
I hope you had a good refreshing time in that land of delights, indicated by Spean Bridge.

---

*Published courtesy of D. M. Sayers.*

*The reference to Spean Bridge indicates that this is a reply to a letter from Woolf which has not survived. Woolf was vacationing in Spean Bridge at the end of June 1938.*
*See also L6 363 (3558) for a later letter from Woolf to Sayers, thanking him for sending his son, A. M. Sayers', book of poetry* Poems of Twenty Years, *privately printed in 1939. Sayers' letter to Woolf about the poetry has not survived. In Woolf's reply she hopes that his son is not "darkened" by the war, writing: "We, as publishers, are hoping that people must read."*

[1] Renée Haynes defended *Three Guineas* in *Time and Tide* on July 2 1938 after an unsigned note had criticized the book on June 25 1938.


**27**
**Handwritten**
**July 4, 1938**

            16 Clarendon Rd
            Cambridge.

4.7.38.

Dear Mrs Woolf.
  I have just read Three Guineas & enjoyed it enormously. Thank you very much for sending it to me; it was awfully kind of you.
  I wish you hadn't let the Newnham treasurer off quite so lightly; I should have thought even bazaars and keeping in with the senate left a certain amount of stretch. But perhaps it is better to hustle a few more girls into Newnham as it is, than run risks of university boycott, by altering it, though alas it isn't as if the dons saw the matter in this way at all; I liked your half pretending that they did!
  I think partly why my generation are such shocking slack feminists is because the forces are divided, our own dons side to some extent with the oppressors, and our energies are sidetracked into nagging at them, instead of

both working to get more women's colleges etc. Three Guineas does bring home how bad things are in every field for us; the trouble is that each profession now has to work on its own; women doctors can't do much for typists.

I wish I thought as you do that free women would mean no war. I can't visualise women ever acting together to prevent it, no matter how educated and independent they were. Except, of course, in the same way as men, through political organisations.

I was very pleased because my husband who isn't much of a feminist looked at Three Guineas and is now going round repeating its stories in horror. Every man and every woman who hasn't come across sex-barriers should be presented with a copy at 18.

I wish you would write an article on Newnham's attitude to marriage. It combines the stinginess both of poverty with the resentment of the unmarried. It is a great shame & disgrace.

If you ever have a spare moment on one of your Cambridge visits we should be delighted to see you.

    Yours sincerely
    Margaret Paul.

---

*Margaret Paul went on to become an economist, lecturing at St. Hilda's College, Oxford, and University College London; from 1969 she was Tutor, Fellow and Emeritus Fellow at Lady Margaret Hall, Oxford.*

28
**Typed**
**July 4, 1938**

---

    *Carradale House,*
    *Carradale, Argyll.*
    *Telephone 34.*

July 4th
Dear Virginia Woolf
  Thankyou so much for your letter, which goes far, I think, to clear up what worried me. It looks as if there were going to be an interesting argument brewing in Time and Tide.[1] I think what Renee Haynes writes is from very much my point of view (except that she is a Christian), though differently expressed. Obviously what bothered us both was the "indifference"; prhaps it is a word which has wrong connotations and should have something else substituted for it.

  I get back from h re at the end of the week (it is rather a good place to work in - at any rate it has a different set of interruptions from London!), and perhaps in the week after I might come and see you, possibly in the middle of the day, as I am apt to get very tired in the evenings these days. I should very much like to.

Joan Easdale[2] has been staying with me, and has re-started on poetry, which is a good thing. Like so many of us, she has been discouraged by the gang of young men who run the poetry racket just now, and needs a lot of encouraging. I think her x long epic poem, Amber Innocent, is extraordinarily good; but that may be that I have seen so much of it's birth. She's a remarkable young woman, anyhow: a bit mad, but then so is everyone who is poetically sensitive. She is lazy too, or perhaps it is that she does things slowly, and apparently can't learn to spell; I spend my time poking and pinching her and making her get on. She's worth taking trouble about.

Yours sin<br>Naomi Mitchison

---

[1] See Letter 26, Note 1.

[2] The Hogarth Press supported the young poet Joan Adeney Easdale's work during the 1930s, publishing *A Collection of Poems, Written Between the Ages of 14 and 17* (1931) and *Clemence and Clare* (1932) in their Hogarth Living Poets Series (Nos. 19 and 23) and then publishing *Amber Innocent* in 1939 (see *L6* 365). Easdale married James Meadows Rendel, grandson of Lytton Strachey's eldest sister and nephew of Woolf's doctor, Elinor Rendel. See *D5* 180 where Woolf notes she must write to Easdale about the marriage.


**29**
**Handwritten**
**July 5, 1938**

Broomcroft<br>Ford Lane<br>Didsbury, Manchester 20<br>Telephone: Didsbury 3368

My dear Virginia,

You then, have noticed that I carefully ration my visits to you - once in six months - because, since you invariably let me come whenever I suggest doing so, the responsibility of not straining your hospitality is on me. But I feel that I can't wait until the Autumn before discussing some of the many points that "Three Guineas" raises, so I am therefore going to suggest, tentatively, that I might perhaps come this month? I shall be in London on Thursday July 14th & again on the 21st & free in the afternoons. But I expect many people are clamouring to discuss "Three Guineas" so I shall quite understand if you can't fit us all in - Also, I have a confession to make.

I am not a complete outsider because, I am just finishing training as an Air Warden. Whilst I agree certainly with you in repudiating any responsibility for the present state of the world, I feel, that if war does come I should prefer to be looking after people rather than to be one of those who had to be looked after. Up to the present my training has had the effect of making me doubt if we ought to risk war under <u>any</u> circumstances - which would mean ~~that~~ I suppose - that I must become a supporter of N. Chamberlain & his policy of letting the dictators do what they like - in Spain, to the Jews & the socialists - However if - as is possible - you feel that I have so far fallen short of the standard of the League of Outsiders - which I admit is the case - that our friendship must cease, I shall acquiesce though with much sorrow. A friend, to whom I sent a copy of Three Gs wrote "It is not a book but an experience" and she is right.

      Yours Shena D Simon

July 5
It was good of you to make time to write to me.

---

*Published courtesy of Professor Brian Simon, Baron of Wythenshawe.*

**30**
**Handwritten**
**July 7, 1938**

Guainville, le 7, 7, 1938
  (7 Juillet 1938)

Madame,

  Merci de votre lettre du 3 juillet, merci aussi de bien vouloir prêter attention à ce que je désire soumettre à votre jugement. Je n'ai pas encore lu "Three Guineas", mais je vais me le procurer.

  Ma lettre est confidentielle, Madame, car je n'ai pas encore toute la liberté pour publier mes souvenirs, mais vous pouvez les utiliser.

  Je laisse de côté les problèmes qui touchent à la Paix. Vous les connaissez mieux que moi.

  Je me forcerai à vous faire un bref récit de mes expériences, de mes observations, puis de conclure par ce qui me parait un moyen de retarder la catastrophe.

  1. En 1931 et en 1932, j'étais à Genève. Je fréquentais le milieu de la P. d. N, mon mari était Sous-directeur, puis Directeur du Bureau Japonais auprès de la P.d.N. J'ai pu me rendre compte comment la Conférence du Désarmement fut sabotée, puis achetée, par les puissances de la métallurgie des

différents pays et des différents continents. Les employés des Banques de Genève, nous ont même divulgué les sources exactes des chèques destinés aux différentes délégations de la Conférence.

2. En hiver 1931, pendant le premier conflit Euro-Japonais, je fis à Genève cette expérience personnelle: connaissant un moyen d'arranger une difficile entente entre deux grandes puissances, France et Japon, j'écrivis loyalement à Briand, pour lui demander une entrevue. Une personne de confiance lui remit ma lettre. à lui seul, il était couché vers 11 heures du soir.Il me répondit qu'il me recevrait le lendemain matin. Mais le lendemain matin, un de ses collaborateurs, à qui il avait du parler, en empêcha.. Il est toujours au Quai d'Orsay. Les vues étaient différentes, de plus il avait une légère rancune contre moi.

Vous savez le reste sur l'échec de la politique de Briand vis à vis de la Conférence du Désarmement et je sais des détails historiques les plus touchants.

3. Ensuite, à Genève, je fis une sorte de croisade, auprès de ceux que je connaissais, délégués ou journalistes en leur disant: "Pourquoi ne faites-vous pas un petit livre, très simple, le même texte en plusieurs langues. Il instruirait les peuples, si vous penser ainsi désarmer moralement?"----- Il me fut répondu: "Mais les peuples ne voudraient plus se battre."(sic)-----Je leur dis alors: "Nauriez-vous pas atteint votre but?--- Voilà pour mon expérience 1932, de Genève.

4. Une personnalité de la Révolution Bolchévique, que j'interrogeais me dit: " Toute propagande pacifiste est inutile, il faut mettre les peuples devant le fait accompli."

5. Aux hommes politiques français, qui font professions d'être des pacifistes sincères, j'ai eu le courage de dénoncer ceux qui empêchent une vraie politique de rapprochement entre les nations très intéressées en Europe, écrivant que telle ou telle personne, à tel poste, jouait un rôle oculte, servant les intérêts des munitionnaires de guerre. J'ai reçu cette lettre: " Nous prenons bonne note de votre letttre, Mais rien ne fut changé.

Devant la mauvaise foi et le manque de sincérité total, je ne crois plus que dans ces hommes. Les uns vendus, les autres intéressés, les autres ignorants. Les masses n'ont ni le temps, ni le désir, ni le discernement pour s'éduqueer et se sauver. C'est une tâche de l'avenir.

6. Comme les peuples, après 1914-1918C ne se battraient plus pour un drapeau ou une frontière, on a crée ce prétexte de lutte sociale: Fascisme-Bolschévisme, qui est une pure hypocrisie.

Il faut reconnaître que les pacifistes et les idéalistes sont vaincus d'avance, leurs scrupules les empêchent d'employer les moyens d'actions qui conduisent au succès.

7e. Il me paraît rester une dernière, faible chance de retarder la catastrophe, ce qui aiderait à préparer des plans nouveaux. Mettre les gouvernements devant cette constatation queles peuples ne sont pas prêts à se battre; en proposant un "Plébiscite de la mort" dans plusieurs pays, ou en parlerait dans tous.

"Devant le drame de l'Espagne sacrifiée nous demandons aux hommes, aux femmes et aux enfants de décider de leur sorts, par le ....., s'ils veulent être anéantis sous la guerre totale, ou organiser un refus passif à cette expérience."

Je crois que cela serait excellent pour les esprits, les gouvernements et les intéressés à la guerre.

Ensuite, il serait nécessaire, que les grands pays qui n'ont plus de visées territoriales, s'ils ont un intérêt et un désir de paix, mettent dans leurs négociations diplomatiques et politiques, les conditions de désarmement moral des pays de dictatures en l'échange des avantages et des concessions à obtenir. Voici, Madame, le résumé très simple des réflexions de plusieurs années de lutte inutile. Je ne développerai pas plus loin, car le plus difficile est dans l'organisation d'une mobilisation des esprits contre la guerre qui approche.

J'ai abusé de votre temps, mais vous comprendrez tout mon désir de vous dire tout ceci.

Me permettez vous de vous envoyer mon travail littéraire, dans un prochain courrier? Ce serait un grand honneur et un grand réconfort pour moi, d'avoir votre critique.

Avec mon admiration, je vous prie de croire, Madame, en mes sentiments très sincères.

Andrée Ito.


July 7, 1938
Guainville


Dear Madam,

I would like to thank you for your letter dated July 3, as well as for giving special attention to what I would like you to reflect on. I have not yet read "Three Guineas", but I am going to obtain a copy.

My letter is confidential, Madam, for I do not yet have complete freedom to publish my memoirs, but you may have use of them.

I am putting aside problems which concern Peace. You know them better than I do.

I will give you a brief account of my experiences, of my observations, then conclude with who seems to me to have a way of putting off the catastrophe.

1. In 1931 and 1932, I was in Geneva. I frequented the P.d.N.[1] milieu; my husband was Assistant Manager, and then Manager of the Japanese office with

the P.d.N. I was able to discover how the Disarmament Conference was sabotaged, then purchased, by the metallurgy authorities from different countries and different continents. The employees from the Banks of Geneva have even divulged to us the exact sources of the cheques intended for different delegations of the Conference.

2. In the winter of 1931, during the first Europe-Japan conflict, I had this personal experience in Geneva; knowing a way of sorting out a difficult arrangement between two major powers, France and Japan, I wrote loyally to Briand[2] to request an interview from him. A reliable person delivered my letter to him. By himself, he was asleep at around 11:00 at night. He told me that he would have me over the following morning. But the following morning, one of his colleagues, whom he was supposed to speak to, stopped him... He is still at the Quai d'Orsay. The views were different. What's more, he held a mild grudge against me.

You know the rest about the failure resulting from Briand's policy regarding the Disarmament Conference,[3] and I am aware of the most significant historical details.

3. Later, in Geneva, I embarked on a sort of crusade with the delegates and journalists I knew by telling them: "why don't you write a short book, very simple, the same text in several languages. It would instruct various people, if you think of this as morally disarming?" — He answered me : "But the peoples would no longer like to fight." (sic) — I then say to them: "Wouldn't you have reached your goal?" —— this is it for my 1932 experience in Geneva.

4. A personality from the Bolshevik Revolution, who was questioning me said: "All pacifist propaganda is useless, and we must put the people before the fait accompli."

5. To the French political men, who make it their profession to be sincere pacifists, I had the courage to denounce those who prevent a true policy involving the uniting of nations which are very interested in Europe, by writing that such and such a person, in such a position, was playing a secret role, serving the interest of multinationals of war. I received this letter: "We are taking note of your letter, but nothing changed.

In the face of bad faith and the lack of total sincerity, I no longer only belive in these men. Some corrupt, others interested, other ignorant. The masses have neither time, nor desire, nor the discernment to educate or save themselves. It is a blemish on the future.

6. Like the people, after 1914-1918 - would no longer fight for a flag or a border, a pretext of social struggle was created: Fascism, Bolshevism, which is pure hypocrisy.

One must recognize that pacifists and idealists were defeated in advance, their scruples preventing them from using means of action which would lead to success.

7. There seems to me to remain a last, weak chance to delay catastrophe, which would help in the preparation of new projects. By placing governments

before this observation, what people would not be ready to fight? By proposing a "Plebiscite of death" in several countries, one would speak about it everywhere.

"Before the drama of Spain, a sacrificed country, we ask men, women and children to decide their fates, by the (....), if they wish to be wiped out by total war, or organize a passive refusal to this experience."

I believe that this would be excellent for spirits, governments, and those interested in war.

Later, it would be necessary that the major countries which no longer have territorial designs, if they have interest and a desire for peace, include their diplomatic and political negotiations, the conditions of moral disarmament of countries governed under dictatorships, in exchange for advantages and concessions to be obtained. Here you have it, Madam, the very simple summary of reflections of two years of useless struggle. I will not continue my development any further, as the most difficult part is in the organization of a mobilization of spirits against the approaching war.

I have already taken enough of your time, but you will understand my desire to tell you all this.

Would you allow me to send you my literary piece in my next letter? It would be a great honour and a great comfort for me to have your critique.
Sincerely yours,
Andrée Ito.

---

*(Translation by Pierre-Eric Villeneuve)*

[1] This most likely refers to the Pacte des Nations, which founded the Societé des Nations (League of Nations) in 1919.

[2] Aristide Briand (1862-1932) was Prime Minister eleven times between 1906 and 1932 and held twenty six ministerial posts. He was known particularly for his support of the league of Nations, and for the Kellogg-Briand Pact (1928) which emphasized the renunciation of war as an instrument of national policy. He won the Nobel Peace Prize in 1926.

[3] The Disarmament Conference convened on 2 February 1932 with the aim of limiting the use of arms among the sixty nations involved, including the United States of America and the Soviet Union. Germany withdraw from the conference on 14 October 1933.

**31**
**Handwritten**
**July 12, 1938**

12.7.38

Mrs Virginia Woolf

Dear Madam
    In reading your most brilliant book Three Guineas, which will no doubt go to a second edition I found two small mistakes which you may desire to alter when reprinting.
    The four men blowing trumpets facing p.39 are not Heralds but trumpeters in (I think) the full dress of the Horse Guards. A Herald in full dress wears a tabard.
    On p. 248 you state that in 1871 married women were allowed to own their own property. Should this date not be 1882 when the first Married Women's Property Act was passed?[1]

                      Yours faithfully
                      David Freeman

---

[1] The Married Women's Property Act was passed in 1870 and amended in 1882.


**32**
**Handwritten**
**July 12, 1938**

Sidcot School
Winscombe
Somerset
12/7/38.

Dear Friend-
    In case you do not know, this is the Quaker method of address to a person whom one has not met.
    I have just finished your book "Three Guineas": hence this letter of appreciation. I'll try and keep from superlatives, but I sincerely believe its a book that should be read & digested by every thinking man & woman. Ever since I read "A Room of One's Own" its been on my list of books that I hand to boys and girls when they leave this school, & now "Three Guineas" will join that list I've underlined with a few others, like "Ends & Means".
    I would ask that you do your best to have a cheap edition published as soon as possible, that it may reach a wider public.

Even if you do no more writing & whenever life appears hard or drab, recall the fact that you have sent out into the world a book that will greatly help men & women of this & future generations to reach a sane vital & joyous life with the barriers of race etc broken down.

  Perhaps you may be interested to know that the writer of this letter - a former educational missionary in India is Senior Resident Master at this Quaker co-Educational School who is responsible for the "Scripture" teaching in the School. Naturally therefore he would have preferred a little more support to what he believes is the only fundamental foundation on which mankind can build a worldwide Commonwealth - the Jesus of the Gospels -.

  I expect you have so many letters of appreciation that I do not wish you to feel you must acknowledge this.

With renewed thanks<br>Yours sincerely<br>R.A.Harman Senr.

P.S. Excuse the form of this letter: written in convalescence in bed; your book has saved the situation of boredom in the last 48 hours.

---

*Published courtesy of I. A. (Bunty) Biggs, daughter of R. A. Harman.*

*After working in Gooty, South India, as headmaster of a school run by the London Missionary Society, Richard Ashbee Harman (1888-1978) returned to England in 1919 to take up a post at the Quaker run Sidcot School, Winscombe, Somerset. He remained there, becoming Senior Master, until 1948. Harman was an "explorer" in education, and a man whose Christian faith underpinned all aspects of his life, including his pacifism. His pacifist convictions led him to withhold the portion of his taxes that would be spent on armaments. His daughter recalls bailiffs collecting from the home such possessions as would make up the shortfall. See L6 255 for Woolf's comment to Ethel Smyth: "I've made some so furious: And then a Quaker or a governess makes up by thanking." This comment most likely refers also to Letter 35.*

**33**
**Handwritten**
**July 14, 1938**

Instone,<br>Pickersleigh Avenue,<br>Malvern Link,<br>Worcestershire.<br>July 14th 1938

Dear Mrs Virginia Woolf.

  Thank you very much for writing "Three Guineas". It is good to have these things said so well; one hopes to persuade one's friends of both sexes to read & ponder thereon.

You mention the London & National Society for Women's Service. I cannot dig up its address in the local library, so may I ask you to send it to me?
I will thank you now - then I need not worry you with another letter. May you long continue to point the way.
                Yours sincerely
                Margaret Amiss

---

*Published courtesy of Joan Smith, friend of Margaret Amiss.*

*Margaret Amiss lived at Instone as companion and adopted daughter to a Mr. and Mrs. Hyde until their deaths in 1949.*

---

**34**
**Typed**
**July 14, 1938**

---

Telephone: 2073                                    *Depot for the S.P.C.K.*[1]

*Charles E. Brumwell*
*Bookseller and Heraldic Stationer*
*Smart Stationery and Useful Presents : A Large*
*Selection of Theological Literature always in stock*
*Die Stamping executed on the premises from Customer's own Dies*
*under personal supervision*

*10 Broad Street: Hereford*

Mrs Virginia Woolf,                                 July 14th 1938
52 Tavistock Square,
London. W.C.1.

Dear Mrs Woolf,
      I am very grateful to you for your letter and for the signed copy of your book received this morning. You may be sure I shall value it. I quite realise that I shall infuriate some of my customers in suggesting your book to them but I am very happy to take that risk as I feel with you there are certain things they ought to know.

                Yours faithfully.
                C.E. Brumwell

---

[1] Society for Promoting Christian Knowledge.

**35**
**Handwritten**
**July 15, 1938**

---

*Tel: Reigate 874*  *The County School for Girls,*
*Reigate,*
*Surrey.*
*15.July. 1938*

**Dear Madam,**
    My Governors and everyone belonging to this school would be most honoured and glad if by any lucky chance you would consent to come down and present the prizes in the Autumn term.[1]

    I have read Three Guineas and noted your veto of Speech Days, and I know that this may seem an impertinent request; but I should be so pleased if it were acceded to, that I am willing to risk making it. I think you might rather like your audience; they are humble - in the good sense - & very appreciative, & don't want platititudes. One of our happiest memories - and saddest - is the address Winifred Holtby gave us not long before she died, when she spoke, in a different way, on many of the things you seem to care for most.

    We generally have our Speech Day on a Wednesday evening in November or early December. If you can spare time, and are willing to spare it, I can send you some dates to choose from. I don't dare to do that yet!

    Please forgive me for taking up your time with this letter; and, if you feel it needs forgiveness, my venturing to send you this request.
              Yours faithfully,
               Jean Aitken.

---

*See Note to Letter 32.*

[1] There is no evidence that Woolf attended a Speech Day at the school.

**36**
**Handwritten**
**July 17, 1938**

20 Puller Road
Barnet
Herts.
17/vii/38.

Dear Madam

I have been reading your book "Three Guineas" with the very greatest interest, and should like to be allowed to write and say what encouragement I receive from your idea of the Society of Outsiders, to which I may claim, I think, to belong. I have always realised dimly, what Archimedes realised in the mechanical sphere, that if you want to move the world, you must be in a position external to it. Some of us who, conscious of having no money and no position, have felt that we were powerless to alter anything, may certainly take courage from your book to believe that we are just the very people who can alter things.

I wonder whether you would be interested (or not) to hear of two ways (among others) in which, as a member of the Society of Outsiders, I work to promote my own aims (though of course they may not be quite your own aims).

For the last four years I have been carrying on in my own person a crusade for equal sunbathing rights for women and men. For three years at a place called Sandy Bay, near Exmouth, and last year at Bognor, I went to the beach which was crowded with people (Boy Scouts, Girl Guides, family parties) and there sunbathed for hours at a time, stripped to the waist as the men do. My experiences in the campaign have been, some unpleasant, others surprisingly encouraging, and in either case illuminating. I have never yet been to the part of the seafront below the promenade where police are on the spot, and so far I have never been spoken to by a police officer. But if I ever am, I shall point to the crowds of men sitting round doing the same thing, and shall say that as we have to put up with them (some of them far from beautiful, covered with hair & so on), they can well be expected to put up with us.

Thousands of people must have seen me at one time and another, but not a word of this sort of adventure ever gets into the papers. Why?

Secondly, I have for years protested openly at the time and by letter, against the habit which bus conductors have of putting, or trying to put, their hands on women as they get on and off the buses. Sometimes when you are half way down the bus, you feel a patronising (and generally very dirty) hand on your back. After I had written on several occasions to the office of the L.P.T.B. in Broadway,[1] I was asked to go up and see two of the controlling officials there & explain my idea. They were both very polite, though I think quite unconverted, for they said, and I was obliged to agree with them, that most women like these attentions from bus conductors. However, I made it quite clear to them that if I was the only woman, among the millions of women who travel by bus, who objected to any attempts by bus conductors to put their hands on me, I was perfectly entitled to object and intended to persevere in doing so.

Of course, I realise that these particular efforts may seem to you a mere waste of time. I have known lots of feminists (I dont dislike the word, as you seem to do), and I think it is a very disheartening experience to find how they all want different things, or seem to. But I have no doubt that it is all working out to some good end when everyone will be satisfied.

Hoping very much that you will at any rate forgive my writing.
        I am yours faithfully
        (Miss) R. Ranken.

---

[1] The head office of the London Passenger Transport Board, in Broadway, St. James' Park, London.

**37**
**Handwritten**
**July 18, 1938**

                                          128 Crofton Rd.
                                          Orpington
                                          Kent
                        £3.3.0        18/7/38

Dear Madam,
        You probably realise that by virtue of your (literary) seniority the newspaper lords have now given orders to reviewers that your work must be treated with respect. This is an old English custom. Accordingly your last work has been praised but obviously not read.

        May I suggest, with deference, that you get some brutal minded opponent to read it & criticise it. In its present form, its disingenuousness, apparent suppression of facts & cheerful acceptance of unverified statements do ill service to the cause you have at heart.

        I will give one instance of the last named fault.

        You quote, time after time, Ray Strachey's "& £250 a year is quite an achievement for a highly qualified woman with years of experience."

        This is untrue.

        According to the Chancellor of the Exchequer salaries in the Civil Service are equal to those paid by a good employer outside - not necessarily the best employer but a good employer. My own knowledge of the labour market supports this view.

        Now the lowest class of woman employee in the Service who can be called, by any stretch of imagination, "highly qualified" is the clerical officer. She enters from a secondary school at 17 years of age. Her salary goes up to

£280 automatically without promotion. Higher clerical posts (up to £420) & staff officer posts (up to £525) are filled from the ranks of these women (there is no separate entry).

Women who enter from Universities, the only ones who really come within the "highly qualified" category, start at £275 & go to £940. They cannot fail to reach £540 - but higher salaries are available on promotion.

                     Yours truly
                     G.H. Bosworth

Mrs. Virginia Woolf
c/o The Hogarth Press
52 Tavistock Sq.
WC1

---

*See D5 157 (July 19 1938) for comment: "Abusive or sneering letters the last 2 days."*

**38**
**July 23, 1938**

---

Letter from Vita Sackville-West
Published in *The Letters of Vita Sackville-West to Virginia Woolf* (London: Hutchinson, 1984: 442) (NY: William Morrow and Company, 1985: 414-15).

---

*Vita writes: "I had never for a moment questioned your facts or their accuracy in 3 guineas, but only disagreed in some places with the deductions you drew from them." In particular, Vita disagrees with Woolf's argument about women's opposition to war, finding that "many women are extremely bellicose." For Woolf's reply see L6 258 (3424).*

**39**
**Handwritten**
**July 25, 1938**

*Broomcroft*
*Ford Lane*
*Didsbury, Manchester 20*
*Telephone: Didsbury 3368*

My dear Virginia

Here are two cuttings to add to your collection. I am sorry that I didn't get the date of the Archbishops. On rereading the Times Leader I begin to wonder if the writer was being humourous after all, but it was the first & not the third leader.[1] & the rest of it was as pompous & serious as always -

Mary Clark, the headmistress of the Manchester High School for girls told me the other day that she was going to use Three Guineas as her Bible - as she is a deeply religious woman, I realized how strongly she felt about it, and though I don't think she agrees with everything you say - however that would be her attitude to the bible also, [       ]

      Yours Shena D Simon

Don't bother to acknowledge this.
July 25th

---

*Enclosures*

Published courtesy of Professor Brian Simon, Baron of Wythenshawe.

[1] See Letter 11.

**The Primate's Hope**

"I may be addressing a girl who will become the first woman Prime Minister," said the Archbishop of Canterbury at St. Margaret's, Bushey, Herts, yesterday.

"But," he went on, "I earnestly and devoutly hope I am not addressing the first woman archbishop. The best business and greatest industry in the world for a woman is the making of a good home."

*News Chronicle -*

corresponds with modern needs.

The Lower House of the Southern Province spent long hours in a debate about deaconesses —their status, their privileges, the character of their ministry, and even their dress. On the whole the temper of the House was against making the concessions demanded, partly because some of those who championed the claims of deaconesses were known to be eager for a feminine priesthood. But it was recognized that deaconesses might officiate at church services of a non-sacramental kind in the absence of the clergyman, and with the consent of the Bishop and incumbent. An amendment to restrict their ministry to occasions when the congregation consists of women and children only was defeated by a small majority. Perhaps this was as well. It would be unfortunate, for instance, if a deaconess officiating at a week-day evensong had begun the service—having carefully ascertained that only a few women were present—and was then compelled to come to a sudden stop because an unpunctual male had appeared in one of the pews. There is no doubt at all that deaconesses in many places are doing work of high value. But there is considerable doubt whether the best of them desire to become clergywomen instead of laywomen. It may be added with some confidence that, whether rightly or wrongly, the majority of educated women do not wish to listen habitually to women preachers.

A question of long standing among Churchpeople is the right method of selecting the diocesan Bishops. In theory the existing system, despite its antiquity, is open to obvious objections. It is anomalous that the spiritual head of a diocese should be nominated by a Prime Minister irrespective of his creed. It is anomalous that a Dean and Chapter should then be invited to select a Bishop, but only after being supplied with the name of the man whom they must choose. Yet, like other anomalies, the system on the whole works extremely well,

**40**
**Handwritten**
**July 30, 1938**

July 30. 1938.

*Telephone: Holborn 7087.*  *From Mrs. Pethick-Lawrence*
*Telegrams "Pethlawro-Holb.London.*  *11 Old Square,*
　*Lincoln's Inn, W.C.2*

Dear Mrs Woolf.
　　May I express my great appreciation of your book <u>Three Guineas</u> which I have read & re-read with delight & which I shall keep at hand for references. I note that in one review it is hailed as likely to inaugurate a new era: and I agree with this opinion: for the greatest of all world-changing influences is thought: and you have brought to bear upon the present state of society an exposition of thought and fact that is unanswerable. I am specially glad that you have made so close a connection between the economic & cultural position of women and the problem which is at present preoccupying the mind of the great mass of the people - how to avoid the menace of war which threatens to destroy us all. I rejoice in the immense influence that you possess in the world of literature and thought.

　　　　　　　　　　　　Yours sincerely
　　　　　　　　　　　　Emmeline Pethick Lawrence
The illustrations are a work of genius - simply delicious!
I think the enclosed paragraph cut from this month's Bulletin of the Women's Freedom League will interest you.

*Enclosure missing*

*See Letter 14 n.2 for biographical information.*

**41**
**Typed**
**August 1, 1938**

Mrs. Virginia Woolf;
63 Marsh Lane, Stanmore, Middlesex.
First August, 1938

Dear Madam,

I have read "Three Guineas" with very great pleasure. The book is certainly worth the amount stated in its title! It is brilliant in technique, amusing in an attractively mordant way; it shows great research. The illustrations are, in modern parlance, "a perfect scream."

BUT…..(of course there is a 'but') Are you not a little too Olympian in your attitude? As the book stands, it is a most severe indictment, making us mortals look the veriest fools (as of course we often are) But there is a method in our madness, which You seem to fail to see. You cannot descend perhaps from your Olympian hieghts to the level of the street

Now I also am an idealist. For the last fifty years I have cherished advanced thought. I was a suffragist at twenty. I have always preached the rightness of woman's claims. But I do seek always to see the other side. And I do feel that you so often overlook it.

Whereas you make Man's opposition to Woman's claims to seem like a piece of the most abject folly, the thing that you overlook, surely, is the economic aspect. It was not really a matter of sexual opposition. (Though it often looked as if it were). It was at base an objection to the coming of a new & powerful rival into the labour market. In fact it was intrinsically the same as the Californian Labourers objection to the incoming of "Cheap Chinese Labour" (see Bret Harte)[1]

When I was a youth, City firms employed male corresponding clerks who were probably married, with families, at a salary of say £3 per week. Then came women typists, ready to do equally good work at a salary of 30/- a week. If the clerk who lost his job said:--

A woman's place|is in the home"
that was not sex domination, but an attempt to hold on to his job.

Form your Olympian point of view I quite agree with you. The woman has a right to enter the labour market if she chooses. But surely you have some little sympathy with the poor devil who lost his job? We must be human, you know, even if our favourite resort is Olympus.

Whitman (whom I adore) says "As if it harmed me, giving others the same chances & rights as myself"[2] and he is entirely right IF our civilisation were an ideal democracy and not a muddled scramble. As things stood, it certainly harmed the male correspondence clerk to lose his job to a woman who undercut him. It would not be the slightest use to tell him he had not been harmed. Obviously he had been.

Take again the case of a medical G.P. who is in the habit of getting a fee of 7/6 per visit, on which he keeps a wife & three children. An unmarried lady doctor comes into the district and charges a fee of 5/- per visit. Down go the male doctor's receipts.

If he then says: — "Women should not be doctors, their nervous systems are too highly strung for such a trying profession" he really means: —— "What the hell made that woman come here to diminish my legitimate profits." His son, who is qualifying at the University says:——
"We men students must boycott those damned women."
But it is not a case of Man versus Woman. It is sheer economic rivalry, intensified by the woman's habit of working for a lower fee.

Of course the ideal is; - Equal pay for equal work PLUS a really adequate family allowance. I have often lectured upon Miss Rathbone's excellent Family Allowance proposals.[3] But till we get a sane system and as long as economic rivalry is sharp between the man & the woman, anomalies must be expected.

Page 133 you quote Churchill as ~~a~~saying that the brain of modern man does not differ 'in essentials' from that of the "Human beings who fought and loved here millions of years ago."

What rubbish. Were there any H man beings "millions of years ago"? I think not. Man, recognisable as Man can hardly reach back even one million years, and the brain of the man of ~~1?000~~ 1,000,000 years ago must have differed in the most important particulars from the brain of modern man. What he means by "essentials" I do not know. It sounds like the politicians' favorite type of vague phrase that may be made to mean anything.

Education. Of course you & I, standing on Olympus, can agree that the girl should have ~~the same education as the boy~~ as good an education as the boy. But come down into the street, and it looks different. A freind of mine, a not too rich professional man had two girls and two boys and at some sacrifice to himself he educated all for professions.

The two girls each married at Twenty-one, never using that training. The two boys will support themselves by their jobs for at least forty years.

As things are, not on Olympus but in the street, a boy's education is a gild edged security, a girl's is a highly speculative venutre.

Here again I agree throughly with you in principle but I see the practical difficulty; and forgive my saying that I wish you had shown a ~~more~~ greater readiness to realise that the earth dweller does not find it quite as simple as the dweller on Olympus may imagine.

Forgive me, again, but you seem to depart from your usual black-and-white clearness of exposition on page 100 etc. "The wife's salary is half the husband's income." Indeed? Who is to pay rent, taxes, food bills, light, heat, children's education? Do they pool these and pay half each? Then at that rate the wife has half the surplus after these bills are paid? Supposing the man is a barrister earning 40,000 a year, & the family lives luxuriously on £16,000 a year; then according to you he should give her £12,000 a year after keeping her in supreme luxury! Forgive my asking Why the hell should he? Are you acting as the giddy gold-diggers' best friend? You don't even stipulate that ~~he~~ she need prove to be a good wife to him. Simply that she has a "spiritual right" to £12,000 a year. (Words fail me here.) "Because her own work is unpaid." I only wish my own work were unpaid on similar terms.

Actually I quite agree that this question of relative shares of man and wife remains a jumble. But it works out better than it seems. No man would like to be thought mean towrds his wife, anyway.

Coming to earth, I find cases where all is, fair, cases where the man may be claiming more than he should, cases where the woman certainly claims more than she should.

I remember one case where the woman married into a richer family than her own. She immediately began to claim, ask, wheedle, coax, obtain far more than her legitimate share. She was ~~I~~ always well dressed. He went shabby.

The man's old father, not really a rich man, was so vexed to see his son so shabby that he scraped up & gave the young man five guineas for his birthday "to buy yourself a new suit."

Weeks passed but that suit was not forth-coming. The wife had scrounged the money for a new dress for herself.

You say that the wife can't be getting her fair share because she has not "money to spend upon such causes as appeal to her." But then has the man money to spend on ~~£L~~ £10,000 pearl necklaces, such as one sees have been stolen from rich women? The wife who ge~~a~~ts money from her man may prefer to spend it on her back, neck or fingers. Perhaps that low-down thought does not occur to you Olympians. I don't find you convincing here.

I am not a rich man, nor do I mix with the rich. Among the persons with whom I mix, people of moderate incomes, I should certainly not say that the man takes more than his share. I could however tell you a few perfectly true tales of Gold-diggers.

I am absolutely in favour of a motherhood allowance for women. Further than that it might be very difficult to go until & unless we completely overhaul our very unsatisfactory capitalistic system. This is bound to come. But when?

Page 314. Surely Mr. Gerhardi does not mean this seriously?[4] He is a wag!

It only remains for me to thank you~~m~~ again & very sincerely for a very stimulating & interesting book.

Yours very truly William Platt.

---

[1] (Francis) Bret Harte (1836-1902) was a writer who moved to California in 1854 where he became the editor of two Californian literary magazines, the *Californian* and the *Overland Monthly*. Platt is most likely referring here to Harte's poem "Plain

Language from Truthful James" (1870) often known as "The Heathen Chinee," which is about Chinese immigration to America.

[2] From "Thought," *Complete Poetry and Prose*, Vol. I: 260. Woolf quotes this passage in *Three Guineas*, Part 3, Note 49.

[3] Eleanor Rathbone (1872-1946) was on the Executive Committee of the National Union of Women's Suffrage Societies and she became an M. P. in 1929. She campaigned for the introduction of Family Allowances and wrote *The Disinherited Family* on this subject, among others, in 1924.

[4] *Three Guineas*, Part 3, Note 18.

**42**
**Typed**
**August 14, 1938**

34 Woodstock Rd<br>OXFORD<br>14.8.38

Dear "Virginia Woolf,"

I cannot but so call you, for your book – Three guineas – has gripped me, fascinated me by the depth of thought that must have preceded it and the experiences that must have brought it to birth.

The part of my identity I will reveal, is that I was at one time organizer and speaker for the W.S.P.U.. was born in the educated class, am favoured as a single woman with small competency..not professional, but find deep interest in metaphysical study. Therefore your searching analysis of the status quo of our sex comes as timely.... presenting points for metaphysical uptake of moment.

Militancy served the purpose of shocking atrophied thought into activity, like breaking the surface of a Rock. Its reactions are largely hidden, but still at work through perhaps more to be discerned by such as I, given as we were unparalleled opportunity to sound the depths of false dominance by personal experience with the background of Publicity. Indeed the word "feminist" has become oldfashioned, and well so, for a broader one awaits coining, as do others that should fill language gaps where feminine outlook is concerned.

Thank you for the stress you have laid on "passing by on the other side" in expected orthodox services to men. I have been gradually taking this line as regards the League of Nations Branch here, having gained a flash of insight at a large male Undergraduates Dinner here –At questions, I asked Chairman –none other than Sir Gilbert Murray[1]- what service women could best concentrate on for Peace..meaning to feel his pulse as to the tireless efforts of women bombarding the League with mass petitions etc. "Help the local Branch" came back, almost with a snap...Ruminating afterwards at his slickness in reply (he had earlier spoken derogatively of certain women who had sought to too soon intrude in clearing the aftermath horrors of war in

Serbia,...... I felt clearly that to continue to be the hewers of wood and drawers of water for the League of Nations, was to indirectly encourage the male ascendency that is the essential of warfare, is part and parcel of it...a wilful refusal of the purging agency of woman..which I deemessential to its cessation....in fact such service can be seen as encouragement to war.
When the subscription toward the male organiser is due, one result of your book will be that I shallwrite in explanation of non-subscription, financial and in membership on your proposed lines..which were indeed simmering for expression in my own thought. I trust my withdrawal will be dignified, with no waste of words, in the spirit of "As long as we women will be hacks, we may". Withdrawal without a grain of resentment, as skilfully made outsiders or of censure, done in wholesale way, would be as a mental stiletto.......bring rightful perspective, and the stern necessity to be their own hewers and drawers.

The greatest amazement on working for W.S.P.U. was their refusal to depend on men save as adjuncts..It proved the only wisdom possible, and this policy of going forward as women independently should be of equal value now,. They must sooner or later bow to our insight in common with their own, and this is obviously the short cut.

Woman as the last creation is undoubtedly the most complete, the highest. When women realise this, without a shade of vanity, but in gratitude to the Creator, conscious of their responsbility, and seize the necessary uptake in their own way apart from men"s organisations where war is concerned, determined never to encourage it by admiration of its honours, or of militarism, or of soldiers; to discount its trappings..to see beyond the so-called cleanness of the sword, they will be doing a dynamic work for Peace.

Rightly seen women are not "dependents" but made so in prevention of their being known as "ascendents". Men as men are cursed with pugilistic tendencies. See films with male casts...one can be sure they will present fights. Thus they need to be saved from themselves. Women are doing the wrong thing in this matter...They should do the opposite. Give up pleading, trying to influence....and hold themselves superior to services of subservience.

Deliberate planning as against women"s influence is obvious, although secretly devised. Men fear women most definitely..and well they may, for they are resting on assumed superiority, which is being challenged more and more.

Women need to pull up the Press, by reminding Editors, that they have women readers who take grave exception to false dominances and sex ascendencies. I make it one of my missions so to do. As I see things, the kernel of war insanity is THOUGHT. If war were out of thought it would not be engineered. Armaments must first be thought. Metaphysically all is Mind and its manifestation. We all have our metaphysics We live by them........Peaceful thought must mean PEACE Warlike thought must mean WAR. Thought is the regenerating Power.. By its side words and acts appear as but vassals. I strive daily to cast out consciously any <true> reality from sex-dominion thought, and rely on the Truth thought of spiritual Unity upholding equality in diversity. Unity in Duity between the sexes. Thus sitting in ones chair at one"s writing desk, one can set going thought force that claimed as linked to invisible forces of Truth and Love can "move mountains" of oppression and false dominance. I love the words "Of the increase of His kingdom there shall be no end"....Thank God the invisible is the Real.

Consciously in your debt<br>Ellen Crockren

*Handwritten*
Thank you heartily for the mental sweat your book must have entailed.
    I guess unlike Compton Mackenzie[2] in Windsor Tapestry you have had no woman hack working for you at the British Museum. It would be interesting to know her total of payment on the 16/book? We women must see our share of blame through over obedience in acceptance of anomalies. I feel moved to write on this point..........womans mental atrophy consequent on false dominance....The womans movement proved that once roused no human being can be more courageously firm. Witness Mrs Pankhurst & the cat & mouse act.[3] What men have subjected themselves in devotion to that monstrous act for any high cause in the interval?

---

[1] Gilbert Murray (1886-1957) was Regius Professor of Greek at Oxford University and Chairman of the League of Nations for fifteen years between the wars.

[2] Compton Mackenzie (1883-1972) was a prolific British novelist. *The Windsor Tapestry* was published by Rich and Gowan in 1938.

[3] The Cat and Mouse Act was introduced by Asquith's Liberal government in 1913. It meant that suffragettes who refused food in prison could be released, but if they committed a further offence, they could be re-imprisoned.

43
Typed
**August 17, 1938**

---

New Hutton Vicarage,<br>Kendal.<br>August 17, 1938.

Dear Madam,
    Although I wish to thank you for "Three Guineas", may I be allowed to make a few comments. I wish to do this because I find that when authors deal with the Church they so often tend to write unfairly or even to misquote. Mr. Shaw and Mr. Wells have both at times misquoted the Church Catechism as "do my duty in that state of life unto which it has pleased God to call me".

Page
221    "He chose his disciples from the working class from which he sprang himself". If the words "working class" are used in the ordinary sense, is this certain? Our village carpenter does not consider himself "working class". Of the disciples, the father of James and John had hired servants. John was known to the High Priest. Matthew seems definitely bourgeois. Judas Iscariot does not seem working class.

224    Emily Brontë. "though not worthy to be a priest". The objection dealt with is surely not on the ground of unworthiness. Would not "acceptable as" be better?

225 "The salary of an archbishop is £15,000..a bishop..£10,000..a dean..£3,000..a deaconess £150.." The indefinite article is here very definite. A parallel use would be, "If you want to make money why not be an author. A novelist sells 1,500,000 copies of a book and makes ten times as much as an archbishop". There is only one archbishop who receives £15,000 and only one bishop who receives £10,000. The average for a bishop is about £4,000, for a dean £1,600.
But in any case there are only about 65 of these people out of 17,000 clergy. Vicars in these parts generally receive £300-£400. The comparison would be more real if made with the opposite number of the deaconess, the deacon, who receives £250. Why this difference?

225 "She mustremain outside the Church".
This is only true if she is excommunicated.
Do you not mean - outside the clergy?

237 and 245 Charlotte Brontë. If she had married earlier, is it not probable that she would have died earlier - not that this affects the principle.

---

*It seems that the correspondent forgot or decided not to sign this letter.*

**44**
**Handwritten**
**August 18, 1938**

*Registered Office:*
*70, Victoria Street,*
*London, S.W.1.*

THE CALL Ltd.
*General Promotion Offices:*
*31, Collingham Place,*
*London, S.W.5*
*Telephone: Frobisher 1566*

*THE CALL*[1]
*THE FIRST DAILY PAPER TO BE OWNED BY WOMEN*

Aug. 18.38

Dear Mrs. Woolf,

Having just finished reading your "Three Guineas" I feel that I may now ask you to grant me the long-desired privilege of meeting you.

Miss Helen Simpson's article in today's Daily Mail, "Women don't understand Science", will, I hope, draw forth a challenge from you which would certainly be accepted even by a man editor coming from so eminent a writer.

Such silly effusions are written by women (who ought to be ashamed of themselves) who know that men are only too eager to publish them. I know of one woman who has made a name and a fortune by such cheap disparagement of her sex. You could pulverise them. O if we only had The Call in which we could broadcast to millions daily the education that would prove an antidote to the poisonous antagonism of the dominant partner - a poison as bad for him as it has been for her.

Your book is wonderful and expresses all that I have wanted to say all my life. If I had only had the co-operation of a few women of the same mind our daily paper would have come into existence years ago. But in spite of the apathy of women and the opposition of men (veiled, of course), it must come.

Do, please, let us have a talk.

Yours sincerely,
Annie Colles

---

[1] There is no record of *The Call* in the British Library Newspaper Archive at Colindale or in bibliographies of women's periodicals. Most likely the newspaper was shortlived, or perhaps, judging by Colles' comments, it never got off the ground at all.

**45**
**Typed**
**August 18, 1938**

*Tel: Barnby Dun 21.* *The Rectory,*
*Station, Barnby Dun.* *Kirk Sandal,*
*Doncaster.*

18.8.38.
Dear Madam,
    Your "Three Guineas" Is very dangerous stuff. Inflammable material. It will re-kindle suppressed and smouldering fires, so painfully damped down and quenched, that are in the hearts (or should I say in the sub-conscious minds?) of many of the daughters of educated men who have married members of the "Procession", in which they are invisible, but yet its bearers! Conscious of their exploitation.

    I had grown so used to accepting the irrelevance of my position that I felt I could do nothing.

    You put fresh courage into our dulled hearts and stimulate us to take action., to assert "the rights of all-all men and women- to the respect in their persons of the great principles of Justice and Equality and Liberty." Therefore I have taken action on behalf of a man treated unjustly, which I should not have ventured to do had I not read "Three Guineas". One has got deadened since those active days of 1911-4, and one feels that so many of the young women of to-day are reactionary, drugged by this aphrodisiacal age with its vicarious emotions and its indifference to the value of life. Please forgive my temerity in thus writing to you. It is an expression of sincere
admiration & appreciation (within my limits) of your lovely writing.

    Your humble admirer & reader - Dorothy Soden


**46**
**Handwritten**
**August 31, 1938**

                      Aug: 31. 1938
*Telephone, Welbeck 7390*            *122, Harley Street,*
                                                             *W.1.*

Dear Mrs Woolf
    I have just written a Review of "Three Guineas" for the Quarterly Journal of the Medical Women's Federation. You will see it in due course I expect - but why I am bothering you with a letter is this. Would the Penguin people not take it as one of their special book series?[1] It ought to be read & reread by every grown up man & woman in the English speaking world & it ought to have a far wider public than it will get as a seven & six penny book.

May I also offer two criticisms?
1. It is very heavy to hold
2. I think the notes belonging to each chapter would be better placed at the end of each chapter instead of altogether at the end of the book
                    Thank you a thousand times for writing it
                                Yours sincerely
                                      Jane Walker

---

*Dr. Jane Harriet Walker (1859-1938) was a specialist in the treatment of tuberculosis. See reference D5 166: "Oh Queenie [Q. D. Leavis' scathing review of* Three Guineas *in* Scrutiny *September 1938] was at once cancelled by a letter from Jane Walker - a thousand thanks...3 Gs ought to be in the hands of every English speaking man & woman &c."*

[1] Penguin Specials were new books on current international affairs which cost sixpence, an offshoot of the Penguin sixpence reprints. They were an important part of Penguin's drive to make knowledge more accessible. Woolf's *Common Reader, Second Series* had, in 1938, been reprinted by Penguin at a price of sixpence.

**47**
**Handwritten**
**September 4, 1938**

---

Sept. 4th 1938.
Dear Madam,
        I have just read "Three Guineas" and should like to say, 'Thank you'.
                      Yours sincerely
                              E. Elizabeth Thornton

**48**
**Handwritten**
**September 4, 1938**

---

                                                    Sept. 4. 38.
Dear Madam
        Your book "Three Guineas" must bring you many compliments & comments, but, admiring it as I do, may I again bring to your notice (as I ventured to do after reading your "Room of One's Own", when you suggested that before the 20th cent. women could only earn their livings as "companions", or (I think) by painting on china) that women were in the medical profession in

some numbers, in the last century, & that we did not ~~earn~~ gain "the right to earn one's living", as you state on p 29, (of "Three Guineas") <& again p.38, you write "Since marriage, until 1919...was the only profession open to us..." Oh! I protest! Quant à moi, I've learnt how to cook, as well as doing other work, having had two boys (not my own) to bring up! & seldom a good servant. I [ ], before the war, on a dress allowance of £30, & a very small private income, living at home, of course.> <Gertrude Bell,[1] whom I knew, walked down Piccad. allright alone, in 1903, & served on our Committee!! May the opinion be expressed that the Law Courts, Mansion Ho., Houses of Parlt. etc are not so important as fields of man's operations as India, the Colonies, Governorships, great pro-Consulates, & the power of our Navy all over the globe? Surely, the Church hasn't much weight with intelligent people, nowadays. Have you read "Impregnable Women" by E. Linklater.[2] Vulgar but good!> only in 1919, when the vote was given to women. I hold no brief for those pioneer-women, but as they are probably too busy to read current literature (or are dead), I feel I must refer to them again. While the suffragists - no doubt most nobly - were working for the vote, these other women had already gained admittance to the medical profession & others were, I believe, sitting on local Govt Boards, & acting as Poor Law Guardians - 'at all events, a few years later; while there was the large body of women educated at Newnham, Girton, Somerville & Lady Margaret Hall,' who were acting as teachers & in other ways; (as you, yourself, indicate) & two Horticultural Colleges (at Swanley & at the Lady Warwick Hostel) were taking many pupils, who learnt chemistry, dairy-work, poultry-farming etc. I was at one of these latter, in the capacity of secretary, part-editor of their magazine, etc, in 1901, not being forced to earn my living, myself, I was greatly impressed by their courage, initiative, & other qualities. <I don't think women worked in the war, because they approved of war, but bec. it gave them chances, & they could clear up the mess! The stage is the only place women can earn fame & money!> As far as I have gone in your book, I feel that women have, on the whole, been rather lazy & stupid, with notable exceptions, but I think it will be found that Scottish women have always shown greater sense & ability than Englishwomen [ ] who, unless endowed with charm, always seem so terrified of being "left", unmarried, altho' you, with your great writing ability, could surely show that to be a wife is usually to be a slave!!

   However, that is by the way; but do, with your popularity & power, remember these pioneer women as you give a wrong impression (of whom there were many hundreds), who were working in difficult circumstances, as early as the late middle of the 19th century, & to whose labours we owe more than to those who obtained the vote - for I can't believe it has been of much use to us. But it is, perhaps, the backward state of foreign women, especially Germans (& Spanish? but I know none), & Chinese, which contributes to the awful state of affairs all over the world, at this moment. <I have often longed

to eliminate competition, but might not slackness result? How few "read at home"!> <Do tear Ludovici's "Women"[3] to pieces!>

> Yours truly
> B.M.Bryson

---

[1] See *Three Guineas*, Part 3, Notes 36 and 38. Gertrude Bell (born Margaret Lowthian 1868-1926) was a British traveller, archaeologist and diplomat. She specialized in Middle Eastern languages, geography and culture. She founded the National Archaeological Museum in Baghdad.

[2] Eric Linklater (1889-1974) was a Scottish writer of comic novels. His *Impregnable Women* was published by Cape in 1938. In the novel France is at war with Britain and 3000 women go on a "general love-strike" by shutting themselves in Edinburgh castle and renouncing men and sex until peace is achieved. *The Times Literary Supplement* reviewer (July 9 1938: 463) sets the novel in the context of *Three Guineas* by writing: "What can women do, Mrs Woolf asked recently, to avert war?" but concludes that Linklater's comic novel is "in doubtful taste."

[3] Anthony Mario Ludovici was an anti-feminist writer and thinker. Bryson most likely refers here to *Woman: A Vindication* (1923) or *The Future of Women* (1936). In his *Enemies of Women* (1948), Ludovici denounces *Orlando* as "a singularly silly novel" which avoids all reference to the "bodily differences" between the sexes "and their concomitant mental differences" (19).

**49**
**Handwritten**
**September 10, 1938**

---

<u>Telephone: 759</u>

122, London Street,
*Fleetwood.*
Lancs.
10.9.38.

Dear Mrs. Woolf -
 I thank you for your kindness in giving me permission to express to you some of my opinions - not that they are worth much; I fear they will introduce to you very little that is new (unless it be a new male folly!). But I have just come in from Football Match at Blackpool where I paid a shilling to see Blackpool beaten by Aston Villa without my seeing much hope for the advance of civilisation in the attitude, outlook, ambitions or intellectuality directions of the masses of our male population. How can any nation that popularly approves of such monstrosities as Blackpool or Southend look with any degree of hope to intellectual progress becoming a national feature. Hundreds of thousands of people at Blackpool have paid or will pay to see the little maid of twenty four summers who has been attending a Blackpool Elementary School this summer

and who presumably gave her date of birth when she was admitted to the School (if so a false date of birth). So its our British love of freedom, liberty and all that sort of thing that makes this sort of thing amusing to us in our English Sunday newspapers which are read by four fifths of our people - read with more interest and intellectual tickling than the political barometer which indicates grave possibilities of a War which would bring us back to Stone Age standards. Your sons and daughters of educated men can do and can hope to do very little so long as our popular standards -social, intellectual, industrial are what they are. It is no use you or Mrs. Rance of Woolwich[1] and all those who may be influenced by such refusing to be Sister Susie knitting socks for soldiers I suggest that the women folks in the last war were more enthusiastic for the killing of British French German etc., soldiers than were any section of our men. How they worshipped the men who went! How they taunted the men who stayed at home. How they enjoyed being "Waacs", "Wrens", munition workers - or even (if you were a "Society Lady) amusing a General in Mesopotamia (in your spare time when you were not doing V.A.D work). "Petticoat" influence had a great time during the last War - at home and abroad. Did I hear something about a promising young Lieutenant losing his Commission because he was ~~unabl~~ unwilling to "play" with a certain Society Lady who had invited him to her house - part of her social service to our men! You mention how Peerages, Baronetcies etc had their cash purchase; quite true - how many of the wives were worrying their husbands' hearts out so that Lady So-and-So might "wish the company of <u>Mrs</u> So-and-So (Green with Envy!) at Dinner on —— "

I believe quite a few thousand pounds a year are still changing hands as the price of Lady So-and-So getting Mrs. So-and-So's daughter presented at Court. A highly cultured civilisation ours is - male and female. You know Mrs Woolf the part that women played in the last War - Write a book indicting them for their blood stained share in it. who have written most strongly against War? Our men poets - many of them died in the mud of Flanders - lousy, rat bitten - and the women (pardon me) who cried over them dried their tears and found another man - although the one that bleached in Gallipoli's glare was always to be "the only one." Oh heavens, Mrs. Woolf let's be fair! I believe most sincerely that you want to be fair.

    You mention my own profession - you comment on someone suggesting that women are not suitable for teaching boys of certain ages (I speak with your book). Surely you know that that is true. When a boy is becoming adolescent I need hardly say that he needs some pretty blunt instruction and direction (<u>not</u> merely occasional) almost constantly in certain aspects of his conduct, habits, mode of life and particularly those psychological features incidental to and inseparable from sex development. Just as in the same way I am not ~~suited~~ fitted to Teaching girls of twelve to fourteen years of age - adolescent girls if you like - and I know sufficient sex psychology to understand that the girl who is becoming mulish, stubborn, having tantrums etc without any external reason is so merely incidentally to her sex periods. Let me be quite clear. I have a large mixed School with boys and girls up to fifteen years of age - I have men Assistants and Women (by the way do you know that most Women Teachers would rather teach under a Headmaster - more psychological harmony and tolerance!). I say without hesitation that in my experience Women Teachers are better Teachers by far than men and are definitely worth at least equal pay professionally. But Equality of Pay and Equality of opportunity for Women in the Professions (and I agree there should be) will never establish Equality of opportunity to be Happy in the two sexes. And mind Marriage (without any desire to continue in her truly professional job) will always be for women the profession they will most desire - and so much the better for man's happiness. The normal man is fool enough even when he has a good wife let alone when without one. My wife is worth more in every way than I am - she was a Teacher and has a better intellect, more common sense, more financial sense and more of every other kind of sense than I have. But she loves best to be running her own home. She is not my equal we are two small interdependent planets.

The Equality of Man and Woman is biologically, psychologically, socially, industrially impossible I do not see undesirable - I say impossible. You know the Folk Story of the Peasant man who grumbled about every thing his wife did in the house and with what results they "changed ends" You don't want women down coal mines or as trawler hands. By the way you say Mussolini speaks of "the world of men" and "the world of women" in general. You would appear to be speaking of or referring your appeal only to "daughters of educated men". It is the Capital and Labour elements that control and always will control Peace, War and everything else. I think Women can never enter either Capital or Labour sufficiently strongly to be able to exercise much influence from those directions on Peace or War. Capital means much more than opportunity to enter the Professions and the Stock Exchange and most women who control Capital (Lady Houston, Mrs Ver der Elst!, Barbara Hutton, etc) are not much help to their sex.

And pray Mrs Woolf unless your appeal about War can affect German and Japanese women as well as English women so that they will refuse to help in War how are Hitler and Mussolini going to act when they know that British women refuse to have babies and refuse to make munitions? It is because so many of our women wish to be "mannish" (God knows why!) and wear trousers and drink beer and play darts and football (I know our 1st and 2nd Division Football is very poor stuff as served by our men today). that they don't want babies - it isn't mannish to have babies The Late Lord Birkenhead said he could do anything a woman could do but have babies. And this frankness that the woman of today so admires; how absurd the Victorian taboo of sex talk between the sexes. Our women will read anything from a novelist without a blush but when I was at Oxford recently and (as an experiment) I read aloud a sex passage (very mild) from Stella Benson's Goodbye Stranger[2] the women were shocked at my indelicacy - but all of them would have been pleasantly tickled to have read the same passage "sub rosa". Why? I do not believe that even educated women want frankness at all - it is a pretence.

I agree with you about the "infantile fixation" chapters. The individual must <u>own</u> her own life and not recognise the right of <u>anyone</u> to possess her - not even her husband. Fathers and husbands of the Barrett of Whimpole St. type were a disgrace to all manly honour. I consider that I have no more right to claim possession of my wife than she has to claim possession of me. In our married life I <u>never</u> claim connubial intimacy with my wife. If she is tired or off form or even disinclined intellectually I would not dream of overriding her wishes. If I want to go to a football match (<u>and provided I am not neglecting my wife socially</u>) I go if my wife wants to go to her mother for a week I don't wish her to ask my permission. I have simply written carelessly, casually, without any previous weighing of what I have said and without troubling about sequence of any kind. I absolutely worship my wife and my three girls - Joan my eldest is just going back to her Science Course at Liverpool University next week. I shall give my daughters absolute freedom - I want neither money nor other return from them except perhaps they may spare me a little affection sometimes.

I want to write you about two or three other points in my next note. - if you will tolerate anymore - Study from the nude does not seem to me to be of much importance.

Sex intimacy ~~without~~ with other than your own husband or wife I cannot recognise as reasonably in the game, or even socially sound.

I love boys and girls - I enclose one or two snaps of my School Camp at Stratford -on Avon last year. Will you visit my School camp next year - I am going to Stratford again next year - Whit - Promise me you will!

      Goodbye - yours sincerely
       Wm Drummond

I dont do any "i") Wm

---

*Enclosure missing*

[1] See *Three Guineas*, Part 3, Note 21.

[2] Stella Benson (1892-1933) was a British writer who lived part of her life in China. *Goodbye Stranger* was published in 1926.

**50**
**Handwritten**
**September 11, 1938**

---

<u>Telephone: 759</u>                              *122, London Street,*
                                                                       *Fleetwood.*
                                                                           11.9.38

Dear Mrs. Woolf -

    After my wild all over the place note of yesterday's date I come to something approximating to particular points with some fact and figure bases On page eighty two, and elsewhere in your "Three Guineas" occurs "to earn £250 a year is quite an achievement for a highly qualified woman with years of experience" You accept this as being a true statement of fact. Now in my own profession: -

1. <u>75% to 80%</u> of the teachers in public Elementary schools (and public Secondary Schools) <u>are Women</u>. I make no complaint; I do not think this is unfair to men.
2. The Salary of a Certificated Woman Assistant at 35 years of age is ordinarily £288 per year (Scale III) - for a Head Teacher, more according to size of School.
3. The Salary of a Graduate Assistant Woman Teacher in a Secondary School, at 37 or 38 years of age is £384 per year - with 3 ½ months Holiday per year. - for a Head Teacher (Woman) £500 per year <u>minimum</u> In the case of the Certificated Assistant Woman in 2. above many of these women have never had any Secondary School or College Education at all - the same applies to the Head Teachers.
4. No Woman Teacher Head or Assistant in a Provided School - Elementary or Secondary - can be required to resign on Marriage - we have three Married Women Assistant in my School.

I enclose official Handbook for verification of my figures.

<u>Outside my own Profession</u> (outside <u>all</u> Professions) many women without anything more than an Elementary School Education are, <u>in business</u> - as buyers in Ladies' Dress Departments and other sections of Trading concerns, earning a thousand pounds per year in London and from £300 to £500 per year in the Provinces.

Whitaker does not give such statistics but Sir Wm Beveridge will verify my figures - Pontings, Barkers, Marshall and Snelgrove, Harrods, Selfridges, Lewis's will also verify. In London business houses thousands of women under forty years of age are receiving upwards of £300 per year. London School of Economics will verify.

In the Board of Education Inpsectorate - Whitaker does give the figures there - Women Inspectors approach the £1000 mark fairly closely.

Yours Sincerely,<br>William Drummond.

About Your Novels.
"Night and Day."

  Catherine Hilbery - delightful young lady - I think she is just ideal and yet true to life. I am charmed with your portrayal of her but how could such a sensible girl ever consent to marrying such a chump, such an empty unmanly conceited ass and typical petty tyrant as William Rodney - and to break and make the engagement two or three times over under trivial circumstances that did not really introduce any new fundamental of Rodney's weakness.

Was it not dishonourable for Ralph Denham to visit Rodney's flat for the purpose of meeting Catherine there and then to accompany her when she left. Not quite playing the game! If he wanted to play for Catherine's affection, Denham should have chosen some other rendezvous than his rival's flat.

Denham used Mary Datchet very badly - there is no justification for a man behaving in such fashion Peter Walsh is a man but Denham is not. Clarissa Dalloway knew that Peter was not the man to make her a husband - Clarissa was very fair to him and Walsh did the right thing to demand to know her attitude to him and to clear out immediately he knew.

  I think your understanding of human nature and real life features has travelled a long way between your "Night and Day" and "Mrs. Dalloway". It seems to me that you were not in the clear daylight of things - that you were groping somewhat in certain essentials of the literary art - when you wrote "Night and Day". Am I right, or merely rude, in my opinion of the development of your powers in the period between these two books?

A little aside: - My wife's reply to Income Tax Form inquiring about her income: - "No income, public or private, professional or otherwise; no salary, no renumeration, no profits from any source; no domestic allowance" - and my wife is educated and well qualified" - she may win a Crossword Puzzle sometime.

Yours Sincerely,<br>Wm Drummond.

*Enclosure missing*

**51**
**Handwritten**
**September 12, 1938**

---

*Telephone*  *7 Grosvenor Crescent,*
*Western 324*  *Glasgow, W.2.*
12th Sept 1938

Dear Mrs Woolf,
 I am the husband of an educated man's daughter. This must serve as my only introduction for my name is unknown to you. It must serve also as my excuse for this letter. Your interest in the educated man's daughter, made plain to all the reading public, would seem to expose you to the approaches of intruders like myself.
 I am not writing to ask for a guinea for this or that. Indeed, seeing I seek an expression of opinion you might rationally demand a fee before reading further. Lest the offer of a payment, however, might embarrass you, a ~~proffesional~~ professional writer, with the professions more usually associated with fees - The Law, Medicine and the like - no cheque is enclosed.
 Were I merely what I styled myself in my opening remarks probably this letter would not have been written. But I am something more. I am the husband of an educated mans educated daughter. I hope one day to read your views on the problem for husbands created by the existence of educated wives. Even if you do tackle this subject with your usual clarity the particular difficulty which occasions this letter is hardly likely to come within your scope. It has too much of the appearance of triviality to prevail among the major problems which clamour for treatment.
 If I could briefly state a question and demand an answer equally brief I would gladly do so, if only to save your time. But no Harley Street consultant, invited to express an opinion, would fail to pay regard to the heredity environment and general circumstance of his case. Equally for you I must sketch a background to my problem as the husband of an educated wife.
 That my wife is educated must be accepted. Certainly an amount similar to that expended on the education of each of her brothers was available for her. As the product of a costly boarding school and as a trained artist she married and became a mother. Her time is now apportioned to running a house, rearing a child and painting infrequent pictures.
 I am in business. From 9a.m. to 5 p.m. I labour at an office.
 These are the relevant facts; now for the problem itself. Of the daily papers published in Glasgow we buy two - one, The Glasgow Herald, (two pence) the other, The Bulletin (one penny). The former is a fair example of the better products of the provincial press. Unlike The Times it is available in Glasgow at breakfast time. The Bulletin is a picture paper, in all respects superior, we believe, to The Daily Sketch or Mirror.

To read The Glasgow Herald is practically essential for those who desire to keep themselves informed on matters of both general and local interest. The pages devoted to local politics, business, sport, art and its personal columns bear an individual stamp.

Our other daily, The Bulletin, has much of the same news in potted form and has numerous photographs. There are undoubtedly too many paragraphs of the type headed "Student Hits Invalid Aunt With Stick", or "Typist To Wed Duke's Heir." Our day's discarded Bulletin is eagerly awaited in kitchen and nursery.

My wife tells me of her astonishment, after marriage, when she first saw me leaving for the office with the Herald under my arm. The inference that the abandoned Bulletin was "good enough for me and the maids", as she put it, was unflattering. After a little she made her views known. Her attitude was, and is, that my train journey to business occupies less than twenty minutes, whereas there are frequently longer periods in her day, notably at her solitary luncheon, when an available Glasgow Herald can be studied. She maintains that in any case there is a copy at the office and several copies at the club where I normally lunch.

My answer to these arguments were, and are, that- firstly, during breakfast she can avail herself of the Herald to examine the births, deaths, engagement notices and such other items as are not provided for in the Bulletin; secondly, that the business pages which are of ~~not~~ no interest to her are to me of occasional importance because of my occupation; and thirdly, that not more than once or twice in a month do I have time to read a daily paper at the office.

Travelling home in the evening I still read the morning paper and sometimes complete its perusal before dinner. My wife urges that if she is to remain an educated man's educated daughter she is entitled to have priority with the Glasgow Herald and that it should remain a perquisite of the house. She does not care to read it in the evening (nor, for that matter, do I) when frequently other occupations intervene. Her daily duties (so many of them like the sending by Mrs Dalloway of ~~hot water bottles~~ air cushions to Continental travellers) tend, she thinks, towards the trivial.

The dispute never reached the status of a family brawl. We had our dignity. But it rankled. After a year or two, and setting aside the crude argument~~s~~ that my father before me had always taken away the Herald which he, and I in my turn, paid for, we reached a compromise. We now work on a basis of month and month about, the ultimate holder of the Herald having no claim upon its columns at breakfast. (It is perhaps not relevant but I have here a difficulty in refraining from a comment on the amazing regularity with which my wife befouls the pages of a newspaper with eggs and marmalade. Education seems to have taught nothing in this respect).

If, as I have stated, a compromise has been reached you may well ask where you come in? If all is well in Czechoslovakia, why Runciman?

Alas, the arrangement does not find favour; revision is sought. My wife claims that the Herald belongs entirely to the home.

In agreeing to seek your arbitration I think I have conceded much, for my wife stakes her claim chiefly as an educated woman whose intelligence is in danger of under-nourishment, while you, I gather, are inclined to champion these Cinderellas of society.

Be that as it may I beg you not to shrink from the duty I seem to impose. The destiny of a tupenny daily, perhaps even of a happy marriage, depends upon a word from you.

I have given up half, - should I give up all?
        Yours faithfully
        Alan D Cuthbert.


**52**
**Handwritten**
**September 14, 1938**

*The Warden's Lodgings,*
*New College, Oxford.*
14.8.38[1]

My dear Virginia

A friend of mine by name Nowell C Smith[1] (135 Banbury Road Oxford) in an effort to raise money from a sale to help the Oxford Branch of the League of Nations Union writes "Do you think you could induce Mrs Woolf to give me say, a copy of her 'Three Guineas' or any other work (signed) for this purpose? I pass on this request - you must receive many such [    ] and may, I hope, be forgiven for doing so.

I wish that there were some hope of seeing you again at New College. My days there are fast drawing to a close.
        Your [    ]
        Herbert Fisher

*Herbert Fisher (1865-1940) was Woolf's first cousin. He was an historian and President of the Board of Education 1916-1922. He became Warden of New College, Oxford in 1925 and received the Order of Merit in 1937. For reply see L6 272 (3444). See also D5 171 where Woolf writes: "HAL Fisher asks me to go & see him. After my remarks on OM's this is conciliatory. He wants me to send a signed copy." She had referred to the Order of Merit in* Three Guineas *on pages 179 and 192.*

[1] Based on the date of Woolf's reply (September 17,1938) and her diary comment (September 16, 1938) it seems that Fisher has got the month wrong here.

[2] See Letter 59.

**53**
**Typed**
**September 14, 1938**

*I.S.J.*

Mrs. Virginia Woolf-
52 Tavistock Square, W.C.1
London.

My dear Mrs. Woolf-

May I take the liberty of expressing to you my delight in your "Three Guineas" which I am now reading for the second time?

Its cool logic, its irresistible and gruelling humor in picturing the cruel absurdities which have always crippled women's efforts in our pseudo civilization, its rapier like thrusts at the smugly complacent - if often unconscious- masculine assumption that judgment and wisdom are a peculiar endowment of the male, make the reading of your book a real and joyous adventure. Withal, you have done it without a trace of the acrimony and acerbity which so often weaken feminine discussion of the roles which men have imposed upon women. It is a masterly performance.

Here in California, we have recently had an incident which-were it not so irritating-would be most amusing. The president of Stanford University - a coeducational institution of over 4,000. students (the number of women admitted being limited) in an address to a body of University women, blandly assured them that many of the woes under which our world is tottering were due to women's failure to do their duty by the children and homes.

It was of course, merely a 1938 version of Adam crooning his familiar apple song, but considering the speaker's position and the anno domini, was infuriating.

Thank you again for doing so perfect a piece of work. Many things which have come from your pen have been a very great pleasure indeed on this side of the Atlantic, both because of their content and the beauty of their English.

                        Very sincerely yours,-

September 14, '38                         Isabel S. Johnson

Mrs. Milbank Johnson
789 South Hudson Avenue.
Pasadena, California.

**54**
**Handwritten**
**September 14, 1938**

*1825 Drummond Drive*
*Vancouver, B.C.*

Sept. 14th
Dear Madam,
      Thank you for that blessed book "Three Guineas" with its lack of heat & clear English. I could gladly send a guinea to your college if I could find a school where a girl might be prepared for it.

My own girl went to Cheltenham from here at great expense to heart & purse. The outcome was rather disappointing. Brilliant results in exams is acheived by blinding work as the entrance to Oxford is so highly competitive. There is no time for adventure, experiment or even thought & an old-school-tie outlook is steadily instilled. Education at such a price seemed too dearly bought. If education for girls is going to follow the public school system, I can't believe it will ~~matters~~ help matters. Why I bother you with this I don't know. Your book roused me so & flattered my self-dissatisfaction. From an inarticulate & very grateful "outsider".

                    Dorothy Mather

**55**
**Handwritten**
**September 14, 1938**

*Marshfield 2.*                                            *Cold Ashton.*
                                                               *Chippenham.*

Dear Mrs Woolf
Your suggestion in 'Three Guineas' that women could stop war by refusing to do a hand's turn for it seems almost the only thing that has not be tried.

Please forgive my writing to you but at a time like this there is not a moment to be lost and there are so many of us who want a lead. ~~and~~

It may be that you have already begun some constructive movement you appear to me to be the obvious person to do so. You know so well what women can do and the driving force they put into what they believe in -

I should be so glad to hear from you
                    Yrs sinly
                    Fanny Mounsey
                    14.ix.38

---

*Published courtesy of Mr. John C. H. Mounsey and Mrs. Frances Conway, grandson and granddaughter of Fanny Mounsey.*

*Fanny Mounsey was involved in music all her life: she was influential in the founding of Glyndebourne. See D5 171: "Mrs Mounsey writes to ask me to head an Outsiders' movement."*

**56**
**Handwritten**
**September 22, 1938**

22.ix.38

15, The Vale, Chelsea. S.W.3.[1]
Telephone. Flaxman 1205.

Dear Mrs Woolf,
Thank you very much for your letter.
It is some comfort to me to know that you too are relying on individual effort - however microscopic and wide of the mark it may seem.

I have already made a nuisance of myself for some time by crying out for non competive festivals as opposed to competitive ones and have refused either to coach or adjudicate on competive lines.

I have just come back from Lewes where a large meeting was held this afternoon for school teachers to discuss the question of holding a noncompetitive music festival for children there next April in place of the competitive one that they have hitherto taken part in
Dr Geoffrey Shaw addressed them.
This letter needs no answer but I ~~would~~ greatly appreciate your promise to let me know after this crisis if anything takes shape although I feel with you that the individual work is more valuable than a society.
                    Yrs sinly
                    Fanny Mounsey
                    (Mrs)

---

*Published courtesy of Mr. John C. H. Mounsey and Mrs. Frances Conway.*

[1] Fanny Mounsey had purchased her Chelsea house (15 The Vale) from Ethel Sands, the American painter (1873-1962) whom Vanessa was visiting at this time in Auppegard, Normandy.

**57**
**Handwritten**
**September 24, 1938**

*The Hill House,*
*87, Redington Road,*
*Hampstead, N.W.3.*
*Hampstead 5419*

Mrs L Woolf                                                                  Sept. 24th
Monk's House
Rodmell,
Lewes

Dear Madam,
    The executive Committee of the Married Womens Association wishes to send you their grateful thanks for allowing & paying for the publication of extracts from your book "Three Guineas".
    The publishers have the text & I have instructed them to go through it again carefully.

                              Yours sincerely,
                              Granita Frances

*In the* Three Guineas *letters' file is a receipt for three pounds and sixpence to Mrs Leonard Woolf from the Married Women's Association dated September 20 1938. The receipt clearly arrived with this letter and is for Woolf's financing of the publication of extracts from* Three Guineas.

**58**
**Handwritten**
**September 29, 1938**

*Estabrook Road*
*Concord, Massachusetts*

                                              9.29.1938

Dear Mrs Woolf,
    Last evening I finished reading your latest book, "Three Guineas". As I neared the end the feeling grew, almost of impatience, that the name which

you propose - the "Society of Outsiders" is so harsh, so negative and so pessimistic. Why not come right out with the 250 year old title, "The Society of Friends." Possibly the new would split the old, and both be spoiled!

In discussing the book (which I like so very much) with the friend who lent it to me, I asked her whether Virginia Woolf ever had knowledge of Quakers. She said, "I do not know, but I believe that she is related to Leslie Stephen." This at once suggested Caroline Stephen, and I hurried this morning to the Library and there found biographical sketches of both Leslie Stephen and his sister Caroline - also the fact that he had daughters, whose names however were un noted.

My question was more than answered, in fact I held in my hand the key to "Three Guineas." The "Quaker Handbook" has been one of my treasures, and I have three lending copies of it in constant circulation for those who ask me about Friends.

I was introduced to Caroline Steven two years ago by a close friend Katherine Page Laing (daughter of Walter Hines Page) who has within the year joined the Society of Friends.

You are working as the Friends are, and a multitude of men and women all over the world are, to avert war. Probably no sharper weapon can be found than ridicule of men and bareing the injustices suffered by women, every word, the unvarnished truth.

Nothing in the world must be more fun than the ability to write a shrewd, humorous and true sketch, which has within it an almost agonizingly solemn purpose.

Thank heaven for the Joan Frys and Edmund Harveys, Baron Cadburys and Janet Whitneys[1] who give the lie to this black picture of English life.

Your book has given at least one reader food for thought, not to mention many a laugh. May I thank you, and also assure you that this needs and expects no reply.

Sincerely Yours,<br>Amelia Forbes Emerson

Mrs Raymond Emerson

---

[1] These are all names of Quakers. Joan M. Fry wrote *The Communion of Life*, T. Edmund Harvey wrote *Silence and Worship*, *Quaker Language* and *Authority and Freedom in the Experience of Quakers* and Janet Whitney wrote *Elizabeth Fry: Quaker Heroine* (1937). Baron George Cadbury was a Quaker businessman and social reformer. He took over his father's cocoa business with his brother and built a model village, Bourneville, for his employees. He also founded various education and welfare trusts.

**59**
**Handwritten**
**October 2, 1938**

*Tel. Summertown 5484.*                       *135, Banbury Road,*
                                                   *Oxford.*
                                                   Oct. 2nd '38

**Dear Mrs Woolf**
     I am very grateful indeed to you for so kindly sending me a signed copy of your "Three Guineas" for our L.N.U.[1] bazaar. I should have acknowledged the gift before but I was away from home.
     May I take the opportunity of saying with what admiration and assent I had already read the book.
     I am afraid the frantic applause which has greeted the Prime Minister's plucking of a very precarious safety out of the nettle[2] which he and the more or less monied classes have been helping to grow all these years, augurs ill for any real attempt - such as women would certainly make - to remove the removable causes of war. I wonder whether if women had the money bags they would become as stupid as men? But this is only a "rhetorical question".
     Once more, please accept my best thanks for your help to our L.N.U. sale.
                                  Yours sincerely
                                  Nowell Smith

*Nowell Charles Smith (1871-1961) was Headmaster of Sherborne School and Chairman of the English Association 1941-3. See Letter 52.*

[1] League of Nations Union.

[2] Smith refers here to the Munich Crisis, brought about by the agreement signed by Hitler, Mussolini, Chamberlain and Daladier on September 29 1938 which ceded Sudetenland to Germany on the understanding that Hitler would not invade Czechoslovakia. In his speech following the signing, Chamberlain quoted Shakespeare's Hotspur: "Out of this nettle danger we pluck the flower safety."

**60**
**Typed**
**October 11, 1938**

                                                        159, North Street,
                                                        Brighton.
                                                        11 October, 1938.

Dear Madam,

                                  "Three Guineas."

    If, as I sincerely hope may be the case, your admirable and entertaining plea for a Society of Outsiders has to be reprinted, I venture to suggest that you should modify two statements which suggest that you share the popular delusion that the remuneration of the clergy of the Church of England is provided by taxation and is a charge on the State.

    Thus, on page 99, you remark that "The work of an archbishop is worth £15,000 a year to the State" and on page 204 you speak of people being "forced to contribute as taxpayers" to the Church. I submit that no part of the Archbishop of Canterbury's remuneration is provided "out of the taxes" and that, apart from the relatively trifling amount which is paid in the form of salaries to chaplains (of other denominations as well as XXXXXXXX the Church of England) of the Forces, and in the Prison Service, etc., the taxpayer, as such, contributes nothing whatever to the support of the Church. In view of the "assumption" (entirely unsupported by evidence) which you make on page 276 (note 21) in the matter of Mary Astell and Bishop Burnet, you may, perhaps, consider that any stick is good enough to beat the Church with. I respectfully suggest, however, that such statements detract quite unnecessarily from the force of the very cogent argument stated so skilfully in a book which has given me much pleasure and which I hope may reach a very wide public.

                                                         Yours faithfully,
                                                         Leonard. J. Holson

Mrs. Virginia Woolf.
P.S. I am not a clergyman.

**61**
**Handwritten**
**October 16, 1938**

1619 South University Avenue
Ann Arbor, Michigan, U.S.A.
October 16, 1938

Dear Mrs. Woolf,

Professor Bredvold is not here, at present, so I am forbidden to do a doctoral dissertation on your works. These other "scholars" say you are too modern to make a proper doctoral subject; thus, I am doing my research on your father, Sir Leslie Stephen. They have granted me that privilege, and I intend to use it as a step to you. I will have my way yet! It will do me no harm to know the works of Sir Leslie as well as I know the works of his daughter. In fact, it will do me much good. When Professor Bredvold returns in February, I am sure he will give my plan a very attentive ear.

I have read <u>Three Guineas</u> and find that it definitely completes <u>The Years</u>. It is sad that the world has not been ready for such a work before - and I am not sure that the world is ready for it now! Certainly the present Italy and the present Germany will never take the <u>Three Guineas</u> to their united bosoms. Furthermore, I fear that the unthinking majority of the critics and the reading public will fail to see the continuity of thought flowing from <u>The Years</u> into <u>Three Guineas</u> - and <u>not</u> because the continuity is obscure and not because you have failed to do what only you could do. You have succeeded splendidly. But the unthinking majority (the reading public enmasse having been taught by critics and pseudo-scholars to put ideas into classifications and categories), this mass Mind, will fail to see a unity in two different classifications. <u>The Years</u> is labelled Fiction - <u>Three Guineas</u> is labelled Criticism; hence, they will see sheets of manuscript separated by a wooden partition!

Fortunately, you are not writing for the mass. You are writing, I believe, for the daughters -and the sons, I notice - of educated men. <u>Unfortunately</u>, however, even among these one must contend with unthinking critics and pseudo-scholars. They <u>should</u> see that the unforgettable doctor of <u>The Years</u> is completely analyzed and made clear in <u>Three Guineas</u> - and we shall hope that they will. Again you have accomplished what has never been done before. You have completed a task which has desperately needed completion - namely, a thorough and accurate analysis of present civilization. The lesson may go unlearned but the knowledge is there to be used. Your part is done just as your part has been done many times before.

I am reminded that you said V. Sackville West thought <u>The Waves</u> utter nonsense. It may be that she will not be favorably drawn to <u>Three Guineas</u>. If she dislikes it may I reiterate what I answered you then? She may be, herself, a victim of such above -mentioned categories. Extrovert, dashing, changeable as she is, her very unconventionality may be a self-imposed classification! If so, her line of vision is only a direct one from her own pigeon-hole. All other views are lost in the darkness of her own partitions.

But, Mrs. Woolf, I still want <u>The Waves</u> to be continued. The new world looms ahead and we need a companion to it to help us meet it. I am not suggesting that you are (any more than your father was) a moral reformer, a Buckmanite, an Anglican, a Non-Conformist, a Buddhist, a Mohammedan, et cetera, but I do believe that you are predominantly Christian in <u>actual practice</u>. I am thankful that you cannot be definitely classified because your works and their results are thereby free to speak for themselves to all classes, sects, or categories. And they do speak. I am conscious of the fact that I did not make my ideas about <u>The Waves</u> very clear when I finally had my interview with you. I admit that I chattered loudly and wildly enough, but try as hard as I could, I simply could not collect myself. I wanted so very much to look at you and talk to you but I was so afraid that you would think I came to stare at you or make use of you for myself - unworthy I - that I looked at and talked to your husband instead! If I am ever permitted another talk with you, I shall be in control of all my faculties, believe me! This incident may amuse you! My father, who has always been able to put my brother and me in close connection with quite worthy and notable personages, was arranging another interview for me. The year before, he had had an audience with King Christian of Denmark, and he was in the process of obtaining a similar audience for me. I wrote father, "The King be hanged - what have we to do with each other? I want Virginia Woolf!" I meant nothing uncomplimentary to King Christian for I do think he is one of the best Heads of State today - but my father's answer was "Then get her!" I got you - and disappointed you, I know!

I say now what I could not say then. I would follow you with the hair-raising frenzy of a suffragette if I did not know that such a following would be most distasteful to you - and that it would be most unsuitable to your kind of stimulation. Nevertheless, if you advised me to discontinue my pursuit of a doctorate on general principles, I should follow your advice immediately for you would never advise unwisely. I do not care for a title - "Doctor" - nor am I seeking fame. I only want to do my part in my way as you have done yours in your way. Since my lawyer brother, three years older than I, has not made his million, and since my clergyman father never <u>will</u> make <u>his</u> million, I cannot buy a press nor pay for printing my ideas or those of others, as you suggest in <u>Three Guineas</u>. I have nothing of my own as yet to pay for anything, either. Therefore, the only path that I can see before me is the "doctorate". It will give me the opportunity to teach others, it will give me my own income, and in America it adds prestige to any written article. If a woman without such a title were to submit an article to a learned magazine, the editors would say, "Hum - another scatter-brained woman! We'll not bother to read it!" And even with the title behind the article, the editor is just as apt to say, "A frustrated woman - but it may be interesting, psychologically." The latter, at least, gets a hearing! May

I ask you just why you say one should not begin to write until he is thirty? You set that limit in your "Letter to a Young Poet", I believe, and you told me that in our meeting. Why exactly <u>thirty</u>?

May I ask you further if you by an chance believe in the world set up by Professor Einstein? I do, in so far as I am able to comprehend him, and I believe you said at the time I saw you that you had not studied him much. Have you, by any chance, had the time to go into his philosophical works since then? You are both, in my opinion, so close to one another in ultimate results. When or <u>if</u> I feel the need to see Professor Einstein as I felt the need to see you, I shall do so, of course. I definitely intend to study thoroughly the lines you have both drawn! At present my goal is another <u>The Waves</u>. I do pray you to give such a work to us!

This is not a very good letter, Mrs. Woolf - I know that - but I am sending it to the "greatest teacher" I know, and it is my best effort. My only purposes in sending it are to give "her" encouragement if perchance "she" may want it and to obtain some help for myself if that be possible. Need I tell you that if you should send another letter to me I should preserve it with the other, I should use it for no purpose but that for which it would be intended, and the letter would be yours again if you should want it?

I know of no closing that would fit this letter as well as that of Dr. Johnson.

"Your most humble and obedient servant",
Elizabeth Nielsen

Postscript: Since writing this letter, I have received a notice that I am to be called upon to speak before the Graduate Club of the University on my ideas of the correlation between you and Professor Einstein. It may be the opportunity I have been wanting!

E.N.

---

*Elizabeth Nielsen was an American graduate student who had visited the Woolfs on May 27 1938. See* D5 *145: "Today I'm had in a corner by a persistent Miss Neilsen, my evening ruined" and 146: "Miss Nielsen came; a daneish bee haunted American Lit. prof., entirely distracted by Einstein, & his extra mundane influence upon fiction. L. threaded the maze to the muddle in the centre. I gave up on the outskirts. Rather genuine, naïve, a little like Christabel; & as usual much more likeable than her letters." See also* L6 *333 (3514) for another reference: "the American professors have started writing about my father now."*

**62**
**Handwritten**
**October 17, 1938**

*Presbyterian Church of England*
Rev. William J. Piggott
*Free Church Minister and Librarian*    *"Torre,"*
*at Claybury L.C.C. Mental Hospital*    *65, St. James' Road,*
*Woodford Bridge, Essex.*    *Sutton, Surrey.*
*and Banstead Mental Hospital,*
*Near Sutton, Surrey.*
*Lecturer, London County Council Evening Institutes.*

October 17 1938

*Telephone Buckhurst 2282-3 Sun. Tues. Thurs. Frid. for Claybury Mental Hospital*
*Vigilant 7668-9 Sun. Mon. Wed. Frid. " Banstead " "*

Dear Miss Woolf,
    My assistant librarian at Claybury, Miss Margery [Neetriss ?] has lent me your book "Three Guineas" and I have read it with much pleasure and interest.
    My dear Sweetheart, who was taken from me by a sudden illness last Easter, and I talked all those things out in our lovely courtship and were working in the great Suffrage and Socialist Movements, so that the things for which you write were the moving passion of our friendship and of over 25 years of our beautiful married life.
    I rejoice to think that where we were pioneers, there stands today a great multitude who will endorse your awakening message.
    There are a few unimportant points on which perhaps you will permit friendly corrections.
    First, you do not clearly enough emphasize the fact that marriage should be a well-paid profession, in which a salary of not less than £3 a week should be arranged for, from her wedding day onward, for every wife for her work in the home <u>generally</u> and for keeping her husband (whom she often discovers to be her first and most fractious child!) employable.
    Remember that more boy babies are born than girl babies, that mothers generally love boy babies most and yet when the age of 21 is reached, there are 14 ½ million women voters of 21 and up and only 12 million men.
    In other words women are <u>not</u> the weaker sex.
    Next, there should be a family allowance to the mother of £1 a week for every child until they reach the age of 18, so as to save the home from the

ravages of want if unemployment or accident or disease met with and cripple the husband.

By this means women gain possession of themselves in marriage and after marriage, and a true free love as compared with bought love, becomes possible.

Also they can then have their own apartment and a holiday if necessary or desirable, away from husband and family, and many need this.

Personally I am in favour of a maintenance young age pension to commence at once after any life or health crippling, accident or disease.

Living human beings have to be kept and it costs no more to keep them in reasonable comfort and freedom than in workhouses, asylums or prisons, and it gives them a fair power of some healthful happiness too.

Then, if you will excuse an ex-architect saying so, I don't think you emphasize the present day needlessness of contracting women's service to the community as narrowly as it is done.

With every advance in machinery and specialization the older differences between male and female skill and output grows less and less. If woman's work lies in the home, then woman's home is the universe, and her work anything that does not hinder the special gifts of wifehood & motherhood, and she as a coequal citizen should freely choose her life.

Turning to far lesser matters why do you say St. Paul was a bachelor.

If, as he said he did, he voted for the martyrdom of the Christians he must have been a member of the Jewish [    ], from which soldiers, butchers and bachelors were, I understand definitely excluded as unlikely to be normally merciful!

He was probably a widower. And one same error slips in about our Lord. which really springs not from New Testament evidence, but from the shadowing authority of St Augustine of Hippo.

Why do you (and Hall Caine too, to demand a good deal!) say Jesus, was a poor man?

The journey to Egypt in [    ] was an expensive one, and the avoidance of [    ] on the return needless, if they were poor but assisted pilgrims. The Greek word TEKVOV is not only carpenter but is used for a contractor.

He was homeless but this was voluntary "though He was rich yet for our sakes He became poor."

His parables etc reveal an inside knowledge of great, worldly affairs, and His disciples had (for they gave up) lands and possessions and good businesses to follow Him.

I think the religious world has forgotten the Divine Feminine as seen both by Isaiah and St Paul in his wiser moments.

So we have a male Trinity and Christians inwardly say Amen, when they hear of the nightly prayer of the Jewish boys "I thank thee Jehovah that Thou has not made me a woman."!

Ours is a man-made world, as Charlotte Perkins Gilman[1] saw in her "Women & Economics and until woman has been <u>economically</u> free for about a 1000 years, none can fairly compare with male man, or predict her real future.

But for the brave work leading up to the revelation and defence of the crowned [ ] equal right of woman, I, a knight in her cause thank you and remain,

Yours very gratefully<br>Wm J. Piggott

*P.S. – Gifts of Books, English or Foreign, especially good standard fiction and illustrated weekly and monthlies, and other magazines, bound and unbound, would be most acceptable for the Patients' Library, and may be sent to me – "<u>CARRIAGE FORWARD</u>" – Banstead Mental Hospital, near Sutton, Surrey. Claybury Mental Hospital, Woodford Bridge, Essex.*

*I am free to accept occasional pulpit supply engagements for Sunday Mornings and Evenings.*

*For terms re Lecturing, Tutorial or Secretarial Work apply as above, noting that certain Lectures are entirely without charge. I am free any evening and certain afternoons in the week.*

---

[1] Charlotte Perkins Gilman (1860-1935) was an American feminist economist. She is best known for her book *Women and Economics* (1898), her short story *The Yellow Wallpaper* (1892) and *Herland* (1915). She also edited the journal *The Forerunner*.

**63**
**Typed**
**November 2, 1938**

Springfield, Massachusetts,<br>122 Marsden Street,<br>November 2, 1938.

My dear Miss Wolff:

Your "Three Guineas" is marvelous. I hope you will hear from many as to just how good it is, for I am hoping you will feel so encouraged - if encouragement is what you need - that you will continue what you have begun in this volume. Your method of presentation leaves one without a doubt as to just what you mean. Your vision is so direct. Your analysis is so just. I would say, from the point of view of this ordinary reader, that you have tackled a new field - one that has scarcely been touched before; that you are a pioneer; that with your particular talents you could spread before us amazing material, and that with help like yours women would at last make an attemptto know themselves. Insofar as I can see, the field is yours. There are few equipped to tackle such a problem. With your intelligence, your ability to free your thoughts from tradition and precedent, your gift to dig for facts and not let them blind you, you could do much, and there is so much to. Most of all, and without it I personally feel what you have to say would sink instead of float, most of all I admire your freedom from complaint. Yourbook is full of material which in the hands of someone else would lead them to raise a hue and cry, to lament and fuss. But there is not the slightest tinge of complaint in your summaries. Your dignityemphasizes the fact that after all a complaining woman does not get very far.

I wish you the best of luck in any new endeavor, and cannot help wondering just what form it will take - you threw out so many possibilities in your "Three Guineas".

Sincerely yours,
Agnes K. Potter

**64**
**Typed**
**November 7, 1938**

Mount Pleasant
Thongsbridge
Holmfirth
Nr Huddersfield Yorks.
Nov 7th 1938.

<P.S. I apologise for the "decorations" - the result of a leaking fountain pen. A.S.>

To Mrs Virginia Woolf.
C/O The Hogarth Press
52 Tavistock Square
London W.C.1.

Dear Madam,

I have just read Your 'Three Guineas' and enjoyed the charm and lucidity with which you write-and agree in the main with points which you put forward.

I think your main points are that women should havethe same rights as men in regard to education, to choice and practice of profession and be paid for the work they do - whether that work be in the home or in the world at large - but that -unlike their male fellows, they should work for the joy of doing worthwhile work, of being occupied and of service to their fellows, of attaining reasonable economic independence-not to attain 'labels' of various kinds, and not to be so immersed inthe work they are doing so as to have no time to really live. In short that women should have, and act on, a real sense of values, not on what the world calls value, for no one who has a real sense of values canallow that war is either worth while and/or permissable.

This is of course a very shallow and badly expressed description of your latest essay - but if I could sum up your book in a 666666 paragraph, I should be better known as a writer than you are yourself- and a good deal better off financially-and so be able to help in making woman what she is yet far from being- a free citizen. I agree too that the word 'feminism' should be swept away=that men and women should contribute their own individual powers to this business of living=and realise as keenly as you can do that what you so aptly put under the heading of 'infantile fixation' suffered by men prevents woman from being a free citizen, and so retards civilisation.

But what irks me about your book is the fact that you write only of and for the Vdaughters of educated men! when the problems with which you deal are those of the working woman also, in fact those problems you outline affect the working woman in a far greater degree.

For the daughter of the working man - the working woman-is and has been as much under family dominance as the daughter of the educated man-being such a one myself I speak from experience.

She has always earned a living one way or another-it is true-but y you overlook the fact that wages are so low that only a combined family income has ever made it possible for the working woman to exist at all & for working people to attain any reasonable standard of comfort.

You say glibly that the working woman could refuse to nurse and to make munitions and so stop the war. A working woman who refuses to work will starve-and there is nothing like stark hunger for blasting ideals. If she can't get work-she will lead a bare existance on unemployment pay-as I am doing at the moment-and have to remain content-or at least accept the fact that she has to accept two shillings less than her unemployed brother.

The real answer to your book would be for me to write a similar one from the working woman's point of view. Perhaps if I had your ability ability I might be able to do so.

And if I had your access to books, the stimulus which you can obtain from conversation, and living, with people who know how to follow a line of thought, and work out its implications-and if, in addition, I had economic freedom I might do so.

I ought I know, to write in impassioned prose of the sick hopelessness of finding myself doomed to begin work as a half timer at twelve, when I wanted to go on going to school (being blessed-or cursed-with an avid and overpowering desire for knowledge.)

I might tell you how I went to sleep at night with factory wheels continueing their grinding in my brain as I slept-how I rose at fivea=m and went out into the blackness of unlighted country lanes or into the whiteness of a howling blizzard-scared sometimes at at the strange shapes I saw as I passed some lighted window=yet going resolutely on-because even strange shapes must be faced if one has to reach the factory at six a.m: and how I sometimes had to return home suffering from the most damnable sick headaches-and yet turn up again next day. How I hated the noise the grease, the whirring wheels, and was too sick to eat my breakfast-and disliked even more the spiritual loneliness of working with warm hearted lasses, who thought only of boy friends of dances, weddings, funerals etc-but had no thought for the beauty of words, of wild flowers and sunsets-or if they had, never let me know it talking only of clothes, of gossip of money etc. All this I endured for 3/6 per week - that my mother might pay rates-rates which were used for the education of my more fortunate fellows-among other things.

When I became a weaver I worked side by side with men, doing as much and as skilled work as they for 10% less. For Trade unionists as well as educated men suffer from "infantile fixation".

Industrial wages-like professional salaries-are supposed to be 'family wages'- (that was the answer to our cry for equal pay - women of course do not have families.) but when-at 17- I found myself wage earner, housekeeper cook and nurse & also earning the sole family income-I did not find myseself paid at a family rate-nor have I ever found any reduction in rent, rates or grocers bills or travelling expenses. As a woman one pays equally-it is in receiving that lower rates exist.

I brought up my sister-(nine years my junior and now happily married) -maintained my mother until her death in 1932-and now at 43-am totally unemployed-and still struggling to keep a roof over my head-with the aid of unemployment pay. 15/- a week to pay rent rates, light, coal gas, food, shoe repairs and clothing etc-and I see from to day's paper that a former Director ofMessrs Fry has left a sum of £590577 from the manufacture of a luxury article beyond my means! The death duties mean that some of that=quite a substantial sum will go in ~~death duties~~ taxes-but as they will be used for armaments-they will not benefit either unemployed or workers. I could nt help thinking of the things I would do with that money. The new library I would give to the Working womens College at Surbiton, the bursaries I would endow there and at the Universities, the nursery schools I would present or set in motion-the pleasant house I would buy for my sister, so that her little boy would be able to have a garden to play in-the addition to her income I would make sothat she could present Edward with a sister or a brother, or both, if she cared to, and which I think she would like to do-as she thinks only children miss something in life. (Beside where are the aunts coming from for the next generation if only c hildren are the rule; Aunts are as necessary as parents to young children-I know because I suffered from the lack of one!) though I fear I am not a very satisfactory one-I have to consider even if I can give a 66666 peice of cake-as I found to my shocked surprise when I called on my nephew this afternoon, and He wanted some of the cuurant tea cake I had just bought! He got his peice of cake - but I found myself thinking that there was so much less for me-so low has unemploymment pay broughtme. But at least I did not have the agony of thinking he was not getting enough to eat-he does get that-it was just the natur greediness of three years old. I have nt been actually destitute myself yet-but I have found myself staying in bed on dark wet mornings until dinner time and thinking I had 'saved' a meal. Which is a rotten state of affairs for any civilised woman to be in.) And my total unemployment is due to the fact that I wanted to give service to my fellows! I served on Courts of Referees-with my employers permission-but nevertheless got victimised for my pains. A working woman should not do public work. Add to the Court of Referees service, the fact that I have stood as a Labour Candidate for the local Urban District Council, as well as various other forms public services, and my crimes, in the view of the average small town employer, are of the blackest dye. And a Woman should not stand anyway -or so many of fellow workers told me. "What", said one dunderhead did I know about property? (he had just bought two old cottages) 'A woman ought to find something better to do' said an old lady whose vote I canvassed.

I have done some broadcasting-taking part in the opening talk of of a series on population Problems.

'A single woman' said some of my working men critics, 'should not take part in a broadcast on population' when she has never had a child'.

I pointed out that four men took part in that broadcast-and I was quite certain that same argument applied to them, as well as to my critics. 'Ah' said my critics,' we are fathers, we know what our wives had to go through'. 'Well,' I countered, 'I am a daughter, a sister I know what my brother's widow, my sister, my mother, and a host of married friends had to go through'. You see what nonsensical arguments are brought up. I was one of the speakers at a Northern listeners B.B.C. Conference. The other four were men, a Director of Education, a Professor of Pshchology, a Professor History and an Author.

Two of these, and almost all the men in the audience said they disliked women broadcasters-some went so far as to say women should not broadcast. In every sphere you see, from the time of Eve the word is, and has been 'DONT'-whatever woman has essayed to do. Only the serpent has ever said NO-and from the time that woman obeyed the serpent-because Eve became the 'Woman who DID' all the evils of mankind have descended upon us-or so the legend goes. If one has the mis fortune (or the luck) to be a spinster those evils will be twice as great. Were I a widow I would have an additional ten shillings a week income. Those widows pensions of course are another bribe to the subjection of women, saying in fact-'Marry and additional security shall be given unto you if you should be unlucky(or lucky)-enough to lose your lord and master.'

What could I not do for the aid of my spinster sisters given such a sum as that left by the late Director of Messrs Fry.

The model flats for single women I would persuade municipalities to build by force of example-and I would never be unemployed any more-would have a little money to spend on books and theatres and travel-would be ab able to arrange for tired housewives and spinsters to have a dee decent holiday, do something for the provision of educational settlements or Peckeham Health

Centres,-but all this is only a 666 dream. I can barely keep a roof over my head, have only a bare sus sustenance to live upon, and am denied the right to use the brains, organising powers, and such other mental and physical qualities as I may have, because of an economic system which is run for profit instead of for service, and which holds both men and women in subjection-though it holds women in greater servitude than men.

With Power Politics increasing-the ideal of a world where men and women contribute equally and together to the well being of the world seems more remote than ever-and while class consciousness continues-they will continue to be far off.

This distincion of caste and class is one which your book emphasisises. I admit these class distinctions exist-but that does not mean that the problems you enumerate are confined only to the daughter of the educated man. It is true that I have to cook my own dinner -while you do not-but that does not make me any more f free from the problems which beset women as a whole, and life in general.

I am afraid I have expressed myself very badly, and have not said one half of what I wished to say-but your book would make some people think that you consider working women, and the daughters of educated men as a race apart.

Do you think we enjoy being 'hewers of wood and drawers of water' that we do menial tasks from choice and are fitted for nothing e else?

Why should all the professional work be done by the daughters of educated men?.

Given the opportunity of either a University education and/or a private income, I also could have served my fellows to a greater degree than I have been able to do. I have always loved words. I too could have written books, given a kinder less strenuous environment. I too could have taken degrees, got into pParliament, studied law or medicine.

Not desire, or ability has been lacking, butlack of opportunity caused by economic inequality. And I am very far from being the only working woman of whom this can be said.

And this lumping of individuals into classes is odious too. It is true I am a woman-and I have to work for my living-or semi starve-but I am an individual-as unique in my way as you are in yours. There is only one Virginia Woolf-and because you have talent, and are lucky enough to be able to use that talent because you arein the right environment, you can impress that individuality on others. There is only one Agnes Smith-but such talent as she has hasnever had outlet and has atrophied and almost died so that she is just one of the unemployed-lost in the general mass-getting up in a morning-and wondering if life is worth living-wondering if after all she is to lose the battle she has waged so long, and go under for lack of something to do.

If one is useless tthere seems little sense in keeping the spark of life in being. It is no good talking of voluntary work. Every contact with one's fellows costs money. I can keep up no subscriptions which means I must lose all contacts-for this is no general depressed area (though there is much short time) most people have a job-or some member of the family has one-which means a shared income. I stand alone, as I have almost always done. I had dependants at a time when most girls of my age were carefree and happy-in middle age I am deprived of work-through no fault of my own.

True leisure I could use, but unemployment is not leisure. I rack my brains to find some way of finding economic independance. Domestic service some people would say-but at forty three -a skilled worker, especially one possessing some pretensions to culture would find it difficult to fit in to living in some one elseVs house-and so the problem continues. I cannot live, I cannot die-all I can do is be thankful that I am not persecuted by physical violence as Jews and others are-which is not a very satisfactory solution.

But I must stop this meandering letter which I have no right whatever to inflict upon a total stranger-except that I resent the fact of any 'educated woman' inferring that working women are of different clay to the 'daughters of educated men' and felt 6666 impelled to say so-though it is doubtful if you will so much as re read it.

With apologies for the infliction, however if you do=,
   I am,
     Yours sincerely, <u>M. Agnes Smith</u>.

---

*This is Agnes Smith's first letter to Woolf, but the two women continued to correspond until Woolf's death. None of Woolf's replies has survived. Woolf suggested that the Hogarth Press publish Smith's autobiography. In fact, Smith's* A Worker's View of the Wool Textile Industry *was published by Hillcroft Studies in 1944. A copy is held in the Monk's House Papers.*

---

**65**
**Handwritten**
**November 17, 1938**

---

*Broomcroft*
*Ford Lane*
*Didsbury, Manchester 20*
*Telephone: Didsbury 3368*

My dear Virginia,
  We had quite a good discussion last night. There were about 50 men & women - Fabians[1] - middle-aged & young. Only one man got up & wholeheartedly agreed with you. He was a teacher & young. He works under a woman head, a strong feminist but evidently he hadn't reacted unfavourably.

What surprised and amused me, was the reaction of the men to your remarks about their dress. Last night they seemed to mind that much more than the "infantile fixation" argument. One young man who tried to explain it away only proved all that you had said - to the merriment of the rest of the company.

Several speakers - men - tried to argue that war was the fault of capitalism & would disappear when socialism came - but I don't think the audience felt that they had made their point -

One criticism that surprised me was that your proposals were negative & not constructive - I should never have thought of that myself & I pointed out that although you may have expressed them negatively they involved extremely positive action. It was a most interesting evening & since the audience was entirely composed of middle class Fabians it was a revelation - to me - to find how amply justified you are in all that you have said.

One young man asked for my own views on your proposals. I said that I agreed with them wholeheartedly but that they involved a very high standard of conduct & that I didn't pretend to live up to them my self - & that is why I wished you could have been there to conduct the discussion because example is of more value than any amount of thought. But I think you would have enjoyed it & would have realized - if you have not already done so - what effect Three Guineas has had even in the few months since it appeared. People are thinking in a different way about the relation of the sexes.

Yours Shena D. Simon

Nov. 17

{The Silent Traveller In London Chiang Yee}[2]

---

*Published courtesy of Professor Brian Simon, Baron of Wythenshawe.*

*For reply see L6 303 (3468). Woolf found it amusing that "the dress charge rankled" and writes: "I'm surprised and delighted that fifty intelligent people should think it worth while to talk about 3 gs."*

[1] The Fabian Society was a socialist movement founded in 1883 by George Bernard Shaw and Sidney and Beatrice Webb.

[2] *The Silent Traveller: A Chinese Artist in Lakeland* by Chiang Yee (1937) is a prose and pictorial description of Yee's travels in the Lake District.

**66**
**Typed**
**November 28, 1938**

> Mount Pleasant
> Thongsbridge
> Holmfirth Yorks.
> Nov 28th 1938.

Dear Madam,

It was good of you to reply so promptly. I suppose the fact that you dealt so exclusively with the 'educated man's daughter" swamped the declaration that ~~you~~ you had declared you would write from this point of view, for the very good reason that it is one of which you have first hand knowledge; which just shows how difficult it is to bear an essay in mind as a whole-though I confess the declaration might not have escaped my memory if I had been more alert. Unemployment atrophies more than the muscles! Mervyn Peake[1] the young modern poet wrote more truly than his readers may gave him ~~e~~ credit for, when he described, in his poem 'Rhondda Valley' how
'At every door a ghost; I saw them lean
With tightened belts and watch the sluggish tide,'
I assure you I do not think writing easy, I know from experience it is not. I have managed to earn about £30 or so by this means and if it were easy there would be no reason why I should not add a couple of noughts to this sum and gain economic independance!
I know you edited the 'Co-operative women's book of potted biographies-I think it is the only bit of writing of yours I have not read.[2]
And I have appreciated what you have written and realised the work you are trying to do. I think I found more stimulation from 'A Room of One's Own' than anything I have read -of late years- and I feel sure that what you have written there and elsewhere will bear fruit-even though-the harvest comes from many small shrubs here, there and everywhere, rather than from one large and splendid tree.
I am not quite sure what a university training could have d done for you though-but perhaps the work you have already accomplished might have been done with less effort.
Anyway, if you did not enter the University, your books are th there, providing matter for criticism for students of English literature!
I enclose one of my own attempts of criticism which may ~~int~~ interest you-though I see now that I ommited the cheif 6666 appeal which your work had- and has-for me.
I think that you feel what you write ~~N~~ and are passionately truthful and sincere. Perhaps if you have read Stephen Potter's 'Muse in Chains'[3]- or even if you haven't , you will have little respect for the study of literature as pursued by the

University-inasmuch as it seems to include so much which has little to do with literature-and teaches criticism rather than encourages creation-but perhaps this will be altered in time.

At the moment I am not suffering from hard work, but from that death in life which comes of having nothing to do-a trouble which would not occur given economic independance & which paradoxally would make the need for work less insistant-though not less necessary. Its a queer world, which has much to be done in it yet keeps willing and able workers idle.

Yours sincerely<br>
<u>Agnes Smith</u>.

*Enclosure missing*

[1] Mervyn Peake (1911-1968) was a novelist, artist and poet. His "Rhondda Valley" was published in the *London Mercury* in 1938 with illustrations. In an attempt to gain employment as a war artist, he had written to Sir Kenneth Clark, Chairman of the War Artists' Commission, about doing a series of drawings inspired by Welsh mining districts. His Rhondda Valley project was an attempt to show his interest in the subject.

[2] Woolf wrote an introductory letter to *Life As We Have Known It*, a collection of autobiographical letters from members of the Women's Co-operative Guild edited by Margaret Llewelyn Davies and published by the Hogarth Press in 1931.

[3] Stephen Potter's *The Muse in Chains: A Study in Education* (Jonathan Cape 1937) is a polemic against New Criticism and the current state of the study of English literature. Potter attacks the "detached criticism" with its "scientific attitude," arguing that criticism is privileged over literature and that the text is divorced from both writer and reader. Literary study, he writes, depersonalizes "the struggle for life, for integrity." Potter also wrote books on D. H. Lawrence and Coleridge.

**67**
**Handwritten**
**December 5, 1938**

Lagora<br>
River Bank<br>
Molesey<br>
Surrey<br>
5th Dec

Dear Madam,

    I have just finished reading "Three Guineas" & felt that I must express to you a little of my satisfaction at finding aspiring woman's case stated so clearly & logically, without irritation or animosity. I hope and believe that your book will have far-reaching influence, not only on the position of women, but in increasing the liberty of the individual - man and woman alike.

    I do hope you will not consider this letter tiresome, but as a woman (I need hardly add semi-educated), as a wage-earner (of course paid less than my husband for similar work) and as the mother of a daughter, still too young to realize the disabilities of her sex, I am profoundly grateful to you for the thought & labour you have put into your book.

                        Yours sincerely
                        Phyllis Preen

*Published courtesy of Hilary Bishop-Preen, daughter of Phyllis Preen.*

*Phyllis Amy Preen (née Cowley 1905-1987) was an English teacher; in the early 1950s she became the headmistress of a girls' secondary school in Barnes, London. Her father died when she was seventeen, leaving her to care for her tubercular mother and to borrow money in order to take a teacher's training certificate in South London. After becoming a teacher, she taught extra evening classes to pay off her debts and studied part-time for an English degree at University College London, which she achieved with outstanding results. She married a fellow teacher, Trevor Preen, in 1935 having waited until the requirement for married teachers to retire had been withdrawn. She was passionately interested in English literature, particularly poetry and drama.*

**68**
**Handwritten**
**January 20, 1939**

                                            Bedales Lodge,
                                            Petersfield.
                                            Hants.
                                            Jan 20th 1939.

Miss Virginia Woolf,
Dear Madam,
                I have just finished reading, with steadily mounting interest, your recent book, Three Guineas.

        At first I felt you were thrashing a dead horse. Belonging as I do to religious body that has to a very large degree practised the equality of the sexes for two hundred years or more (the Quakers), and also not being in your rather limited sense the daughter of an educated man, I had not felt the disadvantages that still cling to my sex in the professional field. It is true that marriage has brought me many limitations. These were not the intention of my husband, who has none of the infantile fixation you describe, but the limitations have come because of our limited income (my husband's earnings of now only £500 a year have to suffice for the upkeep of an "educated man's" home, our medical &

professional expenses & the education of our two children). So that it is difficult simply to keep one's brain functioning when one is tired out with the strain of making ends meet. ('Daddy makes it first, & mother makes it last,' as one of our children put it the other day!)

So, on consideration, & on reading your book further I am satisfied that you are not thrashing a dead horse.

I am particularly interested in your analysis of the infantile fixation that perpetuates the dualism in male-ordered society.

Now may I venture to suggest, dear Madam, that your book doesn't go far enough? It must have occurred to you that this infantile fixation cannot be inherent in male nature, since some, such as Mr Leigh Smith,[1] and numbers of other men since seem to be quite free from it. That our public schools and their imitators, and our older universities perpetuate the fixation if one can use such a phrase, I do not deny, but are not we mothers as well as fathers responsible in a very large measure for that fixation? Will you not now use the influence of your pen to expose and analyse the tendency in women to keep their sons fixed somewhere at the age of six, or is it two?

In the past when the majority of women were limited to the "home sphere" it was not remarkable that they hated their children to grow up mentally, loved their chains, as slaves are said everywhere to do. We are now only partly free of those chains, but as my husband and I have said in a small book we have written on marriage, the upbringing of children, etc. "it may be generations before our children, progressively set free, by parents yet root-bound, but aware of their limitations, may be able to face sex & its strong urges without fear and without reproach from within." The sexual fixations, in a broad sense have, as you have shown, far-reaching influences in society. I am now inclined to think we could loosen up this infantile fixation of men in one generation, with help from people like yourself. There are signs already that it is loosening. There is a growing realisation that dualism is the evil we must eradicate. The conception of the wholeness of life, the oneness of thought & practice is ably dealt with in another book I have just read: "The Clue to History" by John Macmurray,[2] out this year. What is brought ~~up~~ out in this book brings me now to the other point I wish to put before you.

Perhaps I am mistaken, but you seem to assume in "Three Guineas" that men fight because of some fighting instinct that for some reason is inherent in males. Now what seems to me the great weakness of pacifism (I have been a pacifist for twenty years or more) is the assumption that the struggles now conducted by arms, are not about anything vital. The same assumption appears in Eric Linklater's "Impregnable Women".[3] Men are just fighting, like children, for the sake of fighting, and in the opinion of women the issues are negligible.

That men are childishly devoted to dressing up, to assumptions of power, to fatal conservations and precedents, to unreal loyalties I do not dispute. But there is something else moving in history besides these things. Urges towards truth, towards human liberty and equality are not the private peculiarity of women. John Macmurray is of the opinion that these urges and the attempts, however misled and failing in their ~~objects~~ attempted realisation, are the movement of God in history: that the meaning and purpose and realisation of Christianity are to be found there. He has a great deal to say about the origin and meaning of dualism which I believe would interest you, if only in connection with what you most forcefully say about the dualism that permits churchmen to admit only men to Orders on the assumption that their wives can carry the burdens of ordinary human care.

But I ought to be brief & what I want to say is this. The peoples of the world are fighting; not for the sake of fighting, but about real issues. Macmurray would call those issues the struggle for the Kingdom of God to be set up on earth (with all that that implies of social justice, equality and the rule of love) as against the negation of Christianity. My difficulty, as a hater of war, as one who realises its clumsy ineffectiveness, to say the least of it, is that the wars now going on are about something real & vital. How can I work for those ends of equality, justice & the rest and stand aside from the struggle now everywhere going on? I admit the methods you advocate in your second chapter, but there are issues one has to decide every day, as well as in living & working for the future. For instance now - this vote - fought for & won with so much struggle. Now we've got it, look at the alternatives we are offered. I don't want either Chamberlain's double dealing or the Labour Party's programme of rearmament. In a crisis like that of September, only two alternatives, both abominable, are offered. The strength of pacifist opinion made Chamberlain's policy into an undoubted majority. I want some recognition by women that the issues of conflict are vital issues: then I think we shall find our way of pressing for the cause of what Macmurray calls Christianity - by Gandhi's non-co-operative method or something like it. But as long as men and women just ask for peace, as an unwise mother stops quarelling children, without troubling to know what are the rights & wrongs of the quarrel and what injustices have led to the aggression, we shall live to see our generation looking vainly for peace in a world of anarchy and decay.

Perhaps what I am asking for is that women should go ahead with their political education. You are not going to do things politically without being political. Writers such as Vera Brittain,[4] Storm Jameson[5] and yourself might exert a very great influence if you would begin to understand what the struggle is all about.

If you have had patience with all this I am most grateful to you.

Yours sincerely
Frances Barnes.

P.S. One thing you do not mention in Three Guineas is the complete intention & I believe actuality of equality of women with men in Russia? Does it not occur to you that this is politically significant?

*"Sex, Friendship & Marriage" Allen & Unwin 1938.[6]

[1] Father of Barbara Bodichon. See *Three Guineas*, Part 3, Note 38.

[2] John MacMurray (1891-1976) was a philosopher. He held professorships at London and Edinburgh Universities and is best known for his Gifford Lectures, published as *The Self as Agent* and *Persons in Relation* (1953-4). Books published in the 1930s include *The Philosophy of Communism* (1933), *Reason and Emotion* (1935) and *The Clue to History* (1938).

[3] See Letter 48, Note 2.

[4] Vera Brittain (1893-1970) was a writer, pacifist and feminist, best known for her *Testament of Youth* trilogy (1933-57).

[5] Storm (Margaret) Jameson (1891-1983) was a writer, whose novels published in the 1930s include three novellas *Women Against Men* (1933-7) and a trilogy: *Company Parade* (1934), *Love in Winter* (1935) and *None Turn Back* (1936). She was the first woman President of the British section of International P. E. N. 1939-45. She worked constantly for refugee writers. Woolf helped Jameson in 1939 to assist the Jewish Austrian refugees Mela and Robert Spira. Woolf was instrumental in freeing Robert from internment on the Isle of Man. Woolf's letters to Mela and Robert Spira, written during 1939 and 1940, are in the Frances Hooper Collection at Smith College. They have been published in the *Virginia Woolf Bulletin* of the Virginia Woolf Society of Great Britain, Issue No. 2, July 1999: 4-12.

[6] This title refers to the correspondent's book mentioned in paragraph six. *Sex, Friendship and Marriage* by Kenneth C. Barnes and G. Frances Barnes (Allen & Unwin, 1938) was reviewed in the *Times Literary Supplement* 14 May, 1938: 343. The book, complete with illustrations, is a revised series of lectures given by the Barnes' in a co-educational school. In the brief review the reviewer summarizes the book as follows: "The authors feel that it is urgent in these days of free contact between the young of both sexes to give them a clear understanding of biology as it applies to their own lives, and at the same time to show them the spiritual and social implication of biological processes."

**69**
**Handwritten**
**February 5, 1939**

S. Paul's Vicarage,
Spalding.
Feb. 5. 1939.

Dear Mrs Woolf:
I have been reading your book "Three Guineas" with pleasure and profit. I think you rather weaken your argument by over-emphasis but, in general, I agree with it. In fact, my daughter is having a public school education, and is at present a pupil at Cheltenham Ladies' College.

But as regards p.99 and elsewhere -
(a) It is only the Archbishop of Canterbury whose salary is £15,000. Out of that I understand he pays the expenses of his office. The salary of the Archbishop of York is £9,000 and he does likewise. I wonder what an Archbishop can save out of his salary.
(b) With regard to their salaries may I quote the following reply given (to a question relating to the payment of the clergy) by Mr Lloyd George in the House of Commons Dec. 8. 1908.

"I am desired by the Chancellor of the Exchequer to say that, with the exception of those in the direct employment of the State as chaplains, the stipends of clergy of the Church of England are not paid out of public funds." The position is still the same.

So the Archbishops {and clergy} are not paid out of taxes - except, of course, the comparatively few Chaplains to the Forces.

     Yours very sincerely
     J.E. Callister.

P.S: My daughter had spoken highly to me of your book which she read at College last term: so I bought it for her as a Christmas present. Would you very kindly autograph it for her? I will gladly pay postage both ways.

**70**
**Handwritten**
**May 12, 1939**

     The Convent of the Sacred Heart,
     45, Church Rd.,
     Barnes.
     S.W. 13.
     12th May, 1939

Dear Fellow Outsider,
  "Three Guineas", which I could not have bought had Smiths[1] not reduced to 2/-, has given me great consolation & courage.
  All the bees I have been accused of harbouring in my veil, here buzz harmoniously.
  Although all you say about Hon. Secs. & badges & paraphernalia is true- still we can only hustle things along (& why shouldn't they be hustled in these days?) by pooling experiences & profiting by mutual support & advice. I hope you agree.
  I have a romantic suggestion to make: that all who share our views be invited (by something like chain letters to the élite only) to regard a certain place & day as open for meetings: e.g. Any Sunday afternoon in one of the

London parks - no money to be given, for hall adverts, etc., to the enemy: that the rules be simple purity of intention, zeal, & entire willingness to co-operate.

The no-such-[   ] & such like do need fortifying by the knowledge that, as others are also resisting, their resistance will not be vain.

Only one passage in your book merits my disapproval. (I know now that you approve of criticism). I'm sure others have only been too ready to hold it against you - the note on p.300 lines 10-13.[2] It may sound different from what you intended - but to me it seems giving away just a little to the enemy.

One of the pschological causes of "the thing" I believe is the natural male craving after polygamy. He has tried to curb that in himself, & knows that monogamy has taken away some of his power to dominate. The possessive attitude towards wife & daughter is often born of jealousy - for he believes all other men who dare are polygamists.

Let him have his freedom back & women will become "his" & set at one another's throats. From a natural point of view I would prefer sharing to enforced celibacy - but as I cannot have one partner to myself I am remaining celibate in spite of serious temptation; & I experience nothing but a strong feeling of sympathy & benevolence towards the unloved & unloving wife. I believe that bodily chastity is still one of the weapons for good.

I am not of your "class" as perhaps my lack of scholarship shows but a half-educated daughter of a working-class woman.

Nevertheless I feel people of such different upbringing can & must work together.

My favourite way of signing myself needs a little explaining. I am a member of the R.C. Church (fully alive to the defects & omissions in its priesthood) & associate myself with a group who hate snobbery & love honest work. So: -

       Yrs. sincerely in Christ the Worker,
         Constance Cheke.

---

[1] W. H. Smith, booksellers.

[2] Cheke refers to Note 38 to Part Two of *Three Guineas*, specifically the sentence: "Even today it is probable that a woman has to fight a psychological battle of some severity with the ghost of St. Paul, before she can have intercourse with a man other than her husband."

**71**
**Handwritten**
**May 1939**

>45, Church Rd.,
>Barnes,
>S.W.13
>May 1939.

Dear Mrs. Woolf,

It was very kind of you to reply to my letter. I am not asking you to write again but merely to be good enough to consider one point i.e. the possibility of altering that one passage re St. Paul & adultery when your book "Three Guineas" goes into a new edition & I hope it will be soon.

Such a book is so very much needed amongst us Catholics where sex snobbery must be, I think, at its worst: & one mistake of wrong emphasis is enough to make it forbidden to many who would greatly profit by it. I am not suggesting that we are more stupid in our criticisms than others. For my part I would have your book in all school colleges seminaries - but I would expect the students to see for themselves that the author ~~must~~ cannot really mean that St. Paul was the first to forbid adultery. (I know that with others "adultery" can be qualified & that our beliefs are more rigid.)

The book is such good fun*! I haven't enjoyed myself so much for ages. I was not writing to criticise but to ask you to remove a handle from those who would wish to oppose the book because of its philosophy. You know the type, of course!

It will sell like hot cakes I am sure - but I so very much want it to sell like hotter cakes among my co-religionists.

Please forgive my insistence, & again many thanks for your letter, & for your most delightful book.

>Yrs. sincerely,
>Constance Cheke.

I think your typewriting's lovely - I wish I could do it. I was wishing your photograph illustrations had included one of a man au naturel i.e. unshaven - opposed to St. Paul's text about Nature having covered a woman's head with hair more than a man's. Have you ever reflected how "Nature" meant ~~then~~ men to ~~live~~ hide under a bushel?

**72**
**Handwritten**
**June 1939**

598 New Chester Road
Rock Ferry[1]

Mrs. Virginia Woolf.
Dear madam,
    I doubt ever again reading any book written by yourself, from the first page to the last, mainly from the inability to obtain them from the public library partly because you do not write in the manner that fascinates and inveigles the reader of a tale demanding continuity of interest. Margaret Lawrence,[2] I believe it was, in her book "We write as women" described your own inimitable style in such seductive terms as to persuade me to go to an amount of trouble to obtain a volume written by you, the resultant search being rewarded with "The Years", "A room of one's own" and "The common reader", a copy of the last mentioned being in my possession by the expenditure of sixpence, such is the regrettable low standard of the English reader, who will pay many times that price for the work of an author who has only a tale to tell, a parallel can be instanced in comparing those magnificent animals which occupy the King's Stables to a high powered car.
    Enough of this, I write not in order to present any bouquet, rather to criticize, and chide, gently yet assuredly the subjects you present for our study. One book only "The years" have I read completely and I found it beyond, or should it be above, any remarks praising or deprecating a story so delightful, your treatment of the leading character, who was she, Eleanor? I forget, made her so real, so lovely, a lady. Yet you descend to vulgarity; and the effect, the pressure of the teeth against the lips, a shock, a rousing from that state of fascinated dreaminess which you say an essay should produce. I cannot say it irritates, irritation is a petty annoyance, your vulgarities hurt, they jar, they grate like grit on a dusty road on a summers afternoon grate between the teeth, they disgust even as the dirty finger prints I found on many pages of the library copy; they resembled Garbo being forced to display her legs, which I resented in the film "Mata Hari", or the introduction of a muffled trumpet to a rendering of the overture to Tchaikofsky's Ballet, or the debasing of a beautiful carriage horse by using him for rides on the sands at a seaside resort.
    You offer to us your views for the emancipation of your sex, you claim for yourselves equality, and so entirely as a woman do you argue, as at a debating society; and as a debater stating only those instances favourable to your argument, femininely unilateral, unreasonable, biased, ignoring the basic differences of the two sexes: The case of woman by women is privilege and power without responsibility; you complain of being warned off the grass of a college lawn, of being refused entrance to the library, of having to dine of cus-

tard and prunes; yet you never mention that no woman had prepared the velvet green carpet, had subscribed any works to the library collection, had sacrificed a week's dinner to purchase an elaborate dinner set for posterity. Gardening, writing, the creation of beautiful articles are surely within a womans sphere, we are told they are more spiritual than man, are more inclined to aesthetic apreciation; for centuries women of quality and class have had leisure to devote their time and energy in the producing of beautiful and otherwise useless things. To man has been left the fighting, the home making and protecting, the working and providing of necessities. Yet in comparison to women how men have honoured the obligations placed upon them, extending their activities to the designing of beautiful and magnificient buildings often with their attendant gardens, the authorship of books, of poetry and prose, the production of delicate and ornamented pottery and cutlery, the creation of works of art that grace the galleries of the world. Should not then men be granted the privilege of permitting or denying the trespass of a womans foot or prying eye.

You have not admitted the fundamental truth that men and women occupy two seperate and distinct worlds, to you then it must be an insufferable presumption that it is on sufferance that women be allowed to intrude and to share mans' world and activities, just as a wife takes her position, and enjoys the benefits and courtesies due to a wife as the consort of her husband, the man taking precedence.

To women during the War and since have been opened all the occupations, employments, professions, privileges held by men. The men were required for defence, a breach was made in the life works of a nation, would the women fill the breach, keep things going until the men returned, men were urged to fight while the women would keep their jobs going so that the job would still be there to return to. Would the women fill the breach, would they - they gladly stepped in, they jumped in they fought with each other to get in. The men were fooled; they fought for nothing, for less than nothing; the progress made during the previous half century was swept away, smashed, and by the avaricious and irresponsible hand of woman. Of the hardships the men had undergone the fighting was the least, the roughness next, the bestiality was the worst, six million men mixed and mingled together gained an added appreciation of the amenities of a civilized society, they returned softened and sobered expectant of an improvement caused by the soft hand of woman. And the women who during those years had had their virtues praised and lauded to the skies, did they return. If one occupation and one only did they willingly retire from, the most elementary manual work, farm labour; of all the other occupations they had crashed into they held tenaciously on to, grappling fiercely to retain their positions. And the country, the nation, built by a hundred generations of man, how had it fared; for years women had been crying for admittance to engage in the nations life and work, they had been admitted they had the chance to show their merit, to justify their demand. The standard of living was ruined, work and skill had been cheapened, slums had made an appearance and ugliness took the place of beauty in architecture. Where were the great works of art and books by master authoresses where the improvement and softening conditions of a smooth civilization one could reasonably expect of women.

The quarter century during which woman has actively participated with man int he nations affairs has revealed dual accomplishments at which she excelled, and those peculiarly womans, domesticity and dancing; no one ever attempts to deny the lady of the ballet her position, personification of loveliness and grace, performing her art by the only means possible, assiduous study, care, practice and real hard work, tennis, so closely allied to the ballet so ably demonstrated by the prima danceaux Mlle. Suzzanne Lenglen,[3] who for all time remain on a pedestal a woman only can occupy. In the home, woman engaged in domestic economy has proved her ownership of the title "man's consort" which custom of time immemorial has delegated to her.

The professions of medicine, habitations, dress and music she has lamentably failed in. Women are mainly associated with concern of the ills of the body, we associate her with tenderness and a desire to heal, to place all else aside to render aid, to relieve distress, to sympathize. The medical profession was opened to her, following a line of reason a glut of women practitioners should have been the ultimate if not the immediate result, advising and giving treatment to a host of fellow women. A quarter century is not an unreasonable length of time in which to expect results, assuming a girl commenced her studies at the commencement and at the age of twenty, graduating six years later, practicing for the greater part of the ensuing score of years, now in her middle age should have emblazoned her name on the scroll of fame, we still search in vain for any mention of her, either as a member of the Council of the British Medical Association, as consultant to the Royal Family, or even as holding the faith of the majority of the members of her sex, most puzzling of all is the absense of any demand made by her for a general supply of twilight sleep, the anaesthetic administed or should be administed to all women during the process of reproduction of the species.

In dress woman still looks to man for the creation of Fashion and the designing of beautiful dresses to adorn their own exquisite figures, even in the actual making men hold the lead in the tailoring of garments.

We can surely be excused for looking forwards to the working of woman's hand in the matter of the habitation of herself and her family. For many many years she had bitterly complained at mans lack of consideration and refusal to provide her a comfortable place of residence. She wailed that since man forced her to remain in the home, that home should be a fit place to spend her days within. A mocking yell was called after the men those twenty five years ago "A land fit for heroes" in fulfilment of that yell an Act was passed enforcing all housing to be, in the fashion for England to become the land of Garden Cities, the hideous resultant being the outrageous brick boxes, red and two by two sprawling like an angry sore with its ugly tentacles defacing our fair land. Where are the lovely little homes a woman could design and have erected out of the money she herself had earned and saved, where the buildings which should grace our cities, owing their existence and going down to posterity as types of womans architecture, where even the endowment funds for halls, colleges, libraries, galleries of art, subscribed by woman alone. They entered the professions, they accepted the remunerations, and they give in return, what? woman took the power, the privilege, but the responsibility does not that also go with the others, has she nothing to give in the civilizing of society. She demands to place her foot on the path of progress, very well then let her get on the path, let her take her place alongside man and tread and work and do a fair share but not tread on progress and destroy, selfishly unthinkingly a constitution man with effort and patience has built up.

In the evening the day's work finished we turn towards the theatre, the Opera House, the Concert Hall seeking amusement and if not entirely forgetfulness at least relaxation. Members of the fair and gentle sex entertian us by their portrayal of love lorn maidens, gipsy queens and demure ladies with the virtues of angels; we are enraptured by their loveliness, delighted by their golden voices and their seductive charm and grace, they interpret the child born in the mind of the master of Music and unfold the vision in which Man beholds Woman. They interpret only, the rolls of Music contain no work of genius created by woman. From her earliest years a girl is encouraged to be a faithful devotee and attendant to the Goddess of Sound, she is placed at the lowermost steps of the Goddesses Throne with an intrument on which to render faithful service, her supposedly musical spirit, aptitude and talent is her anxious parents continuous care, and those loving parents at the girls' eventual interpretation of the master's genius blindly mistake her for a Mistress of her art. We wearily turn our steps in disappointment towards the Cabaret or Music Hall. Over supper and champaine the Cabaret gives us the reason of our inability to find the mistresses of Music. To our astonished eyes and outraged ears Woman offers her version, dressed in fantastic garments mounted on a small platform which often enough is a tiny pedestal she prances, carrying occasionally a semblance of war dance among her fellow instrumentalists in her own mind satisfied she is conducting the "perfect piece" rendered by her accompanists on the queerest instruments devised which create the weirdest howls and screeches imaginable. Miss Modern steps along hand in hand with hat music". Home ward bound we raise our hat to the lady carrying her violincello from the Philharmonic Hall, we must be thankful for small mercies, at least the last lady is an interpreter of real music; man made.

We arrive home and drop comfortably into the most comfortable of our armchairs, how comfortable these women arrange our domiciles, bless them, now in the privacy of their own rooms they can uncover those exquisite figures they so modestly draped in ankle length gowns for our benefit. We can be at our ease at last, free to speak without restraint; in honour due to the ladies we respected their sensibilities and moderated our speech and our opinions. We start to smoke and give a laugh, what a set of asses our fathers were. They let themselves in for quite a deal of irritations, petty hindrances and small annoyances in their opposition to giving the vote to the gentler sex. To-day our member can enjoy the company and refining influence of a sprinkling of ladies, a contemptible minority perhaps but they did manage to crash in, we have even had one in the Cabinet. Strange that so few of them found a seat, last election the women predominated the voters list, maybe after all politics do not interest them, possibly the trouble was caused by a handful of silly women out of some fad they had at the time, some slight derangement in the part of their fair selves they wore those large hats on, may have caused their loss of proportion. it might have been the ridiculous fashions of the period had gone to the head. The entry of the wealthy Lady Astor[4] had led us to believe and interesting change was imminent in the constitution of our nation. We had looked forward to the views of women being impressed on our lives, even a Feminist Party in office overpowering a feeble Male Opposition was not an improbability and Bills presented and carried by women being recorded on the Statute Book as Acts passed in the venerable Palace of Westminster. We sigh in relief, how barren women have shown themselves in the World of Politics With the almost isolated efforts of Lady Nancy from America to limit our liberty of drinking what we like, women have confined their contribution to the ultra sentimental part of the Labour Movement which they in turn had filched from the Liberals. For the rest of the sex, they have unreasonably supported the leaders of the various parties, propounding no worthy policy of their own, and in spite of their talkative abilities producing not a single person worthy of being entitled Statesman.

It is surely time I tell of the fundamental difference that separate Man and Woman, a difference always over-looked by women and never tolerated by them. They always look at life from a different angle than a man does, they are exceedingly childish and intolerant in their views. Women are as children in many respects; children in their day dreams and in their treatment of animals can be very cruel, they are by no means the tender kind children some writers would have us believe, to give them bare justice they torture cats and birds in ignorance of the possible damage they may do, but whereas boys as they mature learn to oppose, often violently, all forms of torture and cruelty, it is extremely doubtful that women ever grow out of the elementary instinct of cruelty. One little instance will suffice, you must have met on many occasions women who will shed crocodile's tears over the sufferings of a lost or injured animal, yet they gloat over the possession of a costly fur coat, heedless of the intense pain and torture and forfieture of life endured by the numerous creatures whose skins where required to provide them with a covering in which they may imitate the prehistoric inhabitants of our islands. No amount of arguing will persuade her to go without her prehistoric covering, she is entirely immune of all reasoning that she is a member of a community emancipated from a savage state to a civilized society where garments of manufactured fabrics are de rigueur; her final words and ultimate refuge is her statement that she as a single individual could make no impression against the trade which disgraces our civilization regardless that it has been from time immemorable the individual who has formed the march to progress and the mass is merely a composition of individuals.

Children are great day-dreamers, boys well in the forefront in the variety of their imaginations, placing themselves in their various heroes positions and clothing, wrapping themselves in wonderful adventures, glorious scenes and exciting incidents in which they always play the part of the hero who always emerges victorious to receive the plaudits of his associates uniforms and sporting garb take a prominent part in his imaginings although as yet he does not recognize the significations of uniforms, and he often pictures himself splendidly garbed leading regiments of troops, commanding a fleet in an epic sea battle, maneauvring mechanised instruments of war all to be followed by a grand parade and presentation to Royalty; or else he as leader of a famous side wins a strenuous sporting event. With the passing of boyhood the dreams dwindle with an occasional vision of himself captivating pretty girls and compelling their admiration intermingled by representations of himself occupying an elevated position in his favourite sport, until on his arrival to man's estate they have faded to a faint shadow, a shadow of the important personage he wishes he could be. As a reasoning being he accepts the experience of life, that dreams are of no substance, that it is the application of reasoning powers, concentrated study, effort and trained skill alone will make him worthy to be accepted as qualified to occupy the eminent positions. He accepts the truth, general amongst men, the loftier the position carries the higher responsibility and greater service required of him.

A girl dreaming her childish dreams carries them with her into advanced woman hood. How limited is the repertoire of her fancies, as herself the attractive centre of her circle, closely associated to a spiteful glee at the conternation of her vanquished rivals. Beginning in the home circle, where she is the imagined favourite of her indulgent parents, then amongst her near playmates, on through school life, office, shop, or factory, ever onwards until her dominion extends over the whole world, the envy of all women, the queen of the hearts of all handsome, (mostly titled) men who come to pay homage to her ravishing beauty. Seldom if ever in her imaginings does she consider that efforts are required of her in mounting her pedestal, all must be contained in her appearance as a gift of grace bestowed upon her Her sense of value goes awry at the smallest success. She recognizes beauty as the only virtue, her amazing mentality forces her to enter for competitions in quest of Beauty Queen, even in advanced middle age she makes calls on artificial aids to beauty to create impressions on others, mainly to gain mans' attention. During the occasional hours of awakeness to reality her values are all wrong. In her heart every little girl is a snob, she gleefully struts before her envious companions when arrayed in a dress which outshines the others, she boasts her occupancy of a grand domicile, the possession of costly toys, her relation to affluent persons, she is a creature of pride, during maturity her shallow mind takes delight in the display of extravagant dress, glittering jewels, freakish pets, high powered automobiles, dazzling house parties, cruises on luxury liners, the greatest exaltation being yatchs, her male conquests, please forgive me if this paragraph reads like a Labour Party tract, it is not intended to be so, the streak of pride runs right through the whole feminine sex, for some obscure reason a cruise takes precedence. To a woman, her glory is contained within herself, she is concerned only with the effects wealth has in personal display, glory must be a reflected glory of herself, if a consort or daughter, reflected glory of her husband or father, man takes glory only in the effect his efforts have on matters impersonal to himself, a civilized society, traditions, the consitution of a nation, institutions, magnificient edifices, marvels of transport and manufacturing processes, cities suitable for habitation I abhor the practice of setting women to heavy manual labour, I acclaim those men who had them withdrawn from the coal mines and refuse to entertain them as road navvies, any suggestion that they should take their place alongside men in extractive or constructive industries and the conditions of the bad old days deserves the outburst of protest which would receive it. Yet if the sex as a whole renounce all claim to producing of coal or making of highways what claims can they possibly put forward for the comfort and amenities the two industries provide, what right beyond that of man's consort or subordinate have they to warm themselves consume hot meals, drive cars or walk easily and safely We pass quickly along the cavalcade of Miss Moddern, her father has married her mother and accepted the responsibility of providing a home both are accustomed to, of becoming a ratepayer and voter to decide who shall govern our country. He becomes her father, feeds her, dresses her, pays her school fees and seeks a suitable situation for her. She is offered an oportunity of engaging her time and knowledge and ability for a remunerative return which will subsequently render her independent of every other person to keep her. She starts level with her brother, her elder sisters demanded equality, she receives equality. She steps out on to the pavement demanding a smooth road on which to set her dainty feet a highway safe from molestation and injury, a transport system to carry her quickly to her place of work. She expects a courteus reception, a well organised trading establishment, comfortable sanitary surroundings and mechanical devices. She becomes fairly proficient, her salary is raised periodically until it reaches respectable proportions. She is now independant, she works alongside men with equal chances of promotion, she has learnt enough now to specialize in some subject, she has a variety from which she may take her choice, she may even make a break, take a more responsible position elsewhere. The men she finds are on a higher salary than she is, the thought rankles in her mind, there is a society for the welfare of the workers in her profession, she may join it for a weekly contribution of one shilling. One shilling, why I can get a monthly journal for that sum of money it would buy me a box of chocolate, a powder pack, one leg of a pair of art silk stockings. No, no, not me, I can find much better uses for my shilling; she reasons; taking the first step on the sliding scale of evaded responsibility. The junior partner who usually receives the requests of the staff grants her a hearing in her quest of a higher salary, he gently explains to her that all the male members whose salary is in excess of her own engage themselves in some occupation demanding specialized knowledge of the business, does she consider she could become proficient in a particular department which would be to the benefit of the Partnerships' interest. Her work to that moment had been mainly of a routine order; the uncertain strength of her personality wavers at the implied suggestion of accepted responsibility in promoting the Partnerships activities in continuous effort and unwavering loyalty. Beating a retreat she determines on following her favourite pastime of picking her future husband whom she can arrange to marry when she decides to retire from the world of Business. Until then she had considered herself entitled to have her path smoothed for her, for the world to arrange itself in a pleasant, comfortable, easy moving order in which she could occupy herself in some congenial capacity disregarding the various institutions and processes which build up Commerce, monetary systems, foreign exchanges, stock exchanges, banking transport, manufacturing, buying and selling, she passed over as requiring no efforts of hers. She reviews her acquaintances, her immediate superior is a middle aged woman with a medium figure, of no great commanding personality who dresses in a modest style evidently in order to put a fair proportion of her salary in the savings bank. No sane person would consider her one who could create an impression which would advance trade. She was prone to a mild sarcasm in her treatment of juniors, always ready with the threat of reporting them to the partners. The business manager, dressed in a suit he had worn previously a period as his best, a shabby moustache, who arrived every Saturday unshaven since they finished at noon, when he was as prompt at leaving, as he was always insistent on their prompt arrival every morning, in order to be able to attend a football match. His appearance gave the lie to his personality, shrewd in the confidence of the Partners, he seemed to get everything desired from the departments, she compared him with her own superior, he never fussed or threatened, always even tempered, she had never seen him riled, talked to his male staff in a straight manner as man to man without any display of authority, conversing at times for ten minutes on the merits of football, and occasionally passed cheery remarks about the dresses of the female staff offering to mere man an opportunity of admiring their shapely limbs. The man in charge of deliveries who seemed to have an extensive knowledge of the outside trade, a full figure and compelling voice, very much subdued in the telling of riské stories to his fellows, which the whole female staff strained their ears to catch, boasted a complete knowledge of the form of race horses which placed him in great favour amongst the ladies the days outstanding races were contested, and who accepted his betting reverses as unconcernedly as his gains. The cashier, a brilliant and well dressed man still in his early thirties, a genius at figures, anxious to leave as early as possible to get home to his young wife on whom he doted, obviously the reason he avoided the female staff, a player in junior cricket, proud of the garden he tended around his suburban home which he had bought to take his bride to, and from which he regularly supplied the office with flowers. Never did any member of the male staff appeared distracted, irritated or unduly worried at the course of events, taking the affairs of the business in an easy stride towards progress, the days work over engaging themselves in interests beyond pecuniary consideration.

    She is slightly contemptuous of the male staff as men, she mistakes the courteous treatment she receives from them as a sign of their being emasculated, not realizing that grown up men do not act in the manner of robust schoolboys. Her sentiments favour men engaged in manual activities, sailors always take precedence, airmen, builders of bridges, engineers, mechanics. A series of flirtations lead her to an engagement with a young man employed as a car salesman, but marriage is not for her yet, she stalls at the proposal of renouncing her freedom, of planting herself in a home and attending to the needs and comforts of her man so that he may become an efficient member of the profession he follows, she cavills at the cares of motherhood, she refuses the struggle entailed to the purchase of a house extended over a score of years, alternatively she will not entertain the pooling of incomes, both aiming in the marital state, to advance in their respective professions, and so securing a home with domestic assistance. A self centred important little creature in receipt of an income sufficient to supply her necessities she sacrifices love on the altar of dress, evenings out at her mans expense, and daily mixing with amiable working companions, keeping ever in the background the insurance of the promise to marry, assurance against becoming an elderly working spinster, a refuge to enter at a future time convenient to herself. She reflects her satisfaction in her many smiling glances with which she favours the gem studded golden circlet, the ring showing to great advantage her delicate, tinted fingers; any mention that in the staining of those nails she was displaying a mentality not far advanced beyond her naked dark skinned savage sisters, whose notions of personal adornment are based on the art of painting, would arouse her to a state of fury. She is the wearer of an emblem signifying her attractiveness to some member of the sterner sex, and removes all doubt as to her future. No longer need she be anxious over the problem of being proficient to compete with her sisters in the world of commerce, she is assured of completing womans design for living by growing old gracefully in the enviable state of matrimony. She is further assured of the unreasonable sympathy of her sisters should she ever wish to descend to the level of those loathsome creatures who black-mail a former admirer by proceeding against him a breach of promise case in the Courts of Law. It is surely a great renunciation of womans claim to equality for them to seek a monetary salve for injured sentiments when a man honestly tells of his recovery from a bout of infatuation and withdraws from an unsuitable union. I could deal more fully with this topic of Woman and Marriage but to do so here would be out of order. Another instance of self-denunciations of womens claim to equality which also serves as a splendid example of the queer mentality behind their politics is the absurd Spinsters Pensions movement. It is a well known truth that women live to a greater age than men, and also that men, with the exception of coarse manual labourers, are at their best during the seventh decade of their lives, eminent professional men are brilliant even at a greater age, do women desire us to believe they are totally unfitted and unworthy to remain in the world of affairs as early as their fifty fifth birthday and that they look forward with equanimity to another score of years life on the paltry allowance of ten shillings for every week of that period.

The mention of real money sets me off at a tangent and reminds me that you in your delightful composition "Three guineas" so gently satirize men for their apparent inability to perform any sort of work without the accompanying garments, it surely can not be possible that you grievously err over the significance of clothes but rather that you as a woman are looking at them at the wrong angle. Clothes do not honour the man as they do a woman, who adorns herself in conspicuous garments to arrouse interest and become the centre piece. Strange as it may seem woman can not do without clothes, to us in a supposedly civilized community a naked woman would be a novelty, the novelty, once wore off, she would be an eyesore. Theatrical producers soon arrived at that decision, their greatest problem is to dress a scantily clad girl. As I have mentioned a woman must be contained in herself, a man must efface himself, he does not live his works live, the King never dies, the death of a man does not kill an institution. Clothes is the oldest of our institutions, it has from the earliest of times signified the distinction of man and woman, and remains as the distinguishing feature between the two sexes to the present regardless of a few silly women who wish to assert their individuality by wearing a grotesque resemblance of male attire. We have been long accustomed to uniform clothes that only on conspicuous occasions when an unusual form of dress is placed before our view do we ask the reason. I very much doubt if you, even in your most rebellious spirit would wish to see a rabble of men dressed as factory hands march on to Horse Guards Parade to honour the King's birthday, neither would you wish to visit the navy or go on a cruise and be uncertain whether the man you asked to bring your deck chair was a steward or neighbour from the cabin next to your own. Neither would you care to have your car stopped by a man dressed as a clerk and your case tried by an untidy wizened old man. Should that happen you would, I can imagine, rush to your room in a fierce fury of hate (as of a woman scorned) and vent all your animosity against man in a delightful work I would borrow from the library, and cite in it man as your oppresser, it would appear so obviously that it was man who had raised his hand against you, wheras, as it is at the present, it is civilization suppressing any violation of its dictates. Thus has the order of living as a society been forced upon man, and man, applying reason to his judgement, has complied, taking the British policy that armies to be retained as a suppression to agression, and navies to subdue piracy. Force demanded a certain covering and distinguishing mark to the opposing side, fashions have changed but the under lying reason has remained. Appropriateness and convenience had dominated the selection of dress, man in wearing it does not so much add to his own glory as to the institution to which he has been elevated, the institution governs man demanding mans greatest effort in service before bestowing the honour of membership. The Kings' robes signify the regal position of the wearer, I still remember the keen sense of disappointment at the first time I saw King George the fifth on his visit to my home ~~town~~ when I was a school boy. He made the visit in mufti instead of the magnificent uniform I always pictured him in. The robe and full wig of the Judge represent the dignity of the high office of Law, the sparkling dress uniform of General, Admiral, Air Marshal, Chief of Police and various Orders of Knighthood and Office all spell the might and majesty of our Constitution; further in our games we cannot visualise a player of cricket, football, polo or boxing in any other dress than what are usually worn. Even women are awed to obey convention and present themselves in gowns appropriate to the occasions of Presentation at Court, Coronation Service or attendance at the opera, and to some degree in sport such as tennis, swimming, and games calling for team work. Schools can be ruled out as the dress is usually compulsory by order of the Governors' who are mostly male. Convention complied with women are allowed great latitude to express their individuality in the realms of sport and we often see elaborately dressed figures on the courts and lounging on the sands, women using every device to bring glory to themselves. Discipline is mainly obeyed by men in the wearing of dress which is a form of service and are often anxious to discard it, a soldier has to be forced to wear his uniform when off duty, a barrister snatches off his wig the moment he leaves the court sportsmen usually change before leaving the ground, very few seek personal glory by parading themselves, I noticed that the Jew, Marquess Reading[5] gave two of his uniforms of office to a London Museum for all to be aquainted with his dress.

    Discipline, an ugly word, it brings us to a stop and makes us ponder, it has the power of force; that force has to be applied to make us do right, it brings back to the mind one name, a girls' name, Agnes Grey. Strange that a girl should be the cause of bringing two truths to the forefront, discipline and limitation. Herre I must bring in my own condemnation of your writing, you gave to us a lengthy version of the totally unworthy Beau Brummel and inadequately deal with the famous Brontë sisters, who have exposed to us womens amazing mentality and limitations. Strange that the creature born of Anne Brontë's mind, wailing at the lack of discipline forced upon her charges should have brought us up against that rock Discipline and how truly she defines it. Only by the continuous effort by man in the struggle against the elements has she been able to break away from the limited existence of killing wild animals for food and clothing Womens mind is free and inconsistent therefore her thoughts are limited and personal they understand those matters relative only to themselves, mans mind is disciplined and his thoughts unlimited and impersonal Love is a great thing to women, it is most personal to them and affects all their actions, they see life through eyes of love and all women writers are affected by it and very limited in their stories and descriptions. To copy your words to a certain extent, had Emily Brontë lived now in this age of womens independance and earning power she would be a rich woman and best seller. "Wuthering Heights" should be read as the standard work of all women novelists, her characters modernised only, run through all stories written by and for women to this day. Emily Brontë wrote as she saw women and men live and love, all women to day read in the magazines the self same people, they are affiliated in mind with Emily Brontë, and allow themselves to be exploited by an unscrupulous section of the press, who week after week produce rubbish, love stories by the thousand, with practically the only variation of the names of the characters. Heathcliffe to you is an impossible figure, I do not go quite so far since now and then we come across men whose minds have been deranged by the actions of some fickle empty-headed girl, but in the main I agree with you, the man is not a normal type. Yet every woman sees Heathcliffe in every love story they read, strong, manly, rough with all other men, violent and desperate in love, one girl only who can satisfy his yearning and emotions, all other characters being contemptibly weak, of slight frame and no virtues to recommend them. All women writers see them and all women readers see them, character creatures without reason or substance. Compare Eleanor who really lives and moves through, a lovely, natural, sweet even tempered lady, the pages of the years, who do you think followed her career, not adventures by your grace, men or women; it is for sure men who followed her, and accompanied Lady Kitty on her train journey. Eleanor is real and lives with us, but she will not live because you are a woman and no woman will copy you and men will always base the women of their stories on Ann Veronica.[6] I was given to understand the outstanding love story of H.G.Wells caused a sensation before the war, almost to the point of it being barred from respectable homes, yet I found it almost disgustingly modest. As with your works I have read only one of H.G.Wells' works right through, yet I have no hesitancy in saying he will live Ann Veronica is as real to day as she was when Wells created her, a rebel in the home circle, assured, decisive of the man she wishes to marry, timid yet anxious for the adventure, and then with a woman's inconsistently, completely collapsing and placing herself under the mans protective strength. Mr Clissold is a true personation of a man of the world and when we start on Wells' "Autobiography" we stumble on the secret of his greatness, he tells the truth. He sees life as it really is and makes his characters true to life, his stories are not moulded. We have in Priestley[7] another great author, he wraps very little up and adequately describes men and women. Like Wells his stories contain no heroes or heroines, most are working class and he draws the distinction between the two sexes, the men to accept responsibility, the girls stupid, self-centred, unreliable and hopeless in an emergency. Both these great writers neglect the countryside, to my great pleasure I must add in all fairness, they base their stories on people, society and towns, cutting out entirely the sickening sentiment of working in ideal surroundings, this is surprising of Priestley and by it reaches the peaks of excellency, as he is a great lover of the country. In contrast Deeping[8] creates an impossible hero in "Old Pybus" who turns away from life in a community to shelter in the country to write a book. Had I not known the author I would have identified him a woman. The theme was so stereotyped and his hero so ideal, the average man would condemn him for a sissie who had not the back bone to square up to life, work as a man, instead of running away. I think H.G. Wells is a far truer example of a successful author, that many, like him, work hard at the profession in their spare time until they obtain an income to enable them to put on one side their ordinary work. I like H.G.Wells for his honesty in giving to us his "Autobiography" and so eliminating all fictitious Romance that might otherwise be weaved around his name.

    I cite just one more instance of the inconsistency of your sex before making a general summary of my indictment against womens claim to access to every one of mans cherished privileges. You have visited a hospital at some time and gained some knowledge and experience of their work. A Hospital to any person whose thoughts are shallow means a place of illness, pain and suffering, and of the fortitude of the unfortunate patients. We think of it as a great place of silence where one must tread on tip toe so as not to disturb the process of healing, where mercy and kindness go hand in hand with the mystery of surgery, we shudder at the words operating room and dispensary. I ungrudgingly, even thankfully offer from my wage packet and on flag days my tiny contributions, but I offer my mite in no cheap unthinking sentimentality. I know what I will receive in return, the most skilfull surgical treatment and best of care, but I do not ever wish to see inside the doorway of a hospital again, and not out of its most significant meaning, I have no dread of being a patient. It takes most people three guesses to say what really keeps a hospital going before they mention the indispensible nurse. By now it must be obvious that I have no weakness, hold no tender sentiments of the feminine sex, I do not know that there is any great difference between my brother men and myself, yet I seem to read different books, see a different meaning in quite a number of events, and hold a different opinion of matters, it puzzles me slightly when I get talking to people, men and women, who hold a far higher position, are well educated and greatly travelled, dealing in important business matters to discover that these same exalted personages have the same interests and opinions as myself. I must be a misfit somehow, educated at an elementary school, unskilled for any trade, I am only suited for my job as bus conductor, a job whose only advantage is in being able to study people as passengers No words of mine, nor even of yours, could ever adequately describe my sentiment towards nurses. The nearest I can approach it is the term "Wonderful", it is not a word, it is a volume, it tells of all that is highest, splendid, noble, courageous, tender in a lady's being, I never refer to a nurse except as a lady. Well educated, they enter the most arduous profession in the world, it calls for self-abasement, the submerging of personality, hard work, intensive study, discipline, compassion, and to giving the patient unstinting care, a hospital would fall to the ground without her. If you by any chance have not visited the visiting room of a hospital I recommend the experience. Go to a large hospital in London or other town of any size, enter the waiting room or out-patients room and wait for half an hour, it is well worth it. I can well believe you are sensitive, I will vouch the experience will shock you, it shocked me and I am thick skinned. Take no notice of the patients, they do not matter, put all thoughts of their ailments and injuries out of your mind, just in case of ill-placed sympathy. Watch the nurses, doctors are seldom seen and even when they are it is not possible to get a true line on them, they are tough their poker faces and demeaner betray no emotion, but the nurses are well worth watching. The first thing that attracted me was the noise, men were present but they were on their own; each man a few feet away from his neighbour, patiently waiting their call. The shock was effected by the women, they were chatting incessantly to any person who would listen to them. These women had come to the hospital, where nurses strained every nerve in giving patients their care, and laboured diligently to keep it spotlessly clean, I will repeat these women, not all but a great majority, untidy dirty, many with a squawling, unwashed, uncared for brat whom they allowed to run wild around the room, yelling and playing and in turn getting yelled at by their mothers, mothers who had until the moment of injury shown no motherly instinct towards her offspring, too lazy to learn even the elements of child rearing, not even to the finding and tearing of a clean handkerchief to bandage a cut hand. The criticism they directed to the nurses was the worst feature, I regret the appearance of vulgarity in this description yet to be literally exact "A stuck up bitch" was a moderate form of expression to most I heard. They criticized the nurse's work, behaviour, treatment of patients and methods of applying dressing, and passing detrimental remarks about them as they appeared, self-possessed and as a ministering angel smiling to comfort some poor child screaming in her terror at being brought to a hospital. Fully ninety percent of the women present should have gone on their knees at the feet of the nurse to beg forgiveness and then be kicked out, you may be able to guess where I consigned them to, I am not going to tell you. You may be able to explain, but I confess I am unable to understand this attitude of women towards hospitals. Cannot they realize a hospital is the very embodiment of all the latest advancement in the science of medicine and surgery and that the complete staff bring all their skill and training to the benefit of every patient regardless of class distinction. I, myself never wish to cause unnecessary trouble to any one, if I am obliged to call upon any person for assistance I think it is only right that I should make things as smooth and easy as possible for my assistant and later say "Thank you" for the aid they have rendered, it surprises me to find other people take hospitals for granted, even allowing for weekly subscriptions from the wage packet, demanding almost as a right treatment for even the slightest injury offering abuse in return. I think the people behind our hospitals have in mind a far superior purpose, that of dealing with serious cases where treatment is not possible or suitable in the patients domicile, as an experiment I would gladly welcome the closing of the Out-patients department to force those women back on to their own resources with the alternative of meeting a doctors' bill.

To generalize, two main principles are conducive to women's ineffectiveness as mans' equal in the ordering of this worlds' affairs, their appearance and inability to organize. Womans' dress is excellent in displaying her figure and individuality, a well dressed woman is a superb being, not even her naturalness can detract from her loveliness when she has the sense to place herself in the hands of the artist who arranges her coiffure, the complexion plasterer and the male genius who designs her gowns. Given the possession of the virtues of charm and morality she is then very desirable as mans' consort Her features are pleasing and the tone of her voice low, soft and often sweet and modulated, in ordinary conversation she is quite acceptable, when she leaves the chair she occupied as a platform ornament and approaches the rostrum she changes to a most unlovely creature. A woman addressing a meeting is not a pretty sight, the ordinary lovely features become all twisted and her voice has never been attuned for loud speaking, even the gown she wears adds to her uncongruousness. To convince and sway a critical audience a speaker must be the possessor of a strong firm voice, not necessarily deep but certainly not high, set features and composure, a show of undue confidence and assurance can often produce an adverse effect to that the speaker is aiming for. The soft features of a womans' face does not call for confidence in her as a person of will power, method, and able to convince others at a committee meeting, most womens cheeks fall in during early middle age and betray weakness, no woman has features which warrants her entry into an important discussion, those with strong features betray a strong will power, dominant nature and unreasonable conviction. No power on earth and all reason brought to bear on an argument will never persuade a woman to believe what is right if she thinks otherwise. This biased attitude should always disqualify a woman from holding any office of power. This question of dress is a very vexed problem, a gathering of women is never a pretty spectacle, it does not matter what they wear, coat, costume or dress the impression is always the same suggestive of their being unfitted and unsuitable to take a place as a sex equally with men, singly or in pairs they are attractive, in the mass they are horrible. Few women have good choice for clothes despite the great interest they take in them, to say they all dress alike would be an outrageous statement, no two wear exactly the same unless by the incident of birth making them twins their feeble minds induce them to adopt similarly, yet they all ape one another in their endeavour to keep apace with the current fashion, any Sunday afternoon in any town in the country we are shown what is the predominant style. Members of a race of astute business people take full advantage of this caprice of female mentality, filling their shops with a variety of many coloured outrages of all fittings leaving it to the girls' own lack of taste to swell the profits introducing the spirit of farce by providing advisers whose real job is to make a sale no matter what freak the customer becomes. It is not until the girl enters a business house controlled by honest English business men whose honour refuses to allow them to lower their reputation does she become dressed, in the full sense of the term. Unfortunately the girl is too often a victim of two unhappy incidents, mentality demanding incessant change of fashion and an income insufficient to patronise so frequently the house of repute, leaving her to resort to the places run by the aforementioned unscrupulous race. This madness of asserting their individuality often turns them into unsightly beings in business places and they present themselves at office, shop, garage and cafe dressed in coats, jumpers, overalls, smocks that by no means add to the attractiveness of the establishment. You have I expect had the comfortable feeling of having entered a properly conducted cafe when the waitress presents herself at your table dressed in uniform fashion of black dress covered with white apron and cap, you feel that not only is she an attractive and efficient attendant but that behind her stands an organization devoted to your comfort and well being, an organization which will set you at a table covered by a clean table-cover and well polished instruments of the art of eating, provide you with a variety of well cooked courses and place before you delicasies you will be delighted to consume. That girl represents the mystery behind your meal, the board room, investment of capital, purchase of premises, careful thought expended on decoration, furniture, linen, cutlery, apparatus, chefs, attendants, service, all to interest you whether you wish to dine or take a drink of tea. As the girl slides noiselessly back to her recess you have wondered what freak of mentality had caused the woman who served you at the road side halt to consider she was attractive in her flower spotted dress. We see these self same girls working in garages and we experience emotions of a desire to get away as early as possible from the girl dressed as a girl, of disgust if she wears slacks which are slack only round her calves, and of admiration if she has been sensible to don knee breeches. It is an ideal dress for girls working at manual or mechanical jobs and I certainly agree they are capable horse riders and appropriately attired present more graceful figures than most men. The atrocity called slacks are an abomination and my only remark about them, they are beyond all description, any girl wearer of them who views herself in the mirror and then goes out in them deserves a hard spanking where the fitting is least slack. I have little to say against or in favour of shorts, it is an admirable garment for men as well as women for the recreations of walking and cycling. Morality enters our discussion over these although I do not suggest girls wearing shorts are immoral, they must surely be aware of the vast amount of thigh they display when riding, some vie with each other in being original in colour, design, and daring, but their number is so small as to be of no account, what does matter is that women must know that they are attracting attention to their legs by exposing such a length, they may argue that it is not mans' business to look, but since a girls' legs are attractive men will look, the girl knows this side of human nature and when wearing skirts spends any amount of time when in a seated position, pulling at the skirt to prevent any exposure of the knee. Some people try to tell us the reason of the present shortage of domestic servants is the compulsory wearing of uniform that, to me, is exaggeration drawn to a fine point, to use a hackneyed phrase, my own opinion in all probability, as over our waitress, coincides with you own, that the fault rest in mistresses, who are bad masters generally, and decline to supply decent accomodation which in common courtesy every girl is entitled to, do not honour the girl by speaking in a civil manner, long hours and loss of freedom. Certainly the girls will follow their own inclinations in the matter of dress unless authority forbids them, but if instead of viewing themselves from their own inexplicable angle they could look upon themselves through the eyes of a male they would find they were very attractive charming ladies indeed attired in the black and white outfit of the servant maid. I cannot leave this matter of dress without it getting mingled with the principle of organization and it weaves itself around our adorable little friend, the servant maid. She is among the more sensible of her sisters and I do commend her for facing squarely up to life, and bravely as she does not know into what households her profession will take her, the pleasant tasks are few in comparison with the arduous, the work is hard, they work much harder than I do. She is accepting womens true position in life, subordinate to man, and tending to his home and creature comforts. Her choice of occupation is wise, she is preparing for the time when she sets up a home with some man, her wages are often good and give her little time to spend them except on dress, and as she is usually working for people moving among a more exalted state than her own who dress in accordance with their position she becomes enlighted on correct wear. With her limited opportunities for spending or wearing her own clothes, she goes to the excess, buys outdoor wear at a good price and keeps it in good order. Learning the correct order of good housekeeping is priceless knowledge which her sister glean volumes to acquire, and as circumstances take their allotted place, her own little home becomes a joy to live in, raising to a great extent the standard of living for her working husband, and goodness knows even in this emancipated age the working mans' standard of living needs some elevation.

The conducting of affairs has evolved into practice, criticism and reconditioning and all our institutions work on those lines. There must be a leader and confidence and authority vested in the leader. A committee drawn from the members or a board of directors nominated by the shareholders must be trusted with executive powers and what ever the consequences abide on the leaders decisions for the specified period. Britains might has been gained and our great trading reputation secured on those principles, soldiers lives have been wasted by some commanders' error but our Empire has grown by commanders using their initiative under the powers vested in him, our trade expanded by honouring all obligations and the democratic constitution of the Empire based on the

Governments authority. My sister tells me that when she was shop collector for the Union which looked after the interests of the workers in her trade, during a drive for an increased rate of pay the girls became almost fanatical enthusiasts of the Trade Union movement, the wage increase was granted and soon after there was a noticeable waning of interest and in time the girls stopped paying the contributions to such an extent that the branch was closed. The admirable logic of their argument that having attained their objective there was no longer any necessity of continuing their contributions when nothing more could be gained was brilliant. An isolated example you may argue and I am quite willing to agree with you and admit there are numerous projects entirely feminine where the women adherents have remained attached for a score of years or even more. These women agitators take up some project and as she adopts crochet or embroidery the project becomes the hobby of a life-time, she welomes any and every prospective conflict and an emerging triumphant is hysterically delighed, a defeat in combat or any setback she will obstinately reason and twist round to be favourable, the relation of her own movement to affairs in general or even to the Constitution is of no concern to her, she ignores entirely the manner in which the rest of the populace may be affected. At times her particular movement may appeal to women in general and it is then they exhibit their abnormal lack of organizing ability. They never grant to a woman leader a leaders' power they even refuse her the benefit of the doubt never give her their confidence and her detractors are more numerous than her admirers, she usually holds her office by her forcefull talkative methods and by reason of no other prominent member being able to obtain a sufficient number of supporters. The local and sub-committees always have a favourite alternative programme of their own and so add discord to an already dubious or uncertain policy. The obduracy in which they hold to their own point of view and the lack of staying power of the ordinary supporter are, in the main, detrimental to all womens' movements and the reason of their many failures. They limit their activities to very petty causes that only too often can be only of local interest, we all are aware of the pest who collects for hospitals and charities on flag days and enforces the purchase of a ticket for the Church bazaar. This narrow range of vision affects to a great extent womans business activities. There must be many thousand small business concerns run by women and how lamentably small they always remain, the meagre profits are placed in a bank where they remain safe for all time, or what more usually happens are spent by their relatives after she dies, she hesitates to extend her business or enlarge the premisses, never will she speculate, the golden rule of trading, that of returning to the business all that is gained is practically unknown to her. She is devoted to her tiny business, often pathetically so, and serves it faithfully working for many many hours of the day in her fight to keep it alive against the oppressive larger concerns, but she is doing it entirely for herself, for her own livelihood, she sees her business only as it concerns herself giving to the trade she follows no further acknowledgement you may argue that Miss Modern is a very much alive young person in comparison to her brother, that she keeps apace with the times and shows to advantage by the practicable manner she does things and moves about. She can drive a car or an aeroplane, move about and display an energy and knowledge over practical things that astound us yet it is all on the surface. She is merely emulating the street child who becomes hardened to life, tackle any job for a few coppers, displaying an amazing knowledge of his locality, cunning and in time is able to pick up some sort of a living, but that is as far as he goes while the quieter slower boy goes beyond and much deeper into the affairs of life and by his very steady manner of approach forms and controls our whole method of living. Woman has certainly proved her claim to be included in our commercial life, she is excellent in routine work, at machine minding where it is economically necessary to use cheap labour she has replaced boys to advantage and general office work especially as stenographer she is very suitable for, such work being too tedius for an intelligent man. The sudden emancipation of her a quarter of a century ago simply served to accellerate the process of her inclusion, she has always been a necessary member of trades which belonged to womans sphere, doubtless for ages past she has been employed at the making of dresses needing fine fingerwork and for the selling of underwear to their own sex, enlightened and progressive business men were utilizing her in various engagements of a subordinate nature. The whole of the occupations were thown open to her when the shortage of men became acute but she has proved herself fit for subordinate positions only, she is too unreliable, untrustworthy, unimaginative, biased inelastic and self-centred ever to become a force in the steady advancement of our civilization.

When you visit a library and open your note book to put down notes of what man thinks of you instead of stabbing the blank sheet in vexation just gaze at the young student for whose benefit men have built the place in which they can store the books he must read. And read he must to gain the principles of the art of living, sinking all his own free will he passes hour after hour of his adolescent period of training, obeying the law his forbears are explaining for him, the law of obedience and service. His resentment may be great at having to sink himself in study and pass the fleeting golden hours of youth in a sunless room, but reason has over rided resentment and continuing the process of evolution by discarding instinct for intellect. The many books arranged in order along the many shelves that cover the walls explain only the one law to him, that he is man and being a man he is nothing, but the world he must spend sixty or seventy years of his existence on was made for man, and he has been placed on it to make it fit for man to live on. To do that he must read these books to learn the principles of how man lives, whether it be the growing of the grain or the making of the machinery which will transport it or crush it to powder or bake it. No matter what he reads it is all the same, one principle of the law, and a principle only, but by reading and retaining in his mind he is learning how he can serve man and justify his existence, it is the start of his obedience, in a year or two he must obey the law in full and as he reaches mans' estate take a mans' place. He must render efficient service, work he knows how to do and do properly. But the principle he has learnt is only a principle, as a rule is used for measuring, and the world does not keep still, as the world goes round so does the standard of living on it advance. The law demands that he must advance it and as he advances the means also advance the method. He must be moderate towards his fellow man, tolerant, recognise the other mans' equal right to work, to his own opinion, to chivalry and respect. The obedience to the letter of the law is not enough for him and his service to commerce and industry completed his interest is turned to other matters that may possibly make living in a community a pleasure. He takes it for granted that work must come first and has a poor opinion of the man who lays aside his work to seek money and fame in some enjoyable sideline. Any man who frets and cries about his ordinary work complaining it is hampering his presenting to the general public his talent of entertainment and backs out of it is usually condemned by his more level headed brothers. The man of work will give him more than justice, he will show appreciation and offer help and encouragement, the lowest of our working men will always be the first to aid and applaud any fellow worker who shows outstanding merit in either the sport or the fine arts, and be pleased at the prospect of him being able to break out of the rut. Our ex-student will give to him his opportunity, and builds and maintain halls where he may display his gifts. Mans' interests are many and he will always seek out others with similar interests and talking quietly, almost in a manner that could be mistaken as offhanded, but in all sincerity, he will do his utmost in the furtherance of his interest.

We are living in a progressive industrial age and although in this man-controlled world our conditions are far from being perfect we most certainly are far removed from the conditions of the past two or three centuries and on a further reading of your work "A room of one's own" I am surprised at your inferring that past conditions are still responsible for womans' inferiority to man, and also to confining your remarks to your own art, literature. The two sexes to-day start level, the handicap of the girls weaker physique being fully compensated by the opportunities. Her intellect is similar and her senses finer than a boys, she is taught similar subjects, may attend the same colleges and universities and is given preference at lower grade or routine work on account of her willingness to accept a lower rate of pay. Man is very foolish in his attitude he takes towards her, very lenient and extremely chivalrous and she is very unfair in the advantage she takes. It must be impossible that you have never heard the phrase "You are acting like a girl" and just as certainly you are not ignorant of its inference. Put simply and brutally it means childish, acting and talking in the manner of a spoilt child. This attitude that women adopt can only be the result of their mentality and it causes men to believe in what it pleases you to call their superiority. This it is not, it would be more true to call it a sense of disgust and hopelessness at being unable to co-operate with women and being forced to rely on their own reason and judgement You describe well the emotions you felt at being forced to make your living before the legacy fell at your feet, that legacy is your own concern but there are many thousands of women who have been as fortunate and even much more fortunate than you in the wealth that has been bequeathed to them. Finance and commerce are affairs beyond my understanding but it is obvious there is plenty of opportunity for dealing in the open market. The possession of wealth is a great responsibility, not a number of figures on the credit side of a bank pass book and a bundle of shares, it carries with it the obligation of using it to the best advantage and benefit of the community and the worker producer who toil to produce the dividend. Many women are rich and those who have benefited by being the recipients of large legacies are iluminating examples, thinking more about the fur coats they are indecent enough to wear as not knowing how to wear them, than they do about the means of acquiring them. Women can be lovely and delightful beings when they speak softly and allow their adviser to dress them, they can be admirable companions for men to share their pleasures and their homes with and he has opened his gates of work and interests to her, but when she still remains an unrational being who has no true sense of values, who refuses to reason and allow her judgement to be swayed by a biased opinion, who has no deep sentiment, is not reliable nor yet even just; how can we then allow her equality in the great trust of our nations welfare. This world is still a hard rough place and the elements must be matched by the tough stern qualities of a mans personality, the struggle calls for determined persistence force and energy and man must succeed in his purpose of civilizing and I am dogmatic in my opinion that for the centuries to come man only is fit to take control.

 Should you have reached to this page of my letter you have indeed shown a generosity not only of your time but also of your tolerance and it is impossible with my limited qualities to thank you and I beg of you to accept a simple yet sincere "Thank you" as my sentiment of gratitude. I have had no purpose in writing this, the grammar and style fall far below the immaculate and incomparable standard you have set for your own compositions. I claim as you do in presenting your works, honest criticizm, which I extend to "The Years" in regretting that you placed Eleanor above my own working class level. It is as well you did as I am not one of those beguiled idiots who believe there is no class distinction, there is, and as you belong to the elevated educated class you are really ignorant of us, you as a looker on only see us, you don't know us nor understand us and cannot portray us as we truely are. So many futile descriptions of us have been made by authors who do not belong to our class, and we owing to our stinted education and training have not the ability to do it for ourselves, that I am really glad that in "the Years" you did not attempt to and so for Eleanor I thank you.

        Humbly and sincerely.
        Your admirer,
        Ernest Huxley.

[1] Rock Ferry is in Birkenhead, Cheshire, across the River Mersey from Liverpool.

[2] Margaret Lawrence's *We Write As Women* was published by Michael Joseph in London in 1937. A slightly different version of the book had been published as *The School of Femininity* by Frederick Stokes in New York in 1936. Lawrence was a Canadian journalist and lecturer and the book is a survey of various British and American women writers beginning with Mary Wollstonecraft and ending with Woolf. Lawrence treats *Orlando* and *A Room of One's Own*, finding the former "to have little to offer us in the din and confusion of the age of machinery except the peace to our spirits of rest in fine thinking and fine writing" (308) and the latter to mark "the beginning perhaps of a new stage in the story of women," "a philosophy of twentieth century women aware of the baby and aware of the book" (314). Lawrence's book was reviewed in the *Times Literary Supplement* February 27 1937: 153.

[3] Suzanne Lenglen (1899-1938) was a French tennis player. She held the French singles championship from 1920 to 1926, excluding 1924, and the Wimbledon singles championship from 1919-1923. She was known also for introducing a shorter style of tennis dress.

[4] See Letter 5, Note 1.

[5] Rufus Daniel Isaacs, First Marquess of Reading (1860-1935) was a lawyer and administrator. In 1913 he became Lord Chief Justice and between 1921 and 1926 he was Viceroy of India.

[6] H. G. Wells' (1866-1946) *Ann Veronica* (1909) caused a scandal because of its portrayal of an emancipated woman. His *Experiment in Autobiography* was published in 1934. See *Three Guineas*, Part 3, Note 3.

[7] J. B. Priestley (1894-1984) was a novelist, playwright, broadcaster and critic. He is best known for *The Good Companions* (1929). Huxley may be thinking particularly here of *Angel Pavement* (1930), a novel about London life.

[8] (George) Warwick Deeping (1899-1938) wrote seventy novels, the most famous of which is *Sorrell and Son* (1925). *Old Pybus* was published in 1928.

**73**
**Handwritten**
**June 1939**

598 New Chester Road,
Rock Ferry.

Mrs. Virginia Woolf
Dear Madam.
    "And should like to talk on equal terms with the conductors."
    "East is east and west is west and never the twain shall meet."[1]
Two phrases I shall remember and browse over until the end of time, being no liker of phrases, detesting them as hackneyed part-truths associated mainly to the clap-trap and imbecile jargon of political sensations, popular mass movements and womans' morbid sentimentality, two sayings by different eminent

members of the profession of literature, yet so surely do they affect myself one by a realist, the other a spiritualist addressing my unworthy self, that they verge to the level of the invaluable.

To the strains of the Halifax Military Band coming through the loud speaker of a three year old wireless set and with the memory of a service for those who died in a sea disaster I try to form my thoughts in order and set them down legibly, not an ideal state for such an occupation, yet the usual conditions.

Retreating from the hubbub of the living room to the scarcely used sitting room of the flat I share with my wife and ten year old son and gazing at the trees the other side of the wall opposite being shaken and played with by the May breeze with buses, lorries, cars children on their way to school passing along the intervening roadway, and now to the noise of dance records emitted from the wireless I think over the problem of my opening line, written by my most distinguished correspondent. Then I reach for my dictionary and turning to the word subtle I read: rarefied, delicate, hard to sieze, elusive; making fine distinctions; to my mind not a very pleasant array, I read on and passing a few more meanings come to the very unpleasant, crafty, insidious. Laying my pen down I read again my distinguished correspondents' letter, dictated and forwarded by some fortunate stenographer, I had laughed when I came to that line in the last paragraph, not mockingly, nor yet offensively, an amused laugh perhaps, it was a quiet laugh, not much more than a smile, of subtle derision at the utter impossibility of conversing with any person employed on the road staff of an omnibus company. Ten years of swaying, sweating and swearing on the rear platform of double deck omnibuses have convinced me that no outsider can break through the reticence of a bus conductor, the society of busmen is as seclusive as the most exclusive free-mason lodge, I have seen many attempts by people anxious to enter into a discussion with us but the coldness which is always meted must by embarrassing to those good-intentioned people. Over an area of a score of miles I am known to thousands but of these, there are barely a dozen whom I approch on almost equal terms, and they range from barmen, lady hairdresser, school teachers of both sexes to important business men. I have watched them, studied them, gradually approached them and now I can speak with absolute freedom and confidence, it has taken years but it has been well worth it for I can trust them no liberties are taken and no patronage shown, when they are accompanied by husband, wife, friend or business associate I become just a bus conductor collecting their fare but I have yet to be scorned by them, not one of my dozen ever fails to show some form of recognition whatever the circumstances of our meeting, many who know my usual reserved manner must be puzzled by my open friendship with the few, they show their surprise as experience has taught me to be alert for the unexpected occurrence. Unless one is prepared to be a regular passenger and wait a considerable period always extending friendliness a conductor will not be confidingly frank, and it is certainly not worth all that trouble to gain his aquaintance and learn his philosophy, yet in a way the acquaintance is mutually beneficial, we are great students of the general public – the only consolation of our job is getting to know people at their best and their worst – I believe we think deeper than the average working man and to any one friendly disposed we never show sarcasm, often bitterness. Since I have written this much I may as well go on a little further with the subject and try to enlighten the reader on our attitude. To most passengers we appear as ill-tempered, unmannered, brusque, determined to be as unkind and unsympathetic as we dare to be; I like that story of our late King George who above all considerations about his retaining his high position or seeking popularity shewed kindness to some little girl, I liken ourselves to him in that one respect, our work calls only for the collection of fares and stopping the bus on request, nothing more, yet daily, hourly we are assisting, advising, shewing kindness without any thought of pecuniary reward. The tired lady with a baby and the carriage, or maybe loaded with parcels, the small child lost and without a penny, the fellow strange to the district, the lady wearing a new dance dress or carrying a 'cello, the most awkward things to carry I imagine, helping people with luggage and noticing they leave with the same cases. A helping hand, finding a seat, laughing a kiddie's tears away, advising a lady so her dress will not get spoilt or her instrument damaged. A cruel job to any one sensitive. Cursing, growling, sneering, wailing, patronizing, wheedling, fifty passengers and the company all against one, singing, bawling drinking, the bus divided into two seperate camps. Time is all important, the bus must go on, no delay, is the majority in the right, shall a bowling party ending their carnival be allowed to disturb the peace of five decent passengers, shall a busker entertain on his piano-accordeon. Risking the jeering, the threats the cat calls of "Hitler" and "England's a free country" the busker packs his instrument or leaves the bus. Ready reckoning, street and transport guiding, tact needing the training, experience and elusiveness of a diplomat, every passenger a different problem, a situation to be sized up in a split second, is the man with a wrong ticket or no money genuine or a twister, is it being hard hearted to a hard case or missplaced sympathy, many a conductor has paid a passengers fare; insults, accusations, the conductor is trying to make a copper for his own pocket, he is being awkward or funny or will not explain fully, he is not polite, he would not wait for passengers, he has room for passengers, he has overloaded his bus, and all the time the bus must go on, no delay, and an inspector waiting around the next bend, he has not given the correct change, he made the passenger wait for change, he gave too many coppers in the change, the passenger loses his ticket "the conductor could not have given me one" to the inspector, he should have brought a policeman, he cannot manage a bus; fifty people and the company against one man, he is miles away from anywhere, he stands on his own, the man in front must keep on driving, time marches on.

  Some months ago I wrote my impressions of the members of my profession, I mentioned the matter to a fellow conductor who had received ten pounds each for two articles he had submitted to some magazine. He was anxious to read my work up to then an uncompleted work of ten or twelve sheets. He and I were strangers in so far as our understanding each others intimate thoughts, sentiments and motives. We held two things in common, our pastime of writing for pleasure and in being fools – a strange confession. It takes a great man to be a fool, I am not presuming to any greatness but I am sufficiently confident in the efficiency of my work to indulge in mannerisms which evoke laughter and jokes made at my expence. This young fellow offered his criticism opening with "I know you can take it". Those few words were spoken seriously and in earnest, and between us sprang an immediate friendship and mutual understanding, it is not one of those unions where invitations to homes are offered or expected we have never so much as had a drink together, the only occasions we speak is when meeting in the garage or at a terminus. Yet there is something dear, something precious in our friendship, quite unconnected we are both fools in our own seperate fashion, together our foolish manners are shed and we talk seriously and sincerely and mainly on the topic "what" is there really in life, what is beneath the visible and obvious, what the true sentiments.

My contribution to the controversy over women brought me a well deserved and swift rebuke from my distinguished correspondent, she damned my criticism with faint praise. One sentence only, however, distressed me. I am certainly biased against her sex and consider myself justified in being so, but I wrote my remarks carefully, thoughtfully, justly in my opinion, calmly, with no emotion of anger. It worries me that she accuses me of making detrimental remarks against her educated sisters. Had I sacrificed lucidity to brevity to so great an extent for my regard for the educated woman to be unrecognizable. I placed the nurse well in the lead, stressing her value as an educated person and her superiority to doctors, the lady of dress next in order. The educated lady is invaluable, man in his helpless despair turns to her seeking guidance, comfort, inspiration, a lead, any and every thing that will drag him out of the mire of his own conceptions, it is when she attempts to emulate his ways and means he turns from her dropping in despair into a slough of despondancy at knowing he must rely on fellow men ineffective as himself. There is only one pure science and that the Science of Commercialism. Man has perfected it and realises it as his sole accomplishment and strives his hardest to free himself. To escape the coils of that infernal science he turns to the only person who can aid him, the educated woman. He cannot do without her, she is indispensable The talented well-dressed lady had been the centre piece of all mens' imaginations since history records his attacks on culture. A hundred generations ago the Greeks in their conception of her nearly escaped commercialism, she was idealised as being the true representation of life, and life worth living. A society appreciative of beauty, of poetry, of arts, of graceful buildings and the extinction of all forms of aggresion, suppresion and ugliness was created. Their necessity for producing food and clothing without intrusion was satisfied, women gave to them their sons and prepared their meals, beyond that man could not proceed and woman stepped in as an equal, nay, as a superior. She, in her very self, is the incarnation of beauty, he had chosen her to live with because of her lovliness, so he modelled beauty in his style of building, no doubt she directed him in his designs also, her finer senses defining the true outline, her soft speaking voice appealed to his hearing so he cultivated the art of poetry, her gentle manner of behaviour inspired him to good relations with his neighbour and a smooth polite civilization came into being, only to be shattered by the aggresive Romans. The intervening gap since the fall of the Roman Empire to the industrial revolution of the past century is a blank on the record of evolution, mans aggression and oppression yielded no results, the few improvements being those moulded on the Grecian principle, communities gathered into towns of small dimensions, pride in the buildings of their cities, together with the exalted positions of a few ladies. To-day we look to those same ladies, talented, influential and rich to advance our civilization. Our armed forces retained in full strength will prevent any recurrence of the disaster that befell the Greeks, man cannot go beyond the rough work of provision and protection, his methods are too toilsome and wearying to be effective, the educated woman must now enter as an equal and take the lead. She has the examples and as she followed Florence Nightingale, let her follow Dame Laura Knight, Pavlova, Suzzanne Lenglen, Ellen Terry, Conchita Supervia, the author of "The Years"; the Duchess of Kent.[2] I know nothing of these ladies, of their personalities, idiosyncrasies, mannerisms I am entirely ignorant, but all of them possess an indefinable quality that men value. Ever since I saw that construction called Genesis by the sculptor Epstein[3] I have looked at works of art trying to find what is in it. I have looked at ancient Chinese vases and the blue and white Wedgewood pottery, Gothic buildings, statues, paintings. I have stood dumbly before portraits by Gainsborough and Dutch interiors and stared and stared, but with my thick wits I fail to gain more than a faint glimmer of perception. It is in that one respect my distinguished correspondent and I differ, educated as she is, that barrier of education must always rise between us, she as an educated lady could discern and define that indefinable quality in the work of an artist. I know it is there, I know it is that something that makes life worth living, only a person who has been taught can give them to us, and education begets talent, I and every other man therefore looks to the talented woman to give us from her store of truly feminine virtues and accomplishments the amenities of a life worth living. In my minds' eye I see Dame Laura Knights' painting "St Johns' Wood", if I remember right there is in the foreground the wall of a house, trees and beyond tennis courts, a photograph would show it a very ordinary place. I do not know what the artist is trying to tell us but I do believe I can see something that she saw, the wall and courts represent mans' practicability, organization and workmanship, the trees, symmetry, and far distance are just those things that a woman can give, that something more that an educated lady with her finer senses can bring into life. It is not possible to describe in detail the distinctness, especially of classes, even more so of women, they are as the rainbow in a dual sense. Passing over their similarity as creations of beauty and loveliness, they are as the different colours, and as it is not possible to draw a line along the edge of any of the colours so also it is not possible to grade women, we cannot say there is a working woman, there an educated lady, beyond a titled personage, we must take them as a whole and describe them in what they have in common. We must generalize. That accomplished bearer of my family name, Aldous Huxley, in his work "Jesting Pilate"[4] surveys for us half the world, describing in sections of two or three pages a variety of diverse subjects. It is impossible from that book to gain any understanding of the order of the universe, the remarkable author atones in some small way by explaining in a later work how man may extricate himself from commercialism and reach the high level of a peaceful state, he does so at some great length. H.G. Wells aptly sums up in his "Work, Wealth and Happiness"[5] with the visitor to a technical museum who, going to the uppermost balcony looks down and remarks "Now tell me what it is all about." Man is a very dependant being, he is unable to do anything alone. The mention of my relation with a fellow worker may have seemed to have no bearing on this topic, but I believe it enabled me to stumble against reality, the truth that man is a sociable animal, that all of them hold similar sentiments and can understand and sympathize and respect the other mans' view and intentions. Woman is a very isolated individual, even in the process of procreation she is not entirely in unity with her ultimate offspring, the joining is merely a fragile cord which snaps at the appointed time. During adolescence and maturity she is never intimately joined in friendship and understanding with other women, her relations with men and even with her husband are never really complete, she may truly and deeply love a man but no true understanding of sentiment and sympathy are reached.

Leaning against the handrail I gaze out of the bus over the Mersey into the dark violet arc of space dotted with the golden specks of gleaming stars. The glowing shape of some passing member of our planetary system pale the distant suns which reach to the uttermost edge of the arc, beyond those faintly visible the powerful telescope picks yet more stars, fainter and ever fainter they gleam, as the science of astronomy develops space ever extends containing those faint specks in the ever increasing distance. Space and the specks are endless, we cannot conceive the end of space and what lies beyond. And as with space so is our existence, we can have no conception of the extent of our development. The Divine Designer of our Destinies discloses to mans' bewildered senses some pattern to guide him, the symmetrical and ever changing order of the skies. Time and space are our limitations and in like manner work and study are the end of mans' achievement. I turn to look across from the Mersey on to Port Sunlight and I am enlightened, the village resembling men and women comprising a state of perfect harmony. Not two houses are alike, nor two rows or blocks of buildings, each lane lies in a different direction, not one parallel with another, grass plots of uneven shapes, flower beds unfenced and open pools, school, hospital, church, art gallery, tavern, bowling greens, assembly hall, and beyond lies unobtrusively the serious side of the communal state, the works, the cause of the estate, employing thousands of girls and hundreds of men. I visualize the estate as an ancient Grecian and later Roman state in which women were honoured and acknowled as being equal and superior to man. The ensuing fifteen centuries wherein man denied woman her equality, using a rather heavy hand in suppressing her, ended in the terrible state of affairs of to-day. Now man, enriched by his avaricious aquistive tactics in perplexity over the muddle he has caused turns to women to help him straighten things out. The women are having none of it, they refuse to play up to him, and I dare say it looks as if man is crying over it the way he blames and abuses her, but really she can hardly be blamed at walking into jobs, earning as much as she can get and spending it almost as fast on her own fancies. Perhaps we have not given her time to enjoy and satiate herself with unexpected wealth, twenty five or even fifty years is rather a short period for a sex to develop in time she may accustom herself to the changed condition of her position. It is as she is to-day I disapprove of her, and I insist she is unreasonable and looking at life from the wrong angle, she is trying to see through a mans' eye, and the view becomes awry. She is wrong in trying to emulate man, man is a unit and can and must join in union with others to work or play and attain his objective, woman is an individual. It is the educated woman who is chiefly to blame, she has the brains and learns the fundamentals, up to that point the two sexes are equal, but at the end of tuition she should seperate to join him as a sex, as she joins her husband as wife to form the partnership of marriage, so should she in her own sphere join him in directing the conditions of living. To describe her as consort or sub-ordinate to man is to put it badly; she should be subordinate only in mans' limited sphere of work and organization, in directing, her intuition makes her far superior to man, the educated lady, and I include all from the girl who gains her school leaving certificate to the brilliant and accomplished wife of any of our country's representative, should use her intelligence and choose wisely. Let her work and earn her living, she is needed, every occupation has a place for her and work she can do, much of which she is especially suited for, but work is really mans' affair. Man is a working animal right from his primitive ancestors some force has urged him on to expend his energy on useful work, he is well adapted for it his physical strenght enables him to tackles any rough or manual labour, his slow enduring capacities and vivid imagination cause him to study and delve deeply in the sciences and solve the intricasies of mechanics, what he most assuredly has not is intuition. He can dig foundations, make bricks, erect factories, assemble machinery, form armed bodies, organize men, allot work, create states and that is his limit, just sound practical sense. He knows there is something beyond these, these elusive things appear to have little in common with the practical side of life and are unlimited, but in time they will govern materialism, they are the Arts, man is very appreciative of them and when they are brought before his senses attunes his attitude so he can fit in with them. A very limited number of men have been able to grasp them and leave records to posterity and so we have compositions by Chopin, portraits by Gainsborough, verse by Tennyson, prose by Hardy, Greek and Gothic architecture, gardens and woodland. These are not by any means all the arts as some visionary keeps adding to the list. Woman is the greatest of all the arts, Divinely created and presented and man, all men look to her to present the next greatest and important of the arts, the Art of Living.

  I will make a break here and enter to some extent into detail, it may seem to have little in keeping to my topic but I shall gradually arrive to the importance of the educated woman and definitely prove that she can and should lead men if she will just use her intelligence and accept the responsibility of working as a woman. I cite two of my friends. The first a middle aged married lady in business. Two quite young girls, they were of school age were looking at the contents of a manicure set, the open case fell to the floor and I picked it up and handing it back inquired the use of one of the contents, the girl gigled and apparently did not know, with the case still in my hand the lady opposite took it off me and explained the use of the various contents which to me seemed fairly numerous for the purpose of the set. She did not treat the affair as a joke, she was quite serious, she did not talk down to me as if my superior, or in a patronizing manner. This incident happened several years ago, she was before and has been since a regular traveller, now we enter into a discussion on each of our frequent meetings as equals although our stations are far apart. I use my eyes and try to see the best condition to live in, our topics are diverse and she tells me much about the conditions of life on her level, our views are very similar and she is not in great favour of the feminist movement. Practically the only difference between us now is her cultivated voice.

  Before this time I noticed a girl as a frequent passenger, a working class girl, an ordinary girl, neatly rather than smartly dressed, she is not beautiful. Somehow we started talking common places, just a few words spoken in her quiet tone. One night, along with a few friends she was going to a dance, being a hairdresser she knew just how her hair should be treated for such an occasion, she had made use of cosmetics to heighten her pale complexion, I assumed it was her best coat she wore over her long dress. As I collected their fares she gave me a brilliant smile, to my mind flashed the words of a song from the musical comedy "To night's the night:" – "Your lips, your eyes, your golden hair, are in a class beyond compare, You're the lovliest girl that I could see;" she was, she was radiant. Some weeks elapsed before I saw her again, it was a quiet trip and, I was able to speak with her for ten minutes, our longest spell together ever; I told her my thoughts of that previous night, I had pleased her, she thought I flattered her, I did not, it was honest admiration, I have never since flattered her, but I have had cause to admire her more deeply. I am poor at description but I will do my best, of middle height she is slim long oval face, big mouth which her long lips denote, lips that can bear a quick ready smile, exceedingly quiet voice, in tone that of a young girl, gives a frequent silent laugh opening her mouth fairly wide which strangely does not distort her features but mainly talks seriously pleasant, I estimate her age now to be thirty. We are on an equal social level, our subjects are equally familiar to us, we arrive at a ready understanding, her contribution is usually fashion, her own trade, womens' peculiarities, mine of a more virile, every day affairs, matter of fact nature. With a barely perceptible exhibition of feminine gestures she reveals her intelligence and intuition. Ours is a perfect blending of man and woman without personal affection. I can not ask her to meet on other occasions for fear of a charge of infidelity, it is a handicap our class suffers from, greater opportunities for understanding and mingling exist in the circles the educated woman moves in, no comments being made suggesting a passionate relationship.

The houses of Port Sunlight and the trees resemble women, the houses are each a work of art, their combination the design of an artist-architect. In rows as they are, each house has its own distinctive quality, the estate is a composite which presents an evenly-combined and attractive appearance. The trees of our country are very beautiful although of little economic value which is mainly to break the wind and draw rain. Of several families, each member of any variety differs, no two are exactly alike, all have a grandeur of their own, they have that quality along with that of being able to relieve a scene, correctly selected and situated they convert a street into a boulevard and a flat plain to a park. This leads me to my few celebrities, placing first the Duchess of Kent as appearance is womans' most obvious quality, our titled lady seems to be specially talented in the choosing of dress. Men may ridicule women over the way they dress but this is caused by the ludicrous appearance of most of them. Men are really very interested in women dress and spend quite a lot of time and thought over it, a number are absorbed in the problems of creating fashions, skilfully designing garments and at that point man comes to an end. No matter how many various garments he can produce he cannot dress a lady, he must leave it to her intuition and the intuition of the experienced lady adviser he provides to dress herself. If every woman took the same care to develop her choice what a glorious assemblage they would be, it is a responsibility every woman of education should accept. The soft sweet tone of a womans voice must have been the first sound to inspire man to grasp and develop the art of Music. A few Masters have produced for us some exquisite pieces and man has not been dilatory in producing and improving instruments to translate what passed through those Masters' minds. Conchita Supervia had a lovely voice and choice of song. I am not suggesting all woman should try to be opera stars, but they can use the softer and sweeter notes, even in talking and choose only those ballads and melodies worthy of her. Suzzane Lenglen, in my belief, will for all time remain on the pedestal she occupies. The game of tennis is increasingly popular and the prominent players vary year after year, some, especially the moderate players, are stylists, others strive after success by strenuos methods, girls, all of them, should adopt those games and exercises calling for skill and grace. Pavlova was the leading exponent of graceful movement, hers is the most exclusive and exacting profession, millions of women, from the youngest and more dainty to the eldest and incongrous devote themselves to dancing and only one in a myriad can be a prima ballerina. It is posible for them to perform and patronize the more graceful form of the Art such as the waltz and ballet. Beyond dancing all women should develop graceful attitudes of movement and resting, she can present a lovely pose in a seated or reclining position and also when walking. The art of Literature is terribly abused by women who could raise it to a high standard, talented members of the sex could easily transcribe the delightful imaginations using the gentle phrasology associated with her sex, eliminating entirely the sensational, emotional and sentimental, and all women readers should read matter such as the author of "The Years" offer to us and force the publisher of cheap rubbish out of his business banishing him for ever from the trade he disgraces. Most of the characteristics I have just mentioned are what men admire and look for in a womans personality, arts that affect a womans' personal charm, the accomplishments of the author of "The Years" and Dame Laura Knight may be coupled however and are of a different value, a greater value really as talent is a requirement, a wider circle is affected, and the disclosure of a womans' view is entailed. My curiosity was aroused on my second visit to London by the number of women copying the painting in an Art Gallery, some were quite skilful, no one yet has given an explanation that satisfies me, the pictures were worth copying, they have a selling value; that may be so but most of those women were grey haired, why, with their skill and intuition, did they not try to translate into colour those living things they themselves saw.

  Now for it and about time, close to my flat there is a grey stone boys school, in front a large square grass patch, some genius years ago planted trees round the square to form it into a circle, it is a pretty picture on a summers' afternoon when a cricket match is being played, on the farther side of the ground to that where strangers are permitted to watch lady relatives and friends sit in a wide arc, very pleasant. Centuries ago men thought it a fine manly sport to race against each other on horseback, to-day a race meeting is a carnival amidst beautiful surroundings. The boys can play cricket and the men can race just as well without the surroundings but it is more gratifying to do so before others, they invited their lady friends, wishing to please the ladies they decided to hold their passtimes in pretty places. Some years ago I knew a man who courted a pretty and fascinating girl, he idolised her, practically worshiped the ground she walked on, her mean nature caused her to play with his affections, she tortured him to such an extent I have known him to cry. Every man is a poor, feeble, irresolute creature, he can do very little by himself, the world is a hard tough place, and he must be hard too, one mistake, a few faulty decisions may cause his whole world to collapse, his business to crash, his success to be blotted out and his future ruined. Weakness in his dealings may leave just that opening his rivals have been waiting for and they walk right in and over him. He cannot trust his fellow man in commerce, the economic struggle is too strenuous, all knowing their own weakness and unreliableness they have joined together and with their common understanding have formed the laws of Trade. Apart from trading his sentiments are very deep and real, he has a keen sense of justice and goodwill towards others. He will give a fair deal to his employees and customers in return for good work and settlement of accounts, if economically possible he will finance those accessories which do so much to make life worth living. Men working and dealing so much amongst their own selves has somehow resulted in the terribly muddled state of affairs we are experiencing today, it is a pleasant reflection that as more and more women enter into our life and work the situation gets easier. Most men in time turn from the coarse stern fellowship of man to the tender refined nature of a woman. He seeks comfort, condolence and aid, he unburdens himself in confessions he dare not tell a fellow man, he wants to indulge in the pleasant pastime of boasting and preening himself before an admirer, not knowing how to live decently or manage his income he wants a woman to show him and do it for him. He takes her into his employ, in offices and works, he can tell at a glance the practical value of any one of a row of houses, it takes his wife to show him the little differences of one from all the others which will turn it into a home. My love-torn aquaintance of years ago entertained the unworthy subject of his affections as much as his means would permit, he spent a great deal of time in her company, gave way to her and tried as best he could to please her, she mounted the high horse, showed her independence, charged him of lack of affection should he ever demur at her wishes. I am afraid I must be tougher than he is, maybe it is because I have never regarded any person so deep as he did for I would never have accepted the treatment he was subjected to, I want a person to go fifty-fifty with me, and if I do not get it the other person can go to blazes. If this young man had packed his girl off as I would have done she would have backed the loser, he was a good fellow, quite a gentleman and held a good job, most of her friends were shocked at her attitude and would have had no sympathy with her in the event of a break and any other man knowing her would have hesitated to join in with her. Man in our country have been very tolerant to women this past twenty years, giving way to her desires, training her for professions, accepting her in his daily work. Whether the unusual liberty and possession of wealth has unbalanced her and she has not had time to become stabilized is uncertain, but she has not responded well, man-made laws are all in her favour, conditions of working have been made pleasant for her, and all she does is to make a proud show of independance, striding over man flaunting the very laws he made for her emancipation in his face as she passes and makes use of her sudden wealth to satisfy her own selfish desires, leaving him to stare disconsolately after her into the blank space of unrealized dreams. He, poor practical creature who can make a myriad of articles, who on the advice of scientists can change coal to oil, milk to plates, trees to paper, fly four hundred miles an hour, send ships to all parts of the globe exchanging artificial silk stockings for the food of our nation longs for women to emulate Ellen

Terry whose art really only displays good behaviour. He is an assimilative and responsive animal, copying the good manners of his wife and her lady friends in the home circle he extends to them courtesy and greets his fellow man with geniality. Her entry into business life has been all to the good, offices and workrooms have been given a more pleasant appearance, shops designed to attract a lady's custom. Every woman has her intuition, the educated, the talented, the influential, they all individually can, if they will, help man to improve our way of living, the talented can display the peak of excellence of her art, but she does so to countless admirers and onlookers who can never reach her intimately and though she may inspire many she loses most of that personal contact which may be so persuasive. The influential may be the wife or sister or associate of some powerful politician or industrial magnate, she holds a great responsibility in winning his confidence and swaying his decisions to the benefit of all people. It is to the educated lady, ordinary, and simply learned in the essential subjects, enough for her to enter into business and social life, men look towards. Let them cut out all the finer and extravagant points of ettiquette and get down to solid good behaviour amongst themselves, let them dispense with the foolishness such as compels them to complete a round of so called entertainments during the season, let them permit of honest friendship with men without the hideous suggestion of personal intimacy. Every single one of them can help and bring their intuition to bear on some man or object. By her manner gain the respect of all the men she works amongst, by her choice of entertainments, by working an extra twelve months, delaying her wedding day or until the baby arrives, to provide the extra fifty pounds which will buy a prettier home, by looking over her architect friends' shoulder as he draws his lines and tell him the vital differences of a room, guiding a building estate designer persuading him to allow for beauty even against the interests of economy, using their influence in the erection of flats, work-shops and workrooms, guiding an enterprising manufacturer in his choice of products, trying with all her might and brains to gain more understanding and consideration from the employer for his work people. Let man do the rough work and govern labour, he can make now an infinite number of essentials it is for the educated lady to show him which are the best and how to distribute them fairly.

   Shakespeare sums up for us our sentiments in the play with such an apt title for our one-sided discussion.
"We number nothing that we spend for you.
Our duty is so rich, so infinite,
That we may do it still without accompt.
Vouchsafe to show the sunshine of your face,
That we, like savages, may worship it."[6]
\*   For many hours I have meditated over the remarks of my distinguished correspondants reference to my criticisms. To what does she refer, my ungallantry in disparaging her sex, or those compositions of hers which are above esteem. Of two difficulties it is for man to choose, so I take the latter and

admitting to many knuckle rappings against the skull to shape its sluggish grey contents I set down my thoughts to utter what maybe not so vague a criticism.

I do not like to compare but I will mention just a few to help my reasoning to be clear. We have in the H.G. Wells a genius who can dare to add humour to vitality and scientific facts and make a great story of every-day ordinary men and women. He is great enough to theorise about social conditions in these stories and his sting is much appreciated by those who consider they are victims of those oppressions which affected him. W. W. Jacobs[7] is about the only writer who can tell a really funny story without any exaggeration and never deviates from the class of people he knows so well.

The astonishing Aldous Huxley can give us a very clear conception of a man who views the diverse variety of people with amused curiosity, explain with great clearness how man may become a citizen of a perfect civilized state, and turn out a delightful comedy on the frailties of men and women. These three write entirely as men, real live men with a mans' line of view always in their eyes. They are as men who do the rough work and talk in the coarse manner of men, there is no mistaking the vigour with which the lines are written. Priestly should be included to make a fourth, and all of them can deal with the coarser, intimate, animal instincts without causing offence, not one of them attempts to portray that ficticious person, the ideal man or woman.

I do not think my distinguished correspondent has ever had a true criticism passed on her work, her advisers would have guided her on those matters which appeal to the public, her friends would be prejudiced in her favour and if they did notice anything detractive would not be likely to inform her, the same applies to her many admirers who when congratulating her, especially by letter, would be all congratulation, her press critics would be mostly all praise with-holding all detrimental remarks out of respect for the law of libel, their extensive knowledge of literature and the fact that they are required to review so many works must also be a drawback. With me distance and the total absense of personal contact is an advantage, I can say freely in what manner a book appeals to me, and I am not hindered by any training. I am supposing she is prepared to learn the opinions of all classes, the lower and more ignorant as well as the polished. She may have regarded my previous remarks as insolence thickly coated with flattery, it is to erase that possible opinion I offer this criticism. The Hogarth Press valued "A room of one's own" at five shillings, the Pelican Books Ltd assessed "The Common Reader at sixpence, I do not know the price of her other books. I value "The Years" higher than the others, the Pelican issue have a wider circulation than the higher priced editions, it is good commercialism but very unfair. The exquisite writing of "The Years" and "The common reader" caused me to fall entirely under its spell, I am not trying to use extravagant words or phrases. I was enraptured, all outside influences liable to intrude dimmed and vanished as I turned page after page, I read on and on until the various contents come to an end or until I was sated, the subjects in themselves were of little importance to me but the excellent manner they were written caused that state of delighted interest every author aims for. I seemed to be surrounded by an aura of pleasant absorbtion similar to that I experienced during a performance by Miss Frances Day in a London theatre show, the best I can describe her writing and the actress is delicately delightful. "The Years" I read an hour or so at a time, and found it a nice story about nice people who were real, I expected the inevitable happy ending of a woman's story, but I was glad it was missing, as the years passed I seemed to get to know the people quite well and love them, especially Eleanor, and I will admit that I was rather anxious to find out who her husband would be. There was no mistaking that the author was a woman, the manner in which she portrayed the Irishman was entirely the way women view the nationals of his country. Up to then I gave her credit for wisdom she was very consistent in what I had read, my memory had not been called upon, dare I say it again, she had not demanded any continuity of interest, she had, as Hardy did in his short stories, made wonderful splendid and pleasant reading of subjects which held little interest in themselves.

    I wish I had never come across her works "Three Guineas" and "A room of one's own", to then I was satisfied with her skill, and I never would have written to her. She seemed to me to be taking advantage of her accomplishments to propagate womens interests, her artistic style does not warrant such an indulgence and is unsuitable for the subject. Her style is perfect for ensuring delight but when trying to understand her reasoning we miss that delight and it also detracts interest, the two elements oppose each other, it has not the virile quality necessary in dealing with the topic. It resembled feminine weakness and impossibility of forcing an issue against men. Men can always dispense with women, comforts the arts, the amenities of a smooth civilization, they have the strengh, energy and steadiness to enable them to wrest an existence from nature, did they ever choose to they could pass laws, bar women from the professions and business pursuits and beat her back to object subjection and dependance to man, even the wealthy possessors of property could be defeated and deprived by man withdrawing his labour and the use of force.

    To conclude may I mention that to nearly every person living there is some little possession which is absolutely worthless but which has some quality which to the possessor turns it to a priceless treasure. I have a thin white sheet of paper of small dimensions covered from edge to edge with type written letters, underneath is a hand written signature. I value that paper, not for its message nor even for the signature, I do not even think I should grieve if it were burnt to destruction, it is the actual receiving of it I treasure, it is positive proof of the graceful consideration of an eminent lady in deigning to become my distinguished correspondent. I am ready to believe her mail is of prodigious proportions and her time too valuable to deal patiently with the lengthy and worthless epistle I had the audacity to forward to her. For doing so I esteem and thank her, to what degree she herself must estimate. To me however is left the telling of my admiration, I do admire her compositions, indeed I assert I am her greatest admirer for without any literary tuition I fully enjoyed most of what I have read of her works.

I take my final leave of her and beg her not to acknowledge this letter, or to further recognize me as a correspondent. I assure her that to ignore or hurt me does not offend or affect, I am one of those persons insensible to opinions.

With deepest sentiments for continued success,
I remain,
As ever.
Ernest Huxley.
"A woman I forswore; but I will prove,
Thou being a goddess, I forswore not thee."[8]
Shakespeare.


Appendix                                          June 15th 1939.
Dear Mrs Woolf,
I think it is only fair to add these few lines and I am using my ordinary style as I would if writing to my sister. Although I have written the treatise I am asking you not to take the trouble of reading it unless you wish to and have the time at your disposal which you cannot use to better advantage. I do not expect there can be much of interest to you in what I have written, the only section that can concern you is the last five pages marked with an asterisk. I suppose that in some way you are interested in the working class point of view, it probably differs from your own as yours has a wider horizon, I do not want you to think, however, that I have written an omnibus workers' philosophy, as that would embrace much more. I have tried to keep out the emotions of anger, resentment and disdain, which we of the working class generally feel towards a country which keeps us to a low standard of living, a continuous army of unemployed, and spends hundreds of millions on modern armaments yet neglects to provide for an emergency such as the tragedy of the Thetis[9] which we Merseysiders feel so much.

I may have aroused your wrath, scorn and abuse by writing as I have done to you, at first I had no intention of doing so, I just amused myself by writing what I thought of your works, when it was finished I thought I would take a chance and sent it along, I did not ask for nor expect the answer you were so good as to send me. I fully intended to write and send to you this present treatise but I hoped it would be nowhere near as lengthy as the first and I was dismayed as page after page was completed, the first took an hour and a half to read, this will take an hour, I apologise for it being handwritten, I had hoped to have had it typed but was unable to.

You may be annoyed by my action but it may spare you having an abusive opinion of me, if you elegantly abused me I would only return an inelegant "So what", I think I am one of those thick skinned persons with a sulky will power whose spirit can never be really broken no matter what the treatment. I dare say you know the kind of spirit which makes a man say "Who cares I've nothing to gain, and little to lose".

I have not intended to enter into a correspondence of long duration and I will not bother you any more and I urgently ask you not to waste any of your precious time considering a reply, I beg you not to.

My last word must be that I hope there will be class distinction for a considerable time to come, I personally like to know there is someone better than me I can look up to, heredity as well as training goes far in forming personality, our trade union and labour leaders are a fine sample of the emancipated worker, although a past member of the I.L.P[10]. and a firm believer in their policy I vote Liberal. I prefer a rogue who tells me straight he is going to have the best end of a deal to a dishonest rogue. Now good-bye.

Ernest Huxley.

---

[1] The first quotation is from Woolf's reply to Letter 72. Her replies have not survived. The second quotation is from Rudyard Kipling's "The Ballad of East and West."

[2] Florence Nightingale (1820-1910) was a British health reformer; Dame Laura Knight (1877-1970) was a British artist known for paintings of circus and gypsy life; Anna Pavlova (1881-1931) was a Russian ballet dancer; Dame Ellen Terry (1847-1928) was a British actress and Conchita Supervia (1895-1936) was a Spanish mezzo-soprano who appeared at Covent Garden Opera House in 1934-5. For Suzanne Lenglen see Letter 72, Note 2. In 1939 the Duchess of Kent was Princess Marina, the youngest daughter of HRH Prince Nicholas of Greece. She married the Duke of Kent in 1934.

[3] Sir Jacob Epstein (1880-1959) was a sculptor. His "Genesis" is a stone carving of a pregnant woman made in 1931.

[4] Aldous Huxley's (1894-1963) *Jesting Pilate* is a travel book published in 1926.

[5] H. G. Wells' *The Work, Wealth and Happiness of Mankind* (1932), along with *The Science of Life* (1929), was an encyclopaedic compilation about history, biology and economics. The two texts were companion volumes to *The Outline of History* (1920) and *A Short History of the World* (1922).

[6] *Love's Labour's Lost*, Act 5, Sc. 2, ll. 198-202.

[7] William Wymark Jacobs (1863-1943) was a writer of many volumes of comic stories. He also wrote horror stories, the best known of which is "The Monkey's Paw."

[8] *Love's Labour's Lost*, Act. 4, Sc. 3, ll. 61-2.

[9] The HMS *Thetis* was a British submarine which sank in Liverpool Bay during sea trials in June 1939 killing 99 of the 103 men on board. It was the worst submarine disaster in British history.

[10] Independent Labour Party.

**74**
**Handwritten**
**July 5, 1939**

5.7.39

Dear Virginia Woolf

  I have been "itching" to write to you ever since I started to read "Three Guineas" (which I have just finished,) & only hope you will not breathe a sigh of utter boredom at the egotistical outpourings of one of your admirers!

  Its hard to know where to begin: really, as you have such profound knowledge, such a keen intellect & logical brain, I want to ask advice, but to do that, I will have to talk a lot about myself, I fear.

  I am 45 years of age, & all my life, except for the usual handicap of limited means, since marriage, I have done what I liked (more or less) all my life. As I am 45, I was (naturally) born in 1894, 6 years before Victoria died, therefore, in the eyes of my daughter, I am a Victorian. My father, whom I adored, was killed in a railway accident in the U.S.A. in 1905 when I was eleven years old, with two sisters & a brother younger than myself. I was naughty, selfish & self-willed, & was spoilt by my sweet mother who found it very hard to adjust herself to life as a widow! We were all spoilt as a matter of fact, & were probably the nastiest set of children you could have found in the reign of Edward VII! My father, my mother told me many times, was a complete believer in the "equality of women" (one must use that phrase!) & said constantly the girls must have absolute equality of opportunity & education with the boy - & he left his money to us all equally. All honour to him! Mother carried this out as much as was humanly possible (actually, my brother's (lack of) education cost more than ours, but we were better educated, & were, in any case, blessed with the grey matter he lacks.) & gave us training in the professions we fancied. I went to a school that was modern for the period "(play the game, girls! "The honour of the school, girls, - behave like ladies, girls!) but, this comes to the crux of the matter; since the age of 14 (1908) I developed, from where I can't imagine, a positive fixation <u>against</u> men, & a violent partisanship for my own sex. It annoyed, amused, & exasperated everyone, but <u>I have never lost it</u>. I still have the reputation of the bee in the bonnet, & I see smiles begin all round if & when the subject crops up -("ah! she's off!") I hung round the edge of the suffrage movement all the time I was at school, tried to make converts, got into trouble - was hauled on the carpet by the Head - all suffrage literature was confiscated - I was well-muzzled. But in the holidays I ran riot! All my mother drew the line at was speaking at street corners & militancy! Anyway I wouldn't have been allowed to use militant methods by the W.S.P.U. at 15-16 years of age. There was nothing in life for me during my adolescence but the "Woman question" = people found me an unmitaged bore!

  Then came the great war, & like all the other suffragettes, I did war work.

Then, 1918. I entered my chosen profession, the stage. On the stage, I found for the first time, a true equality between men & women. What counted was Box Office, & if a woman was better Box Office, she drew a better salary! (I admit, in one company, chorus boys got £4 & girls £3, but that was only one company, otherwise it depended on the part, or the personality, in other words, I repeat, Box Office!) Even then, though this regrettable insistence on sex appeal was rampant, & still my sex-antagonism persisted. But I had "boy-friends" = with them, relationships were <u>equal</u>; we paid for ourselves - we got the same wage. It was <u>right</u>, somehow.

Well, I got married, to an actor-vocalist.

When we married, I was in work, he was out of work, I supported him for some time. I found the relationship ideal, but I fear he suffered from my fixation. I <u>would</u> have my own way. He was (& is) very much in love with me, we worked together for a time - still on all equality!

But I became pregnant....

He has never been able to support me - I have <u>never</u> reproached him. He would if he could, he wants to. He <u>hates</u> the fact that he can't - & also, probably, that I am (tho' poor) independent by means of the small income my father left me. I keep myself & the two children in the bare necessities of existance, & tho' I have <u>tried</u> to <u>get work</u> of any sort I find it impossible, as I am neither a spinster or a widow but that execrable object - a "Mrs"! I write, plays, articles, poems, but have never had success. I love my husband - we are apart, we can't afford to live together as he <u>will not</u> live on me, & his work is in the Midlands. We would like to be together, but circumstances, at the moment, render it impossible.

Now, what I would like to know is, <u>why</u>, when I adored my father, love my husband, & have my own small income, rendering me blessedly independent, was a member of a profession that ignored the difference in sex as regards salary – why have I still got this definite fixation against the male sex? Its a handicap - they feel it, & therefore I get less out of life than I should. I despise the great majority of women for their spineless, supine dependence on men, but I don't dislike them! I feel the greatest compassion & love for them, poor dears. But men, I've no use for them, though, paradoxically, I have some men friends! Is there anything I can do about it? How can I prevent infecting my daughter with it? How treat my son? Would a psychiatrist be of any use? It can't be ~~write~~ right, I feel, & I do try to fight it, reason with myself, & try to make no difference in my behaviour to men, but its difficult.

Life is a great struggle, bringing up two children, housework, cooking etc. etc, & all the financial managment & responsibility as well; all the decisions rest with me, I have "last word". I look upon it as my debt to Society for my small income, & my husband doesn't come into it - I don't feel I'm working for <u>him</u>, but for the next generation. Marriage has stopped my career, frustrated my talents, stopped my social advancement & impaired my health, but I do not regret it. It has been a bar to my husband's progress too, I well know. &

don't regret it, because it has developed character, sympathy, understanding, &, after all, humanity is incomplete without marriage & children. Though the price we women have to pay for that completeness is very stiff! My regret is that there is not enough to give my children anything like the education they need, or the educated environment that I had myself, & would willingly work to give it them if society would only <u>let</u> me work.

Give me advice, please, most understanding person, & bear with this long rigmarole!

Philippa Tristain

**75**
**Handwritten**
**September 18, 1939**

The Wilderness
Upper Winchendon
Nr. Aylesbury
Bucks

18/9/39
Dear Virginia,

My conscience has been pricking for some time, because you asked me to write to you when we were in France, and I didn't. Therefore I am writing to you now.

I decided these holidays to read some of your books, so that I might judge for myself, wether the staff at school had any reason to rave about you, as they did! I have come to the conclusion that they really did have a very good reason, so I shall be more tolerant next term, when Miss Sikes, who never speaks to me, as a rule, except to blow me up, asks if you really smoke a pipe & hate cigars, or some equally futile question. I read "The Years", "Three Guineas" and "The Waves". I think I liked "Three Guineas" best because the people in The Years were so unpleasant, and the "Waves" puzzles me. I expect this will annoy you, as it is as bad as admiring a picture and then asking what it's ment to represent, but I couldn't make out, if, when you wrote the Waves, you wrote it with a special meaning like "Three Guineas",[1] or just to create something beautiful. If it was the latter, which I rather feel it was, I think you succeeded very well.

Our headmistress is very stupid about what I read. When I told her I had read Tolstoy's Peace and War, she murmered "Rather advanced", and looked as if she didn't quite approve. But when I suggested reading "Brave New World", she nearly had a fit, and begged me not to, so of course it was the first book I read these holidays! I'm longing to see her face when I tell her that I read it, liked it, and understood it.

You asked me to tell you if the beds in Douarnenez[2] were " hopping with fleas and lice". None of them could have hopped if they'd tried, as they had no springs, but there weren't any lice, and only a few fleas. Douarnenez was lovely, and simply swarming with artists, and we had a lovely time while we were there. The batheing was super, and the food pretty good too, but we three & Daddy always missed one course in each meal, out, as we belong to the A.B.A.B.A.Bs, and they always gave us crabs or shrimps or lobster or crayfish at every meal. A.B.A.B.A.B. means the Anti Baking Alive of Beasts Associated Bretherin – I expect Uncle Leonard belonged when he was small.

We were very lucky in getting over to England again, with so little bother. We left the car at St Malo, and were fetched at Southampton by one of the Manor cars. But our car came over about a week later.

We go back to school this Thursday, and Marie & I will board in Oxford during the week, because the petrol rationing will not allow us to be fetched every day, by car, and the bus would be too tireing. I don't quite know how every one will fit in at school, as the building is already rather small for the four hundred of us, and now Kensington High School has joined up with us.

I am riding down to the office to meet Daddy, so I will stop now.
With love from
Pip [Philippa Woolf]

[The Artist at Douarnenez]

*Published courtesy of Dr. Philippa Woolf.*

*Philippa Woolf is the daughter of Philip Woolf, Leonard's youngest brother. She was fifteen when she wrote the letter. For Woolf's reply see L6 360-1 (3554), in which she writes: "I'm purring all over like a Siamese cat to think that you liked some of my books."*

[1] In her reply Woolf writes: "Must a book have a special meaning? Three Guineas was a pamphlet to make people angry and say irritating things."

[2] In France, on the coast of Brittany between Quimper and Brest.

**76**
**Handwritten**
**December 12, 1939**

*Y.M.C.A.*
*With His Majestys Forces*

*Please Address Your Reply To*
No. 2050943 Rank: Sapper Name: Heffer
Address: 318th AACoy, 30th Battn. R.E. Mirley Lodge, Farnborough, Hants
Date: 12.12.39

Dear Mrs. Woolf,
    I read your book "Three Guineas" - and felt you were right; I worked for the League of Nations Union; I was a pacifist. I am still! Yet I could only think of searchlight work when the time came. I lost my only Brother - my hero - in 1916; they may get me & leave my wife & children without me - & still get my boys later. But I have faith my creed is perfectly expressed in Rupert Brooke's "Second Best"[1] - yet my vanity - I suppose - made me perpetrate the enclosed . "Perpetrate"! - the truth is that I'm childishly proud of it. However, subject to this confession, I sincerely believe what I have written & wonder if it's any use as Propaganda?
    I should not have dared to write to the author of "The Waves" but now I am bored to desperation - lonely & so I've come wagging my muddy tail and snuffling at your doorstep; forgive me!
                Yours sincerely,
                    Ronald Heffer

*Enclosure missing*

*See L6 375 (3574) to Shena Simon: "I'm encouraged [...] by two letters today, one from a soldier in the trenches who says he's read Three Guineas and 'feels that its true;' and is apparently so 'unspeakably bored' that he'll tackle any more views on the same lines: and another from a middle class provincial lady, who asks distractedly for help, and wants to start an outsiders Society among the women of Yeovil. She's shocked to find them all in uniform, greedy for honour and office." See also D5 250: "Yesterday I was, I suppose unnecessarily [?], cheerful. 2 letters from admirers of 3 Gs; both genuine: one a soldier in the trenches; the other a distracted middle-class woman at Yeovil." Heffer was evidently in Hampshire rather than the trenches.*

[1] In *The Complete Poems of Rupert Brooke* (Sidgwick & Jackson,1933). Heffer's creed is as follows:

'[...] *as of old*
*comes Death, on shadowy and relentless feet,*
*Death, unappeasable by prayer or gold;*
*Death is the end, the end!'*
Proud, then, clear-eyed and laughing, go to greet
Death as a friend!
[...] Yet, behind the night,
Waits for the the great unborn, somewhere afar,
Some white tremendous daybreak.

**77**
**Typed**
**December 13, 1939**

From Mrs I.G. Bartholomew

13 Dec
Dear Madam
    I am hoping that if you read this letter, the reason for my addressing you will be|clear without apology, and that if you cannot give the leadership asked or indicate where su such might be found, that you will al least excuse my having applied to you.
    A sincere admirer of your work, it is actually on the pamphlet 'Three guineas' that I hoped from you, because this shows you interested in the practical work of women as well as the what must of course come first, your work as a poet in the fre-french sense.
    The question in my mind and which I have discussed with a few women, rather exceptional women I fear, is of some kind of organisation among women for XXXXXXXXX after the peace and of course towards it...as opposed to the absurd degrading and damaging regimentation of women on 'military' lines which has sapped our influence entire...Woman's status could hardly be lower than that of merely C3 men....A hermit by choice I have since last war gone on thinking and studying quietly by myself, writing occasionally, under the impression that other women were doing the same...those to whom I have rarely mentioned my thoughts have seemed responsive....It was not until the crisis of '38 that I realised that the mentality of most ordinary influential women was pre-war and pre-vote...so that in the when emmergency that a at last arose; the tentative enquirer, the doubtful and even the definitely antagonistic, were swept into the 'military' organisation...
    I realise that it is women like myself who have had intellectual training and inteest who are to blame, we who have no poetic output to excuse our lack of action..One cannot retrieve lost opportunity but one may be able to create fresh opportunity?

Nobele women won the vote and the rest of us have let the whole benefit go...for the few who seem to have made use of it, with I suppose a few exceptions, have done so simply as neutral individuals, men or women, in the ordinary conevntional ~~al~~ ways...and if to increase the ranks of this kind of worker and careerist was all we could do.. we were in better position and more useful as ~~the~~ mere amusers and comforters of men...I still think that no bad role for some women all the time amd for XXXXXX all~~w~~ women part of the time, because in itself it is an illuminating occupation....And I think that if we are to be any use as constructive workers, it must be from another angle to that of the male. That, brains being equal, in the ordinary sense of the word, it is our different angle of view and of understanding which is so vitally important ~~and~~ and the desire and the opportunity to use this ~~which was~~ the real urge towards the vote.. it was on this point that I would have liked to join issue with '3 Guineas'....the lack of those extra peticoats etc so that the boys might have all, ~~which~~ forced attention to this other outlook and made the drab fact of education a real glory to women...I have indeed no right to talk having never suffered deprivation for the sake of my menkind, so please forgive me where I am probably horribly wrong!

We are fairly helpless here in the country with the usual 'war-work' and fussing going on, among those who are not rushing round saluting each other and being terribly efficient...chasing O.B.Es

No use in my saying any more you will know so much better, if anything can be ~~do~~/done and what. My own conviction is for conferences and peace, but I am open to correction so that it is not of the glorious war type..But ~~t~~ in any case|I doubt if anything can be done in this way at present, but I think and hope we might prepare for peace - for having the vote, it is that much power -

    I am yours admiringly gratefully
    XXXXXXXXXXXXXXXXXand sincerely and with|all apologies for addressing you
    Mrs Bartholomew

**78**
**Typed**
**January 8, 1940**

                Broomcroft,
                Ford Lane,
                Didsbury,
                Manchester 20.

       January 8th 1940.

My dear Virginia,
    When you asked me to give you my views on Women and War I said that it would be merely handing back to you in rags and tatters the arguments

in Three Guineas which you have clothed so gloriously. But you persisted and I am grateful because, although I cannot pretend to any wide knowledge of women's views, I have found since war started, that my own were in a muddle and I am glad to have to try to sort them out.

After the last war I felt that war was the greatest evil and that nothing justified it. When, however, Hitler rose to power in Europe I felt - largely I think because I am a woman - that war would be better than a world dominated by his ideas and his practices. So I criticised the government for its retreat before the dictators and as I realized that standing up to Hitler involved the risk of war, I felt that it was only logical for me to be ready to take my part in it, if it came. So in the summer of 1938 I trained as an Air Raid Warden. I must admit that during those days before Munich when I was feverishly fitting gas masks on children I found myself wondering whether it would not be better to let Hitler take Czecho Slovakia rather than have children all over Europe gassed - so you see I am very infirm of purpose even when I have thought the matter out as clearly as I can.

After Munich I criticised the policy of appeasement, and welcomed the pledge to Poland, although I again realized that war was possible. When it came I did not feel that under the circumstances we could have done otherwise. I do not mean, of course, that we might not have avoided war if we had been able to come to an agreement with the U.S.S.R.

But since war started I have been frankly appalled by the general attitude towards it, especially of men. I was partly prepared for this by "Three Guineas", the truth of which has been proved over and over again since September 1st. On the other hand we say that war is terrible, "a hideous evil" the Archbishop of York calls it, and at the same time we heap praise and honours on people who take part in it. Our airmen do their best to kill German airmen, and when they succeed and when the bodies are recoverable, they send wreaths and give them a splendid funeral.

The commander of the Graf Spee[1] is reported to have said to one of the English Captains, prisoner on his ship, after the engagement "You English are tough. When people fight like that, all personal enmity goes." There is evidently a feeling of comradeship between men who are engaged not only in trying to kill each other but in what the Archbishop calls "a hideous evil". Now, as a woman I find this all very confusing. War, I agree, is a hideous evil, but I am not a pacifist and so I am ready to admit that it may prevent an even more hideous evil, just as although nobody likes shutting up a human being in prison, it may be necessary to shut him up in order to prevent his doing damage to other people. But we do not make heroes out of prisoners nor do we load honours on the Warders of our prisons, nor on our police. We consider that they are only doing their duty, - however unpleasant it may be at times. Why then do we speak and act as if men who are killing one another - not merely shutting them up - are doing something wonderful and glorious? Is it because they are risking their own lives, whereas policemen and warders are not usually doing so?

But miners risk their lives in the course of their work which is essential to the country, and they are not given splendid funerals, nor are their wives or mothers consoled with statements about the "supreme sacrifice" and "giving his life for his country".

Ought we not to say that if a question between nations cannot be settled except by war, one side may be more to blame than another, but neither side ought to be allowed to think that it is behaving in a noble way, - both are engaged in a beastly undertaking.

The only answer is the one you give in Three Guineas namely that the average man enjoys fighting or at any rate thinks that it is praiseworthy, and therefore instead of regarding it as a necessary evil - which I am prepared to admit it is, at present - and treating it as such, makes out that it is fine and glorious and gives rise to noble qualities. Now this seems to me completely inconsistent. If war is a hideous evil nothing can make it anything else, however much courage it calls forth.

The old sayings that you cannot touch pitch without being defiled, and that it takes two to make a quarrel, are surely true. The allies are not blameless, although not nearly so blameworthy I believe, as Hitler, but we cannot get out of a certain share of responsibility for a situation that has resulted in an appeal to force.

Hitler, of course, glorifies war, but we - especially since 1918 - have professed to abhor it. Why then does the Church give it its blessing? I should have thought that the only line for the Church to take up when a Christian nation is involved in war is to say that however unavoidable war may have been, so long as people are engaged in killing one another, so long they must consider themselves outside the Christian community. Chaplains should not be sent to the army, men in uniform should not be allowed in Church, etc. The attitude of the Church to war has always seemed to me so inconsistent. Regimental banners are hung in Cathedrals, war memorials are placed there. In spite of what it says the Church evidently thinks that some wars are to be blessed.

This confusion of thought is not confined to the Church. Did you hear a broadcast by Sir Ernest Swinton[2] the other night in which, speaking of the attacks by German aeroplanes on our trawlers he said with great indignation "This is not war, it is dirty murder". The distinction is a nice one. The Oxford dictionary says that murder is "the unlawful killing of human beings with malice aforethought" whereas war is a "quarrel usually between nations conducted by force", and of course, although the Oxford dictionary does not mention it, war involves killing, but it is killing which is organized and sanctioned and is not done for any personal motive. Now, in so far as the trawlers were unarmed, the attack on them by German planes was despicable, but nobody accused the German Commander of the ship that sunk the Rawal Pindi[3] of "dirty murder" although some time before she sank, the Rawal Pindi was practically unarmed and completely at the mercy of the bigger and stronger ship. But, it will be said the men on the Rawal Pindi were prepared to be killed, whereas the men on the trawlers were not. Well, it is all the same to their wives and children. If my son had been killed on a trawler I do not think I should have felt that it would have been better if he had been killed on the Rawal Pindi. It seems as if we lose all sense of the importance of individual life when we engage in war. Personally, I should have thought it much better if the Commander of the Rawal Pindi had surrendered when he had done all the damage that he could to the German ship, and saved the lives of at least the remainder of his men. but everyone spoke of the magnificent exploit of going down fighting, glorious traditions of the Navy etc. as if there was something meritorious in sacrificing those lives.

In the same way the scuttling of the Graf Spee was sneered at by the Times as inglorious, whereas I was thankful - weren't you? - that at least the men on that ship were saved. Of course, it is only natural that women should attach more importance to individual life than men, so much of their work has always consisted of caring for children and the sick, and I cannot believe that if the woman's point of view were stronger all over the world, war would not have been dismissed as an impossible solution before now. But, as you have explained so convincingly, in Three Guineas, although we have now had votes for twenty years we have not yet got into positions of control, and the prospect of our doing so seems remote.

It is this universal acceptance of force as the final sanction that I find so depressing. I am quite ready to admit that, given the world as it is, force cannot immediately be abandoned, but while recognising the fact, I feel that we ought to admit that that fact is a disgrace that all of us must share, and that no plans will be successful for avoiding war until we recognize it as "murder" as taking killing lawfully - instead of unlawfully - with malice aforethought. We can, and often do, call capital punishment "judicial murder", so I do not see why we should talk about war as something more glorious and give it all the trappings which make armies and navies and air forces appeal to the public.

I find it difficult to believe that the sole reason why the League of Nations failed was because the principle of national sovereignty was not surrendered, and that Federal Union will succeed because there will be an international force. Even if we get to that point after this war, unless something is done to strip the international army, navy and air force of any virtue or glory, you we may, by enthroning the idea of force, make the countries who do not wish to come in to the Union, concentrate on trying to get together a greater force, just as the nations who wished to defy the league of Nations built up their own forces and xxxx then left the League. And although the Federal Union may have the stronger force, it may mean a series of wars before this is proved.

Somehow or other surely we must discredit force whilst admitting that it may be necessary for a time; and I suggest that an analogy might be found in our attitude towards the police. Their uniforms are sombre, the various ranks do not wear more splendid clothes - except the Chief Constable - and Sergeants and Superintendents do not wear swords as part of their dress uniform. (Do you realize that in this war an officer in a Territorial Anti-Air Craft Battery has to provide himself ith a sword?) They are paid sufficiently but no gentleman's son goes into the Police Force as he goes into the army, navy, or air force - for many generations, of course, the only possible career for a gentleman's son.

If the international force were dressed and officered like the Police Force, if they got no more honours than does the police, if service in it were not regarded as any more honourable, if their work in time of war was considered as necessary but extremely unpleasant, like a scavangers then I think we should have taken the first step to debunk war.

But can we get people to regard physical force as something beastly in itself, even if necessary - as a "hideous evil"? As you have shown, fighting means something to men which women cannot really understand. It goes very deep and ~~have~~ has many manifestations. From the beginning, boys are brought up to hit back if they are attacked - little girls are scolded for doing the same - A fight between boys is considered "natural" and "manly" - a quarrel between girls which develops into a fight is considered disgraceful. Are men afraid of the effect of encouraging physical courage in girls, or is it merely that they want boys later on, to be ready to fight, and girls later on, merely to weep? In Manchester there is no woman head of a Senior School - children between 11 and 14 - even when the school is mixed, and there is usually a fight to get half the Junior Mixed schools - ages 7 to 11 - staffed by Women Heads. Partly this is due to the dislike of putting any man teacher under a woman, but still more, I find, it arises from the idea that Woman heads would make the boys effeminate. Now, I am more and more convinced that we shall never abolish war until the so-called "Womanly Virtues" are inculcated in boys all through their school life and I would begin by insisting that all boys should be taught by women teachers - provided the women would treat them as if they were girls. As the men teachers would have to do something, I would put them to teach girls. They could not do much harm - because I am sure that it would go too much against the grain for them to try to inculcate the manly virtues in their pupils, and they are excellent teachers in other respects. After some generations of feminine upbringing, it would probably be safe for the boys to be educated in mixed schools with mixed staffs.

Of course, it will be said that this would result in a race unwilling and unable to fight if necessary. But I do not think the combative spirit and certainly not the defensive spirit is so easily ~~pulled when~~ quelled. We find that a third of the men who are conscripted choose the air force, and we realise that there is plenty of physical courage and love of adventure in the present generation of Englishmen, which has certainly not been brought up to regard war as glorious and manly as were their fathers. Neither do they seem any less competent fighters than the German youths who, for the last six years, have been brought up to look upon death in battle as the best of all deaths. You remember the fears aroused by the Oxford Union resolution not to fight for King and Country? It always seemed to me ridiculous to think that, so quickly, a nation that had always taken a fair share of fighting, would not fight again, if the necessity arose. I certainly think we could take the risk, especially as if Germany is defeated, the women of that country will get the chance of making common cause with us.

What encourages me to think that it is not completely Utopian to ~~think~~ talk of really abolishing war, is that we seem to have moved slightly in that direction during the last 25 years. There is not the same enthusiasm shown by those who are joining the forces today, even when it is voluntary, as there was in 1914. Yet on the face of it there should be more. Germany under Hitler is a much greater danger than she was under the Kaiser, and although Poland is farther away and not so well known to Englishmen, Hitler's invasion was an even worse act of aggression than the Kaiser's march in Gelgium. Then, too, our attitude to conscientious objectors is much more tolerant.

I think, don't you, that the reasons for this change are partly that many who feel that we had got to such a state that war was inevitable, are sceptical after the experience of the last 25 years of the possibility of building a new world on the ruins of one destroyed by war, and partly that the intensive League of Nations propaganda in the schools has at least had its effect on the youth of today? Unfortunately the people in whose hands the power lies did not have the advantage of this education.

Men - for the most part, I think - are going in to this war as a necessity not as an adventure, and if we could get over that war is not merely a "hideous evil" but something like cannibalism that just isn't done by civilised nations, I believe we might begin to get somewhere. I imagine that if a shipwrecked crew were faced with starvation unless they killed and eat the weakest member, they would not talk about it if they survived; and if it became known they would not be feted as the Ajax[4] is being feted in South America.

The actual steps that I can think of are a development of your "Outsiders Society". Women should not attend processions like Coronations, etc. which consist largely of troops, or military Tattoes, and should use all their influence to prevent children from being taken. They might protest to the Cinema managements of News Reels showing too many military events, and also to members of Parliament about the expenditure of their money as taxpayers on grand uniforms for the forces. They would not themselves accept honours for any war work that they might have done, and might protest against honours being given to men for exploits that involve the death of other people. On the other hand, I don't see any reason why they should not be conscripted as men are for national service in an emergency. Those who are physically strong enough might be sent to the front line. What they experienced there would surely only strenghten their desire to put war outside the pale.

It may be said that I have only been repeating what conscientious objectors have always felt. That is not quite correct. I don't go so far as to say that force is wrong in itself and that under no circumstances should people fight. As I explained earlier, in the present state of the world, I am prepared to support war against Hitler, in fact unless he is defeated our chance of discrediting force will be put off for a long time. Also, I do not notice that C.O.S.[5] make any sustaned effort in between wars to get rid of the idea that force is the final sanction, and this sort of idea cannot be produced suddenly in the middle of a war.

Hitler and Mussolini glorify force, we on the other hand not only recognize it as the final s anction but consider it quite respectable, if regrettable. Since the last war we have certainly put more emphasis on the regrettable aspect than did previous generations who regarded it as something to be easily resorted to - in the Boer War, in Ireland, etc That is a distinct gain, but we must I suggest now take the next step which is to consider war as "dirty murder", something which decent people ought not to engage in and which no cause can make anything but beastly and uncivilised.

Well, Virginia, if you have had the patience to wade through all this, you will not even have your reward at the end. You asked me to give you some ideas for the article you are to write for an American paper,[6] xxxx on Women and War, and I have only given you the views of one woman and they are practically your own. But now that I have thought out my own views I will try to find out whether any other women share them.

As to America, I have only been there once for three weeks. I have always heard that women's views are more regarded there than here, and as your reputation there is very high, I am delighted that you are writing the article.

      Yours ever,
      Shena D. Simon

P.S. This war has already given us two delightful footnotes to Three Guineas. 1, the announcement by the B.B.C. on the day that war was declared that the King and his Household had donned military uniforms, and 2, the picture of the King broadcasting on Xmas day wearing an Admiral's uniform! Even war gives an excuse for dressing up, for nobody can suppose that the clothes worn by the King and his Household can help - or hinder - the prosecution of the war.

---

*Published courtesy of Professor Brian Simon, Baron of Wythenshawe.*

*For reply see L6 379 (3580). Woolf found Simon's letter "useful, suggestive and sound" and asks her to "cast your mind further that way: about sharing life after war: about pooling men's and women's work: about the possibility, if disarmament comes, of removing men's disabilities."*

[1] On December 14 1939 the German battleship *Graf Spee* stopped in the harbour of Montevideo after it had sunk nine British ships between September 26 and December 13 1939. The ship was given seventy two hours by the Uruguayan government in which to leave. Under threat of British cruisers, however, on December 17 the boat was unloaded and blown up.

[2] Sir Ernest Dunlop Swinton (1868-1951) was a British soldier, writer and inventor. He was one of the originators of armoured fighting vehicles and he coined the word "tank." He was Professor of Military History at Oxford University 1925-39.

[3] The *Rawalpindi*, under Captain E. C. Kennedy, was sunk by German battleships in November 1939 south east of Iceland. There were many casualties and many men were taken prisoner.

[4] The *Ajax* was a British ship used to hunt enemy vessels off the coast of South America during the war. It was one of the ships involved in the attack on the *Graf Spee* in 1939.

[5] Conscientious objectors.

[6] See *L6* 375 (3574) where Woolf writes to Simon: "if you would sometime write down any views you've come to about women and war I'm sure it would be a great help to me. I've promised to write something for America." She is referring to an article requested by *The Forum*, an American monthly review, which she never actually wrote. Later, in October 1940, Woolf was to publish "Thoughts on Peace in an Air Raid" in the *New Republic*, New York.

## 79
**Typed**
**Date unknown**

*Mrs. Smith Ely Jelliffe*
*64 West 56th Street*
*New York City*

Virginia Woolf.
Atlantic Monthly.
My dear Mrs. Woolf:

    I like your articles[1] very much, and want to tell you so. It is encouraging to know that others, of some power, are with one in spirit. I am glad that you have written as you have, and that I have been able to read them. I am asking all my women friends to read your articles, and although at the moment everything seems futile, still one must constantly renew ones courage and go on.

                      Very sincerely yours,
                            Belinda Jelliffe.

---

[1] A summary of *Three Guineas* was published in the *Atlantic Monthly* in May and June 1938 as "Women Must Weep, Or Unite Against War." This letter is undated.

**80**
**Typed**
**Date unknown**

*Belinda Jelliffe*
*Huletts Landing*
*Washington Co., N.Y.*

Mrs. Virginia Woolf.
Harcourt, Brace.[1]

Dear Mrs. Woolf:

    Thank you very much for your reply to my letter, telling you that I liked so much your article in the Harpers.[2] Now I am reading your book, and it has stimulated me more than I am able to express, just now. I am so pathetically lacking in the simplest fundamentals of education; i have nothing but Feelings, and that won't get me anywhere. The review of your book in the Times was done by, I think, their BEST reviewer, Katharine Woods. She also was kind enough to speak very well of a book I wrote,[3] at the instigation of Mr. Maxwell Perkins, at Charles Scribners. In my book, I have told of my fight to secure an education, and how I failed; at least academically. In an article in Harpers, a Mr. Wilson criticized my book, along with Huxley and De Voto,[4] to my surprise, and I wrote a letter which they published in the front there where they do publish letters, in defense not so much of me, or my book, but of Mr. Perkins, who is, I'm told, the finest Editor in this country. All this is of no importance, but if you had the time to read the two, you'd see what I mean about education in this country, for all its vaunted opportunities. The whole thing is such a mess as would strangle the breath in your throat. Sometimes I think that of all countries in the whole world, this is the MOST hipocritical. We are such fakes in so many ways. For instance, the only women I know who have anything to THINK with at all, are working women who work so hard that it is an extreme effort for them to remove their clothing to fall into bed at night. Those who are on top, who have money, become molluscs, or something revolting..Of course there ARE a great many who are doing something, that is are acting, as well as thinking. But how can women be got to co-operate? I've often felt that if if if women stuck together, they've the whole world right in their hand. They REALLY and truly can control the universe, once they SEE what power they have.

    You can, I believe, imagine how your beautiful, lucid, intelligent writing makes me feel, -hopeless. I'm right up against a well, and though my book got wonderful reviews, and sold well here, not so well in England where Hurst & Blackett took a chance on it, still I KNOW that I know nothing; that it will be nearly an impossibility for me to ever learn to write. I've lived in a world of Psychiatry for the past 20 years, and that too gives one a different outlook on the universe. There is that MENTAL consideration and I think things I wouldn't

DARE to write..concerning the CAUSE of so much idiocy..which is all that WAR is, really...a mental idiocy when you sift it right down. Indeed, I wouldn't be at all surprised to see even you draw back from me in distaste, if I say to you that I believe the BASE of all such stupidity begins in the home. It is horrible nauseating FAMILY emotional stuff that clutters people up. Here in America, everyone will Kill, Steal, Sweat, Lie, Anything in order to get money, so THEIR children need not work; that they may Advance Socially, and anyone here who GETS money, it doesn't matter HOW, are worshipped, and I've been around Europe a lot, and that obtains everywhere. The only place I didn't feel it inx the air, was in the Scandinavian countries. I swear that the very AIR felt more free, in Denmark, Sweden and Norway.

Do forgive me for taking so much of your time,-that is if you have read this. But I think your book is so fine, so wonderfully done that I am all keyed up and bursting with chaotic energies that can scarcely be called thoughts....I am reading it slowly, for I want to get it, and I am going to make a few of the women I know BUY it and READ it. I say BUY because from the thousands of letters I have had from readers who liked my book, at least half of them TELL me that they Borrowed it..that is a great habit over here..

With the best of possible good wishes to you, and appreciation of your book.

         Sincerely yours,
         Belinda Jelliffe.

I'm in the country, so have not your address.

---

[1] Harcourt and Brace were the American publishers of *Three Guineas*. See *L6* 268 (3436).

[2] Woolf's article was actually in the *Atlantic Monthly*. See Letter 79 Note 1 and Letter 81.

[3] Belinda Jeliffe's book *For Dear Life* was published in 1937 in America and Britain. It was an autobiography about her upbringing in a large family on a farm in North Carolina, her fight for education and her career as a nurse. Jeliffe's book was reviewed in the *Times Literary Supplement* on October 2 1937: 717.

[4] Bernard Augustine De Voto (1897-1955) was an American novelist, critic, essayist, and editor. He was Professor of English at Northwestern and Harvard Universities. Between 1935 and 1955 he occupied the "Easy Chair" at *Harper's*. He was Literary Editor of the Mark Twain estate.

**81**
**Typed**
**Date unknown**

                              Mrs. Smith Ely Jelliffe
                                  Huletts Landing
                               Washington Co., N.Y.

Mrs. Virginia Woolf.
c/o Harcourt, Brace & Co.
Dear Mrs. Woolf:

    I've read your book over again and still feel that I can easily read it again, because there is so much food for thought in it. It is a fine book, and I am going to do all in my power to get females I know to read it, and to BUY it.

    Though it is not important, I want x to tell you that in my haste, in my letter to you, I said a letter of mine had been published in Harpers, and I MEANT Atlantic...or I THINK I did. I've been working against so much confusion for months that I am not sure of much. I'm trying to finish a novel that is not important; I had wanted to say Something in it that seems important to me, but having absolutely NO education, it is difficult. When you speak of 'infantile fixation', I thought you were Very considerate, very diplomatic....and it is that that I have not got...I'd like to slash right and left and kill! Oh, the destruction that is wrought by Family Complexes...I'm of the opinion that Hitler is Hitler because of frustrated libido, some hatred of his Family, overcompensatory....Oh well, I won't take your time; you know all these things, and what is behind them...and thank god you know how to write it so it will get over. I'm sending you a little leaflet that comes to me ever so often; they have had some Very good advertisments in all the papers, and I've contributed. But I feel that they don't know AT ALL what Causes War...<I've told them to read your book - > and while I think of it I do want to ask you if you've read two little books by Dr Edward Glover,[1] there in London...one of them I think is VERY good on What Causes War...I may easily be wrong, but I feel he is aware of reasons that certainly are not aired...the one called War, Sadism and Pacifism..the other is The Dangers of being Human....You MIGHT like to look them over.

    Forgive me for taking up so much of your time, if you have read this far. It is due to my enthusiasm for you book, and my lack of ability to say so neatly, completely and be done with it.

                          With great admiration sincerely,
                                Belinda Jelliffe.

*Enclosure missing*

[1] Edward Glover was a psychologist. His books *War, Sadism and Pacifism* and *The Dangers of Being Human* were published in 1933 and 1936 respectively.

**82**
**Handwritten**
**Date unknown**

From Mrs Le Blanc-Smith
Dear Madam
      I have just read your book "Three Guineas" which has interested me very much. I also feel that the question of "Peace" comes before everything else in the world, and is the only thing that matters at present, but it seems to me that you confuse our approbation of re-armament-for-defence, with a desire for war, whereas the two things are exact opposites. Everyone in Britain, women <u>and</u> men loathe war, but they want defence against aggression. The objective of modern war as we see it now in Spain and China is no longer the killing of enemy troops, but the destruction of all that equipment of national life which is essential to civilised populations. This sort of warfare has put an end to Britain's island-security, and has made peace, and armament-for defence, almost synonymous terms, as the aggressor countries fear nothing but well armed defence. There is no doubt that with a very few, negligible exceptions there are no people in Britain who do not hate and detest war, but the ~~the question but the~~ desire for adequate defence ~~for~~ at the moment for our population, is a very different thing to a desire for war, and entirely opposed to it in my opinion. The only people who appear to wish to fight, are the Opposition in the House of Commons who are constantly suggesting that we should fight Spain. This is to me inexplicable as a very short time ago they were hotly opposing any form of re-armament, and now demand aeroplanes and battle ships instead of arbitration to deal with Spain. This is inviting war for certain. Your suggestion that educated women should stand aside indifferently from the whole question is a "counsel of perfection" when bombs are killing their families and destroying their homes I am afraid that advice would certainly leave you in a minority of one. I like your book because I loathe war, but it is not practical really, and you are over critical of men and in some ways very unfair to them, but that would mean a long argument and this letter is too long already.
                Yours very truly
                (Mrs) Amy <u>Le Blanc-Smith</u>

# Guide to Library Special Collections

This guide updates the information in volume 5.

**Name of Collection:** The Beinecke Rare Book and Manuscript Library

**Contact:** Vincent Giroud, Curator of Modern Books and Manuscripts

Patricia Willis, Curator of American Literature

**Address:** Yale University Library
P. O. Box 208240
New Haven, CT 06520-8240

**Hours:** Mon.-Fri. 8:30AM-5PM

**Access Requirements:** Register at the circulation desk on each visit.

**Holdings Relevant To Woolf:** General Collection includes autograph manuscript of "Notes on Oliver Goldsmith." Comments on Edward Gibbon, William Beckford Collection. Letters from Virginia Woolf in the Bryher Papers, the Louise Morgan and Otto Theis Papers, and the Rebecca West Papers. Related material: 41 letters from Vita Sackville-West to Violet Trefusis; files relating to Robert Manson Myers's *From Beowulf to Virginia Woolf* in the Edmond Pauker Papers.

Yale Collection of American Literature includes typewritten manuscripts of "The Art of Walter Sickert," "Augustine Birrell," "Aurora Leigh," "How Should One Read a Book?" "Letter to a Young Poet," "The Novels of Turgenev," "Street Haunting." Dial/Scofield Thayer Papers: manuscripts of "The Lives of the Obscure," "Miss Ormerod," and "Mrs. Dalloway in Bond Street." Letters from Virginia Woolf in the William Rose Benet Papers, the Benet Family Correspondence, the Henry Seidel Canby Papers, the Seward Collins Papers, the Dial/Scofield Thayer Papers, and the *Yale Review* archive. Material relating to translations of Woolf in the Thornton Wilder Papers. Related material: Clive Bell, "Virginia Woolf" (Dial/Scofield Thayer Papers); 43 letters from Leonard Woolf to Helen McAfee (*Yale Review*); 11 letters from Leonard Woolf to Gertrude Stein.

**Name of Collection:** The Henry W. and Albert A. Berg Collection of English and American Literature
**Contact:** Rodney Phillips, Curator
**Address:** New York Public Library
Fifth Avenue & 42nd Street
New York, NY 10018
**Hours:** Tues./Wed. 11AM-5:45PM
Thurs.-Sat. 10AM-5:45PM
*Closed Sun., Mon. and legal holidays*

**Access Requirements:** Apply for card of admission at Office of Special Collections. Traceable identification required. Undergraduates working on honors theses need letter from faculty advisor.

**Restrictions:** Virginia Woolf's MSS are now made available on microfilm. N.B. *All the Berg's Woolf mss. are on microfilm published by Research Publications and available at many research libraries.*

**Holdings Relevant To Woolf:** Manuscripts of *Between the Acts, Flush, Jacob's Room, Mrs. Dalloway* (notes and fragments), *Night and Day, To the Lighthouse, The Voyage Out, The Waves, The Years*; 12 notebooks of articles, essays, fiction and reviews, 1924-1940; 36 volumes of diaries; 26 volumes of reading notes; correspondence with Vanessa Bell, Ethel Smyth, Vita Sackville-West and others. Su Hua Ling Chen's Bloomsbury correspondence.

**Name of Collection:** The British Library Manuscript Collections
**Contact:** The Manuscripts Librarian
**Address:** 96 Euston Road
London NW1 2DB
England

**Telephone:** 0171-412-7513
**Fax:** 0171-412 7745
**e-mail:** mss@bl.uk
**Hours:** Please inquire

| | |
|---|---|
| Access Requirements: | Must be a graduate student and/or over 21. Letter of recommendation required from a person in a recognized position, along with proper identification. |
| Restrictions: | Photocopies of selected items available upon receipt of written authorization for photo duplication from the copyright holder. |
| Holdings Relevant To Woolf: | Diaries 1930-1931 (microfilm); Mrs. Dalloway and other writings (1923-1925) three volumes; letter from Leonard Woolf to H.G. Wells (1941); two letters from Virginia Woolf and three letters from Leonard Woolf to John Lehmann (1941); letter written on behalf of Leonard Woolf to S. S. Koteliansky (1946); notebook in Italian kept by Virginia Woolf; notebook of Virginia Stephen (1906-1909); A sketch of the past revised ts (1940); letters from Virginia Woolf in the correspondence files of Lytton and James Strachey; letter from Virginia Woolf to Mildred Massingberd; letter from Virginia Woolf to Harriet Shaw Weaver (1918); letters from Virginia Woolf to S.S. Koteliansky (1923-27); letter from Virginia Woolf to Frances Cornford (1929); letter from Virginia Woolf to Ernest Rhys (1930); correspondence of Virginia Woolf in the Society of Authors archive (1934-37); letter and postcard from Virginia Woolf to Bernard Shaw (1940); three letters (suicide notes) from Virginia Woolf (1941); two letters from Virginia Woolf and three from Leonard Woolf to John Lehmann (1941).

Collection of RPs ("reserved photocopies"—copies of manuscripts exported, some subject to restrictions). |
| Recent Acquisitions: | "Hyde Park Gate News" 1891-92, 1895 (add. Mss 70725, 70726). Letters of Virginia and Leonard Woolf to Lady Aberconway, 1927-1941. Letter from Virginia Woolf to Frances Cornford. |
| **Name of Collection:** | Harry Ransom Humanities Research Center |
| Contact: | Research Librarian |
| Address: | The University of Texas at Austin<br>P.O. Box 7219<br>Austin, TX 78713-7219 |

| | |
|---|---|
| Telephone: | 512-471-9119 |
| Fax: | 512-471-2899 |
| e-mail: | reference@hrc.utexas.edu |
| Hours: | Mon.- Fri. 9AM-5PM |
| | Sat. 9AM-NOON |
| | *Closed holidays; intersession Saturdays; one week each in late May and late August.* |
| Access Requirements: | Completed manuscript reader's application; current photo identification. |
| Restrictions: | Photocopies of selected items available upon receipt of written authorization for photoduplication from the copyright holder. |
| Holdings Relevant To Woolf: | The manuscript collection includes the typed manuscript with autograph revisions of *Kew Gardens*, and the typed manuscript and autograph revisions of "Thoughts on Peace in an Air Raid." The Center holds 571 of Woolf's letters, including correspondence to Elizabeth Bowen, Lady Ottoline Morrell, Mary Hutchinson, William Plomer, Hugh Walpole and others. Further mss. relating to Virginia Woolf include letters to her from T. S. Eliot and reviews of her work. A substantial collection of first British and American editions of Woolf's published works, as well as 130 volumes from Leonard and Virginia Woolf's library and a collection of books published by the Hogarth Press, is also housed. An iconography collection holds a landscape painting of Virginia's garden and a series of Cockney cartoons in a sketch book, signed "V.W." The center also has extensive holdings of materials related to Leonard Woolf, Ottoline Morrell, Mary Hutchinson, Lytton Strachey, Dora Carrington, E. M. Forster, Clive Bell, Roger Fry, Vanessa Bell, Bertrand Russell, Elizabeth Bowen, William Plomer, Stephen Spender and Hugh Walpole. |

# GUIDE TO SPECIAL COLLECTIONS 173

**Name of Collection:** Archive Centre
Contact: Jacqueline Cox, Archivist
Address: King's College
Cambridge CB2 1ST
Telephone: 01223-331444
Fax: 01223-331891
e-mail: jc10021@cam.ac.uk
Hours: Mon-Fri 9:30 AM-12:30 PM
and 1:30 PM - 5:15 PM.
Closed during public holidays and the College's annual periods of closure.

Access requirements: Proof of ID, letter of introduction, appointment in advance.

Holdings Relevant to Woolf: Woolf mss and letters: Minute book, written up by Clive Bell, of the meetings of a play-reading society, with cast lists and comments on performances by CB. Dec, 1907-Jan. 1909, Oct. 1914-Feb. 1915. Players included variously Clive & Vanessa Bell, Roger & Margery Fry, Duncan Grant, Walter Lamb, Molly MacCarthy, Adrian & Virginia Stephen, Saxon Sydney-Turner. *Freshwater, A Comedy*—photocopy of editorial typescript prepared from the MSS at Sussex University and Monk's House; photocopy of covering letter from the publisher to "Robert Silvers," 1.29.1976. Papers relating to the Virginia Woolf Centenary Conference held at Fitzwilliam College, Cambridge, 9.20-22.1982. TS with corrections of "Nurse Lugton's Curtain." Typed transcript of R. Fry's memoir of his schooldays. Correspondence with Clive Bell, Julian Bell, Vanessa Bell, Richard Braithwaite, Rupert Brooke, Mrs. Brooke, Katharine Cox, Julian Fry, Roger Fry, John Davy Hayward, J. M. Keynes, Lydia Keynes, Rosamond Lehmann, Charles Mauron, Raymond Mortimer, G. H. W. Rylands, J. T. Sheppard, W. J. H. Sprott, Thoby Stephen, Madge Vaughan. Woolf-related archival collections held: Charleston Papers; Rupert Brooke Papers; E. M. Forster Papers;

Roger Fry Papers; J. M. Keynes Papers; J. T. Sheppard Papers; W. J. H. Sprott Papers.
Various works of art by Vanessa Bell, Duncan Grant, and Roger Fry, held in various locations around King's College. Access via Domus Bursar's secretary.

Recent Acquisitions: Roger Fry Papers: sketchbooks, 1880s-1920s

**Name of Collection:** Archives and Manuscripts, University of Maryland at College Park Libraries
Contact: Beth Alvarez, Curator of Literary Manuscripts
Address: McKeldin Library
University of Maryland at College Park
College Park, MD 20742
Telephone: 301-405-9298
e-mail: ra60@umail.umd.edu
Hours: Mon.-Fri. 10AM-5PM
Access Requirements: Photo ID.
Holdings Relevant To Woolf: Papers of Hope Mirrlees contain five autograph letters and postcards (1919-28) from Virginia Woolf to Mirrlees. Also in the collection are 113 letters from T. S. Eliot to Mirrlees, and three letters from Lady Ottoline Morrell to Mirrlees.

**Name of Collection:** Monks House Papers/Leonard Woolf Papers/Charleston Papers/Nicolson Papers
Contact: Elizabeth Inglis, Manuscripts Librarian
Address: University of Sussex Library
Brighton
Sussex BN1 9QL
ENGLAND
Telephone: 01273-678163
Fax: 01273-678441
e-mail: Library@UK.AC.Sussex.Central
Hours: Mon. - Fri. 9:15AM -5PM

Access Requirements: Letter, to be received *before* visiting.

# GUIDE TO SPECIAL COLLECTIONS 175

Restrictions: Photocopying strictly controlled.

Holdings Relevant To Woolf: The University of Sussex holds two large archives relating to Leonard and Virginia Woolf: The Monks House Papers, primarily correspondence and MSS of Virginia Woolf, including the three scrapbooks relating to *Three Guineas*; and The Leonard Woolf Papers, primarily correspondence and other papers of Leonard Woolf. (Monks House Papers are available on microfilm in many research libraries.) The Charleston Papers consist in the main of letters written to or by Clive and Vanessa Bell and Duncan Grant which had accumulated in their home; the library houses Quentin Bell's photocopied set. Also included are c. 900 letters from Maria Jackson to Julia and Leslie Stephen (Charleston Papers Ad. 1); letters from Roger Fry, Maynard Keynes, Lytton Strachey, Virginia Woolf, Vita Sackville-West, E. M. Forster, T. S. Eliot, Frances Partridge and others. The Nicolson Papers complement these three Sussex archives relating to the Bloomsbury Group, and consist of Nigel Nicolson's correspondence relating to his editorial work as principal editor of the six-volume *Letters of Virginia Woolf*, published between 1975 and 1980.

Recent Acquisitions: The Bell Papers. A. O. Bell's correspondence relating to her editorial work on Virginia Woolf's Diaries. A parallel collection to the Nicolson Papers.

**Name of Collection:** Archives & Manuscripts
Contact: Michael Bott, The Archivist
Address: The University of Reading
The Library
Whiteknights
P. O. Box 223,
Reading RG6 6AE
UK
Telephone: 0118-931-8776
Fax: 0118-931-6636
e-mail: g.m.c.bott@reading.ac.uk

| | |
|---|---|
| Access Requirements: | Appointment needed to consult material. Permission required to consult or copy material in the Hogarth Press and Chatto & Windus collections from Random House, 20 Vauxhall Bridge Road, London SW1V 2SA, UK. |
| Holdings Relevant to Woolf: | Hogarth Press (MS2750): editorial and production correspondence relating to publications of the Press including Woolf's own titles. Production ledgers 1920s-1950s. Correspondence between Leonard Woolf and Stanley Unwin about progress with his collected edition of the works of Freud.

Chatto & Windus (MS2444): small number of letters 1915-25; 1929-31.
George Bell & Sons (MS1640): 5 letters from Leonard Woolf 1930-66.
Routledge (MS1489): Reader's report by Leonard Woolf on George Padmore's "Britannia rules the blacks" (1935); "How Britain rules Africa."
Megroz (MS1979/68): 2 letters from LW, 1926.
Allen & Unwin (MS3282): Correspondence with LW 1923-24; 1939-40; 1943; 1946; 1950-51, including letters concerning a reprint of *Empire and Commerce in Africa*, and concerning ill-founded rumors about the Hogarth Press. |
| Name of Collection: | Frances Hooper Collection of Virginia Woolf Books and Manuscripts/Elizabeth Power Richardson Bloomsbury Iconography Collection. |
| Contact: | Martin, Antonetti, Curator of Rare Books |
| Address: | Mortimer Rare Book Room
William Allan Neilson Library
Smith College
Northampton, MA 01063 |
| Telephone: | 413-585-2906 |
| Fax: | 413-585-2904 |
| e-mail: | mantonet@library.smith.edu |
| Hours: | Mon.- Fri. 9AM-5PM |
| Access Requirements: | Appointment to be made with the Curator. |

Holdings Relevant
To Woolf: The Hooper Collection emphasizes Woolf as an essayist but also includes many Hogarth Press first editions, limited editions of Woolf's works, and translations. The collection includes page proofs of *Orlando*, *To the Lighthouse*, and *The Common Reader*, corrected by Woolf for the first American editions, a proof copy of *The Waves* that Woolf inscribed to Hugh Walpole, and proof copies of *The Years* and of *Flush*. The Collection also has one of the deluxe editions of *Orlando* that was printed on green paper. Other items include twenty-two pages of reading notes from 1926, three pages of notes on D. H. Lawrence's *Sons and Lovers*, thirty-three pages of notes for *Roger Fry*, a six-page ms. "As to criticism," a five-page ms. of "The Searchlight," and a fourteen-page ms. of "The Patron and The Crocus." The Hooper Collection also owns 140 letters between Woolf and Lytton Strachey as well as other correspondence, including a 13 February [1921] letter to Katherine Mansfield and ten letters to Mela and Robert Spira.

The Richardson Collection is a working collection of books and materials used by Richardson in preparing her *Bloomsbury Iconography*. It includes Leslie Stephen's photograph album, ninety-eight original exhibition catalogs dating back to 1929, clippings and photocopies of such items as reviews of early Woolf works, and Bloomsbury material from British *Vogue* of the 1920s. The Collection also has three preliminary pencil drawings by Vanessa Bell for *Flush*.

The Mortimer Rare Book Room also owns Woolf's 1916 Italian ms. notebook and her corrected typescripts of "Reviewing" and "The Searchlight." In addition, there is a 1923 photograph of Woolf at Garsington. The Mortimer Rare Book Room also has a Sylvia Plath Collection that includes eight of Woolf's books from Plath's library, several of which are underlined and annotated, as well as Plath's notes from her undergraduate English 211 class at Smith (1951-52) in which she studied *To the Lighthouse*.

**Name of Collection:** Woolf/Hogarth Press/Bloomsbury
**Contact:** Robert C. Brandeis
**Address:** Victoria University Library
71 Queens Park Crescent E.
Toronto M5S 1K7
Ontario
CANADA
**Hours:** Mon.-Fri. 9AM-5PM
**Access Requirements:** Prior notification; identification.
**Restrictions:** Limited photocopying.

**Holdings Relevant To Woolf:** This collection, the most comprehensive of its kind in Canada, contains all the work of Virginia and Leonard Woolf in various editions, issues, variants and translations; all the books hand printed by Leonard and Virginia Woolf at the Hogarth Press, including many variant issues and bindings, association copies and page proofs; a nearly comprehensive collection of Hogarth Press machine printed books to 1946 (the year Leonard Woolf and the Press joined Chatto & Windus) including presentation copies, signed limited editions, page proofs, variants as well as substantial amounts of ephemera. The collection is also very strong in Bloomsbury art, especially the decorative arts, and contains important examples of Omega Workshops publications and exhibition catalogues. Vanessa Bell correspondence/MSS; Leonard Woolf correspondence; Ritchie family materials and correspondence re: Anne Thackeray Ritchie/Stephen family.

**Recent Acquisitions:** Vanessa Bell dustwrapper designs for Woolf novels; Quentin Bell correspondence; S. P. Rosenbaum mss.

# GUIDE TO SPECIAL COLLECTIONS

**Name of Collection:** Library of Leonard and Virginia Woolf (Washington SU)

**Contact:** Laila Miletic-Vejzovic, Head Manuscripts, Archives and Special Collections

**Address:** Washington State University Libraries Pullman, WA 99164-5610

**URL:** http://www.wsulibs.wsu.edu/holland/masc/masc.htm

**Hours:** Mon.- Fri.  8:30AM-5PM

**Access Requirements:** Letter stating nature of research preferred; student or other identification.

**Restrictions:** Materials must be used in the MASC area under supervision. Photocopying or photographing is permitted only when it will not harm the materials and is permitted by copyright.

**Holdings Relevant To Woolf:** WSU has the Woolfs' basic working library including many works which belonged to Virginia's father, Sir Leslie Stephen, and other family members. Over 800 titles came from their Sussex home, Monks House, including some works bought at auction soon after Leonard Woolf died in 1969. Later additions include: 1,875 titles from his house in Victoria Square, London; 400 titles from his nephew Cecil Woolf; and over 60 titles from Quentin and Anne Olivier Bell. WSU has been actively collecting: all works in all editions by Virginia; all titles by Leonard; works published by the Woolfs at the Hogarth Press through 1946; books by their friends and associates, especially those by Bloomsbury authors and about Bloomsbury artists; relevant correspondence and original works of art. Original artwork by Vanessa Bell; scattered letters by Vanessa Bell, E. M. Forster, Roger Fry, Leslie Stephen, Lytton Strachey, and Leonard Woolf. Original artwork by Richard Kennedy for illustrations in his book *A Boy at the Hogarth Press*; scattered letters by Roger Fry, Leslie Stephen, Ethel Smyth, and Leonard Woolf.

**Recent Acquisitions:** Virginia Woolf's initialed copy of *Cornishiana*; Leonard Woolf's annotated copy of *An Anatomy of Poetry* by A. William-Ellis; Leslie Stephen's copy of *Lapsus Calami and Other Verses*, inscribed by James Kenneth Stephen. Several letters from Virginia Woolf, including two written in 1939 to Ronald Heffer, and a letter to Edward McKnight Kauffer. New in the Hogarth Press Collection are a copy of E. M. Forster's *Anonymity, an Enquiry*, bound in cream paper boards, and what Woolmer calls the third label state of Forster's *The Story of the Siren*.

**Name of Collection:** Yale Center for British Art
**Contact:** Elisabeth Fairman, Associate Curator for Rare Books
**Address:** 1080 Chapel Street
P. O. Box 208280
New Haven, CT 06520-8280
**Telephone:** 203-432-2814
**Fax:** 203-432-9695
**e-mail:** elisabeth.fairman@yale.edu
**Hours:** Tues.-Fri. 10AM-4:30PM
**Restrictions:** Permission needed in order to reproduce.

**Holdings Relevant To Woolf:** Rare Books Department: 94 letters from Vanessa Bell and Duncan Grant to Sir Kenneth Clark. Prints & Drawings Department: 2 designs by Vanessa Bell and 2 studies by Duncan Grant. Paintings Department: 1 painting by Vanessa Bell, 2 by Duncan Grant (including a portrait of Vanessa Bell).

# Reviews

## Reading Alcoholisms: Theorizing Character and Narrative in Selected Novels of Thomas Hardy, James Joyce, and Virginia Woolf
Jane Lilienfeld, (NY: St. Martin's Press, 1999), xii+292 pp.

In *Reading Alcoholisms: Theorizing Character and Narrative in Selected Novels of Thomas Hardy, James Joyce, and Virginia Woolf,* Jane Lilienfeld provides innovative and provocative readings of familiar novels by joining intellectual disciplines normally kept separate: literary and medical studies. Lilienfeld adopts what she defines as the "biopsychosocial" model of alcoholism because it takes into account physiological as well as biographical and social factors of addiction. She selects from a wide range of scientific theories as she studies the impact of addiction on three novels: Hardy's *The Mayor of Casterbridge*, Joyce's *A Portrait of the Artist as a Young Man*, and Woolf's *To the Lighthouse*.

Lilienfeld provides biographical information supporting her contention that *The Mayor of Casterbridge* reflects Hardy's intimate knowledge of alcoholism and its effects on character and community. She notes that his mother's childhood poverty was caused by her father's alcoholism and that heavy drinking was an expected masculine ritual among the men Hardy grew up with. More important yet was the influence of Horace Moule, Hardy's tutor and role model, whose alcoholism destroyed his promising career as a scholar and led to suicide. Moule, Lilienfeld notes, is the probable model for Michael Henchard in this novel and the inspiration for Hardy's compassionate study of the damaging effects of alcohol on the addict and those who love him. Thus, Lilienfeld adds to available readings of Henchard's tragic flaw a convincing argument that his life story is inseparable from his alcoholism.

In her introduction, Lilienfeld tells us that this book originated in classroom discussions about alcohol drinking following the deaths of two students in alcohol-related accidents within two weeks of each other. This close tie between literature and "real life" issues is sustained throughout the book. For example, Lilienfeld isolates facets of Henchard's personality as characteristic of alcoholics: his habit of blaming others; his extreme emotional dependencies; and his uncontrollable rages. Lilienfeld's comparative approach foregrounds similarities in Henchard's relationship to his step-daughter, Elizabeth-Jane; in Simon Dedalus' relationship to his son, Stephen; and in Mr. Ramsay's treatment of his wife. Addiction and abuse of various sorts are familiar aspects of most students' lives and this book offers ways to make the world of these novels more familiar and relevant to contemporary students.

In her discussion of James Joyce's *Portrait of the Artist as a Young Man*, Lilienfeld relies on Stanislaus Joyce's memoir of their father's alcoholism, *The Complete Dublin Diary*, to prove that Simon Dedalus' alcoholism is a primary determinant of narrative and character in this novel. Lilienfeld faces a more difficult task in this chapter because Simon's alcoholism is less overt than Michael Henchard's. Nevertheless, by combining close readings of the text with contemporary narrative and medical theories, Lilienfeld ably defends her thesis. She identifies disparate events in the overt narrative which only make sense when the repressed narrative of Simon's alcoholism is discovered. Interestingly, Lilienfeld compares this narrative suppression to "the psychological phenomena of 'splitting,' dissociation, and alcoholic denial. These textual 'blackouts,'" she adds, ". . . serve as an 'unconscious' narrative response that can eliminate Stephen's, Simon's, and the reader's recognition of Simon's increasing dependence on alcohol and the havoc it causes in his life and that of his family" (108).

These indications of alcoholism include the physical decline of the family; Stephen's offhand references to his father's innumerable jobs, two of which include alcohol, and the signs of his father's drinking to excess at the Christmas party and during the trip to Cork: his shaky hands; sentimental sobs; and abusive shouting. Like Michael Henchard, Simon's impulsive rage, his inability to take responsibility for his own actions, and his neglect of his wife and children are typical of alcoholic behaviors. One of the most interesting of Lilienfeld's insights is the link she makes between Stephen's psychology and the coping strategies of children in alcoholic families. With characteristic verve, Lilienfeld does not isolate Stephen as mere victim, but shows how his repetitive imaginative escapes evolve into healing rituals as they are transformed by his writing endeavors.

In her chapter on Virginia Woolf and *To the Lighthouse*, Lilienfeld shifts her focus from alcoholism to opiate addiction. Lilienfeld reads the "opium narrative" she finds in this novel as an indirect commentary on the relationship of Julia Jackson to her mother. Julia Jackson was nurse-maid to her own mother for much of her adult life. Due to rheumatism, Mrs. Jackson was prescribed morphine and chloral, which although medically sanctioned, were addictive. Lilienfeld suggests that Julia carried over these early habits of self-denial into her marriage with Woolf's father, Leslie Stephen.

Lilienfeld adopts the term "codependence" to describe the psychology of Julia Stephen as represented in Woolf's version of her mother's life story in *To the Lighthouse*. Although, as Lilienfeld admits, this nomenclature has been justly criticized by feminists and others for its use as a therapeutic tool for victim-blaming, Lilienfeld defends her use of the term by redefining its meaning. She defines codependent behaviors as strategies of survival and resistance typically adopted by victims within abusive family systems. For Mrs. Ramsay, these codependent behaviors might include her low self-esteem; her obsessional focus on placating her husband; and her need to manage the behaviors of her husband and other family members.

Lilienfeld identifies a number of narrative strategies by which Woolf represents codependency in both Mrs. Ramsay and Lily Briscoe, but the most unexpected and intriguing is the narrative parallel she finds between Mr. Carmichael's and Mrs. Ramsay's escape strategies. Like Stephen Dedalus, both of these characters devise ways of escape from unbearable family environments—Mr. Carmichael through opium and Mrs. Ramsay by day-dreaming. Lilienfeld writes, "Mrs. Ramsay's necessary reliance on self-suppression may mirror his reliance on opium. . . . [H]er dependence on manipulating or serving others and his supposed opium reveries serve much the same purpose: escape from self" (208). In a close reading of Mrs. Ramsay's "'waking revery,'" (214) Lilienfeld shows how Woolf discovers that female codependence, opium, and empire are interlinked in Mrs. Ramsay's fantasy as well as family life.

Some readers accustomed to more conventional literary modes of analysis may have difficulty accepting Lilienfeld's use of medical theories for literary analysis. Nevertheless, I urge such readers to read past any discomfort with addiction terminology to the core insights of this book which are essential to understanding the impact of abuse phenomena on the authors she studies. Clearly, as Lilienfeld has now illustrated, Hardy, Joyce, and Woolf were much preoccupied with depicting abuse patterns. Whether we identify this concern, as Lilienfeld does, in terms of a specific addiction to alcohol or opiates, or more generally in terms of abusive patterns in private and public life, this is a topic in literature which needs to be further explored and accounted for. Most exciting for modernist studies is Lilienfeld's suggestion that "narratives . . . can behave as if they had an alcoholic mind-set" (233). Thus, Joyce and Woolf's narrative innovations, she suggests, may reflect these authors' attempts to capture the emotional experiences and point of view of those trapped in abusive family systems.

In conclusion, I would like to especially commend Jane Lilienfeld for the breadth and range of scholarship which informs this exciting new work. Throughout this book, Lilienfeld engages with a wide range of medical, narrative, feminist, and postmodern theorists, as well as scholars of individual writers. By integrating her respectful engagements with these theorists throughout the text, readers are privy to the debates within these fields as well as Lilienfeld's responses to them. Thoroughly documented and bold, *Reading Alcoholisms* invites further development of the new ways of reading this study initiates.

—Patricia Cramer, *University of Connecticut at Stamford*

*Women in the Milieu of Leonard and Virginia Woolf:*
*Peace, Politics and Education*
Wayne K. Chapman and Janet Manson,eds.
(NY: Pace UP, 1998), xviii + 266pp.

When, in *Downhill All the Way*, Leonard Woolf assesses his wife as "the least political animal that has lived since Aristotle invented the definition" (27), he can not have foreseen the extent and heat of the critical controversy his remarks would later engender. In adding to his remarks the caveat that Virginia Woolf "was not a bit like the [woman] who appears in many books written by literary critics or autobiographers who did not know her, a frail invalidish lady living in an ivory tower in Bloomsbury and worshipped by a little clique of aesthetes" (27), he only fans the fires of later theoretical debate. His partner, he concedes, did indeed participate in the "pedestrian operations of the Labour Party and the Co-operative Movement," penned "political pamphlets" such as *A Room of One's Own* and *Three Guineas* and was "the last person who could ignore the political menaces under which we all lived" (27).

Nonetheless, in following the lead of Aristotle, valorizing involvement with actual cases rather than with an elucidation of the ideal, with the practical or "real" over the abstract, Leonard Woolf summarily rejects Virginia as "political" (something she herself admittedly tended to do on occasion)—despite his admission of her consistent "grass roots" involvement in political causes. Devaluing his wife's political contributions, especially when compared to his own, he appears to assume an insurmountable gulf between the worlds of art and practical politics. Obliquely, he begs the question as to whether art, or the artist, can be firmly linked to what we, in the latter half of the twentieth century, like to designate as political or social "activism," and answers, as many of us would *not*, in the negative.

Taken as a whole, Wayne K. Chapman and Janet M. Manson's informative *Women in the Milieu of Leonard and Virginia Woolf: Peace, Politics, and Education* tackles similar issues, albeit more obliquely. This text itself is a collection of essays describing the socio-political workings and publications of a number of activist women, all known to the Woolfs during their marriage (1912-1941): Margaret Llewelyn Davies, Lady Strachey, Alix Strachey, Ray Strachey, Marie Stopes, Winifred Holtby, Beatrice Webb, Margaret Cole, Margery Perham, Eleanor Balfour Sidgwick, Octavia Wilberforce. Individual articles focus primarily on those, in contrast to Virginia Woolf, whose work took a "hands-on" form and brought them consistently and designedly into the political trenches: onto the streets, into foreign countries, into factories, universities, Houses of Parliament, as well as into clubrooms and committee chambers and private homes. While nearly all of the women examined were published writers, only a few, like Marie Stopes, retained the conviction that art, *their* art, could and should launch political movements. Most, like Leonard Woolf, with whom a number of them worked directly, generally found themselves more comfortable in various public or social service arenas than in the realms of imagination. So, by default, rather than by intention, the accent of Chapman and Manson's text might appear to fall on the side of Leonard Woolf's practical brand of political endeavor. Since the editors focus their attentions on the contributions and activism of *women*, Virginia Woolf's far more introspective kind of life work must necessarily be thrown into some sort of relief, with the results of which the individual reader of Chapman and Manson's text must ultimately come to terms.

Nonetheless, Chapman and Manson state clearly in their Preface that the overall purpose of their text is not to illuminate any individual person (or approach) but, rather, to expose a *milieu*, a working background. They accomplish such a task with considerable success. Leonard and Virginia Woolf, then, are not intended as the subjects of the various studies (with the possible exception of Patricia Laurence's "A Writing Couple: Shared Ideology in Virginia Woolf's *Three Guineas* and Leonard Woolf's *Quack! Quack!*") but, rather, serve as "integrating agents" (xi) for the text as a whole. The text competently serves to illuminate the considerable efforts of the wider intellectual community from which the Woolfs drew nourishment, and to which they gave much in return. And it does so most effectively by concentrating on studies of women whose truly extraordinary efforts in political, social and educational arenas have been too long neglected or underreported in the annals of British history.

Interestingly, in the midst of the work's larger context, two essays in *Women in the Milieu of Leonard and Virginia Woolf: Peace, Politics and Education* do substantially tackle the somewhat vexing but always interesting question of Virginia Woolf's relation to the world of politics, and they take somewhat opposing positions. Sarah Bishop Merrill's contribution, "Eleanor Balfour Sidgwick and Henry Sidgwick: Collaborators on the Fourth Guinea," provides valuable information on Nora Sidgwick's work as co-founder of Newnham College (Cambridge), pacifist, university lecturer and overseer of the publication of her philosopher husband's works. In the course of her examination, Merrill directly compares Woolf's brand of political service to Sidgwick's. In Aristotelian fashion, she asserts that Woolf's "political activism through art may have failed to give her an active and satisfying participation in the *reality* of social change and progress" (196, emphasis mine). And thus she implies that Woolf lacked the gratification of seeing her ideas "work" on individual parties in an everyday world.

Thus relegating Woolf's perceived form of politicizing to secondary status, she counterbalances what she calls Woolf's (and by extension, Bloomsbury's) "clear Platonic elitism" (196) with Sidgwick's overriding practicality, emphasizing Sidgwick's attention to ethics, morality and anti-egoism, her direct work with people. She goes on to suggest that Sidgwick's work in education enabled her to link the worlds of art and politics that Bloomsbury and Virginia Woolf, with her "creative introspection" (206), "so often held apart" (197). Sidgwick, Merrill asserts, wrote and lectured tirelessly, modeling appropriate behavior by continually placing herself in "active service" (meaning, it would appear, to do one's work primarily in public view rather than meditatively, to cultivate the "'outer'" (196) acts without entirely sacrificing inner visions). Sidgwick, Merrill says with a comparative eye to Woolf, is *the* "woman of independent means, a woman with the fourth guinea of independent wealth, leadership, and a professional career."

Patricia Laurence, on the other hand, in "A Writing Couple—Shared Ideology in Virginia Woolf's *Three Guineas* and Leonard Woolf's *Quack! Quack!*," takes a contrasting point of view when it comes to Virginia Woolf and the political. As she examines the shared ideologies present in the Woolfs' somewhat parallel writings, she reaffirms both Leonard *and* Virginia's preeminent position as questioners and elucidators of contemporary political matters, emphasizing Virginia Woolf's feminist and keen sense of the alliance of the personal and the political. Such an alliance surely means that the feminist writer can scarcely avoid being political. While not denying Leonard Woolf's pragmatic approach as compared to his wife's more markedly philosophical one, Laurence finds Virginia her husband's ideological soulmate, a fact illuminated when the two noted political treatises are adequately compared.

Each of the twelve articles in *Women in the Milieu of Leonard and Virginia Woolf* passes on important, and often new, information about an essential female figure in the Woolfian era. Of particular interest is Diane Gillespie's article "Marie Stopes: Her War for Peace." Gillespie captures the vexing complexity of Marie Stopes, Ph.D., scientist, educator, playwright, League of Nations activist, "controversial pioneer" (97) in the areas of birth control and sex education. Feisty, confrontational, Stopes was, as Gillespie puts it, "imbued with the conflict model of human relations" (97), a woman whose intellectual energies remained radically diverse and unrestrained. Her commitment to eugenic theories seems troubling, off-putting in the glare of historical events as we now know them but rather oddly congruent with her range of views and, perhaps, with her own life experience.

Janet Manson's "Margery Perham, the Fabians, and Colonial Policy," about another extraordinary woman, outlines the major contributions of Perham to Africanist studies and to a new colonial view in Britain. An academic of respected standing, Perham made numerous trips to Africa throughout her life and greatly influenced British colonial affairs, becoming the "'godmother' of the Colonial service" (176). "'I live on one plane,'" Perham would say, "'it is Africa always for me. I work, sleep, seek personal encounters, play games, enlarge my general knowledge, save my strength and money for Africa'" (175). In her seventies in 1968, Perham flew to her beloved Nigeria to help settle the civil war there, and, to her great dismay, found her peacemaking efforts unsuccessful. Sadly, had she not been a female, Perham most certainly would have been a colonial administrator, but as Manson suggests, her role as expert but outsider probably served to increase her ultimate effectiveness.

Overall, *Women in the Milieu of Leonard and Virginia Woolf: Peace, Politics, and Education* illustrates persuasively the crucial roles played by women in formulating political agendas and the various "isms" of the Woolfian era: feminism, suffragism, socialism, pacifism, anti-imperialism, internationalism, to name a few. Surely an extraordinary mix of persons and personalities, all operating with extraordinary gusto in an extraordinary time, provided rich soil for works so important to us now by Leonard and Virginia Woolf. Further, Chapman and Manson's illuminating text makes a significant tangential point. The Woolfs were clearly admired by their contemporaries and they, in turn, responded to those around them in a most productive way. Associations within and without Bloomsbury proved enriching and dynamic. Collaboration proved "felicitous" (xi) within the Woolf marriage (a fact which the Chapman and Manson appendices reiterate), and within the marriages of numerous others like the Coles, the Webbs, the Sidgwicks, the James Stracheys, the Oliver Stracheys. The success of such working alliances counterbalances some of the more negative ideas about collaborative tensions that prevail in much current critical theory. *Women in the Milieu of Leonard and Virginia Woolf* provides a fascinating, if admittedly incomplete picture of the *milieu* in question, throwing significant light on the Woolfs through a lens which magnifies unexplored territory in their surrounding culture.

—Susan Hudson Fox, *California State University, Hayward*

*Virginia Woolf and the Great War*
Karen L. Levenback (Syracuse: Syracuse U P, 1999), xvii+208 pp.

This book is an important addition to the movement, beginning in North American criticism in the 70s, to present a politically engaged Virginia Woolf. Levenback acknowledges what has been done to take Woolf seriously as a "theorist of war" as Mark Hussey calls her, but insists that more needs doing before the common assumption that war is about masculine combat is altered to validate the civilian experience (2-3). To help in the revision of both Great War history and Woolf studies, Levenback focuses on "Woolf's war-consciousness," evolved in response to newspaper and other renditions of the war combined with, or contrasted to, actual experiences. Although Levenback shows how Woolf blurs the line between soldiers and civilians in a wide range of her writings, the readings of *Mrs. Dalloway*, *To the Lighthouse*, and *The Years*—if not always entirely convincing—are certainly always thought-provoking.

In her first chapter, "Myths of War, Illusions of Immunity, Realities of Survival," Levenback discusses Woolf's *TLS* reviews (from 1916 on) of books dealing with the Great War. She traces Woolf's developing realization, especially following the quickly mythologized death of Rupert Brooke in 1915, that the common civilian "sense of immunity from the effects of the war...was an illusion" fostered by the newspapers (9). Against this propagandistic mythmaking, Woolf weighed realities such as the death in 1917 of Leonard Woolf's younger brother Cecil and the wounding of his youngest brother Philip; the threatened conscription of Leonard himself as well as Duncan Grant and David Garnett; the glorification of the dead after the war; and the guilt felt by both survivors like Philip Woolf and civilian outsiders like Virginia Woolf who could identify with them. Out of this discrepancy between illusion and reality, Woolf linked the experiences of soldier and civilian through the use of irony, her way of seeking the truth about the Great War.

"Life and Death, Memory and Denial in Postwar London" focuses on *Mrs. Dalloway*. Challenging facile definitions of sanity and insanity through "Kierkegaardian indirection" (82), Woolf creates an ironic narrative voice to communicate "distance from both the war and its experience" (47). Clarissa Dalloway is "untouched" by the war and the resulting deaths of "anonymous others" (48). Peter Walsh seems equally oblivious. At the center of this chapter, however, are the characters who are more easily dubbed outsiders and survivors: Doris Kilman, Rezia Warren Smith, and especially Septimus Smith. Within the contexts of trench warfare and post-war society, Septimus has no visible badge of service (like an amputated limb). His war experiences are not memories; they are present realities with which he copes, as did Philip Woolf, by repressing emotion in general yet fearing death in particular, his talk of which reminds and threatens those around him. If killing enemy soldiers as part of a "communal effort" during the war is evidence of manliness worthy of reward, then, according to the post-war vestiges of those values, an isolated survivor who kills himself is dubbed cowardly and insane. "The social system" of civilian life, reflected in the trenches, meant that the relationship with Evans, whatever Septimus may have felt for him, must have been the "avuncular" or fatherly one of commander and enlisted man. Because the relationship could not have transcended the war is perhaps one reason why his war-time experience "has not ended for Septimus" (68). His death, then, is an "affirmation of a life that was impossible in the postwar world." Its indifference to and denial of the war and of "human cruelty" render him powerless except to take his own life (71-2). Although some of the arguments about feelings of powerlessness and suicide agree with Elaine Showalter's discussion of "male hysteria" in *The Female Malady*,[1] Levenback prefers the theories of Durkheim, Buber, and Freud, as well as a tongue-twisting "Kierkegaardization" of Montaigne. Although such links and anticipations are often illuminating, one occasionally wonders how much this buttressing with prominent masculine names really strengthens the structure of the argument.

Some aspects of Levenback's interdisciplinary approach may be cumbersome, but the extent of her research is a virtue all too rare in this age of premature publication. Not only is she knowledgeable about a number of relevant Woolf studies, critical and biographical, but she is also well informed about the Great War and its treatment in several twentieth-century genres (from the journalistic to the literary), both early and more recent. Thanks to Syracuse University Press's obviously generous policy, she is able to place Woolf's responses to the Great War in a variety of contexts both in her text and in footnotes sometimes as interesting to read as the argument itself.

The third chapter, "The Language of Memory as Time Passes," deals primarily with the center section of *To the Lighthouse*. Among the contexts Levenback creates here are Rose Macaulay's *Non-Combatants and Others* (1916), an anti-war novel negatively received during the war; Beatrice Webb's direct treatment of her past in *My Apprenticeship* (1926); the ten-day General Strike of 1926 to which journalists and historians applied Great War imagery; and Woolf's own "strike diary." Rather than reading "The Window" as nostalgia for a pre-war past, Levenback usefully relates it to Woolf's awareness of a

---

[1] Levenback cites Showalter only once in this chapter, to disagree with her about the real-life model for Septimus Smith (57).

sentimental "prewar mythology" embodied in language similar to that which "invited participation in and support for the Great War, but disallowed its reality" (93). By means of a narrative voice that uses war imagery, bracketed reports that parody the language of the war-time newspapers, and Mrs. McNab, the "Time Passes" section provides the civilian experience of shortages, high prices, difficult travel, and reports of deaths. The references to Mrs. McNab and Mrs. Bast as well as to the General Strike in this chapter, however, also invite more awareness of the class context in which Woolf responded to the Great War. Knowing, for instance—through a substantial number of studies on the subject—what women not only enjoyed but also endured when they did manual labor, including the often dangerous work in munitions factories, one wonders to what degree Woolf's responses to the Great War were characteristic of the upper middle class intelligentsia. In the final section of the novel ("The Lighthouse"), Woolf emphasizes the degree to which "postwar life picks up where prewar life (almost literally) stopped" (109). Lily Briscoe the artist, however, remembers what has been lost, and Woolf suggests that not just the experience of war and not just the memory of it are essential, but also learning how to live with the changes war has caused.

"Remembering the War in the Years Between the Wars" juxtaposes *The Years*—where, in the raid scene, Woolf finally confronts directly and painfully the memories of her own civilian experiences—with her work on *Three Guineas*, with Vera Brittain's painful memories in *Testament of Youth* (1933), and with Woolf's own war-time diaries and letters the rereading of which "merged with portents of World War II" (124). Seeing a recurrence of the "illusion of civilian immunity" so prevalent from 1914-1918 (143), Woolf made short the 1918 section of *The Years*, Levenback says, focusing on the "Present Day." North returns after having been in the Great War (and then to Africa) to try to find a place in a society that aids his desire to forget by ignoring his past experiences at the front. Only Eleanor, like Lily Briscoe, is aware of changes that are war's aftermath. Confronted as she is with the death of her nephew in 1937 in the Spanish Civil War, Woolf is similarly aware.

As an efficient method of dealing with the large "cast of characters" and preventing identifications from impeding the development of her argument, Levenback includes an appendix of biographical notes. Given her emphasis on the cultural context for the war, however, it is curious that there is only one visual illustration. Although it is well-chosen, it is not integrated into the argument. She mentions her frontispiece, Roger Fry's *German General Staff* (1915), only in the appendix entry on Fry. Yet Woolf mentions the painting in "The War Years" chapter of *Roger Fry: A Biography* (1940). There she quotes Fry as saying that "most of the critics are very cross" with him except Sir Claude Phillips who "found a moral, unintended by me, in the Kaiser picture" (162 and 341 n.). As Spalding explains, "to Fry's surprise" the *papier-collé*, initially a joke based on a newspaper photograph in which the generals' feet are hidden, combined with a chance encounter of a passage from Nietzsche[2] subsequently included in the exhibition catalogue, "was praised in the press for its patriotic sentiment" (199). Yet Levenback deals with this important war chapter in the Fry biography in only a couple of sentences in connection with the "Time Passes" section of *To the Lighthouse*. She notes Woolf's comment in the biography that "a break must be made in every life when August 1914 is reached." She notes Woolf's emphasis on Fry's "detachment" and her method of providing "scattered and incongruous fragments" to sum up his war experiences (102-3). How detached was Fry, really? Woolf provides much evidence to the contrary, similar to some of the evidence Levenback provides for Woolf herself. Fry, for example, not only railed against British hypocrisy, criticized the illusion-creating Northcliffe press, and supported the conscientious objectors he knew as Woolf did; he also housed a family of war refugees at Durbins, struggled to pay his Omega artists as the war eroded sales, wrote to Lord Curzon as the Omega artists were being called up begging him to put "the men whose abilities make them national assets" under government protection (Roger Fry, 163, 342 n.), mourned the death of one French artist friend and tried to visit another at the front, and comforted another friend who had lost her family on the *Lusitania*. As Woolf wrote this substantial chapter—in intervals between her work on *The Years* and *Three Guineas*—she again must have had to relive some of her own experiences of the Great War. Conversely, work on the biography also provided Woolf with an antidote to reports of new violence on the continent: "How I bless Roger, & wish I could tell him so, for giving me himself to think of—what a help he remains—in this welter of unreality" (*D5* 161). Yet writing "The War Years" chapter is one of Woolf's own anti-war acts. When Benedict Nicolson said of Fry that "he shut himself out from all disagreeable actualities and allowed the spirit of Nazism to grow without taking any steps to check it" (quoted in *L6* 413), Woolf bristled. On the contrary, she said, Fry spent "half his life, not in a tower, but traveling about England addressing masses of people" and making them understand and enjoy painting. "And wasn't that the best way of checking Nazism?" (*L6* 414).[3] Woolf, a civilian like Fry, waged mental warfare during the Great War, and after it as well. In "Thoughts on Peace in an Air Raid," she quotes Blake. "'I will not cease

---

[2] "I cannot tolerate the neighbourhood of this race. . .which has no sense in its feet and doesn't even know how to walk. . . .All things considered, the Germans have not got feet at all, they have only legs" (qtd. in Spalding, 199).

[3] What, one wonders, might Levenback have to say about Duncan Grant's degree of detachment and engagement in his elegant war poster, "Musical Instruments for the Front," recently reprinted in color in Bradshaw (plate 10). With a large, stylized trumpet in the center, the poster, with "Wanted! Wanted" at the top, says, at the bottom, "If you have any musical instruments to give the soldiers at the front write at once to the Secretary Chatham House 13 George Street Hanover Square W." A copy is in the Victoria and Albert Museum.

from mental fight'" which "means thinking against the current, not with it." Unfortunately, she notes, matching Levenback's concern with popular myth-making, everyone is told daily that they are free and that they are "fighting to defend freedom." If we were truly free, she protests, we would not have to worry about "Hitler's bombs." Tyrants like Hitler "are bred by slaves" (*CE4* 174).

Levenback uses this essay briefly to show Woolf's "understanding of how official language finally deprives the word 'war' of its horror." Fry's efforts to make the visual arts a part of people's lives and his efforts to protect artists, along with Woolf's own creations in words for common readers may look like detachment, however ironic, and Woolf's comments on art in relation to war are not always consistent. Still, creative acts and their dissemination are counter-movements to destruction and death, commitments to "making art, not war" (Gillespie 155)—often futile, yet utterly worthwhile. Does Levenback misread as "naive," therefore, Lily Briscoe's assertion that "nothing stays; all changes; but not words, not paint" (113)? Woolf glosses such a comment herself in one of the last essays she wrote. Art "is indeed the instinct of self preservation. Only when we put two and two together—two pencil strokes, two written words, two bricks <notes> do we overcome dissolution and set up some stake against oblivion" ("Anon" 403). Even if Lily is right about the quality of her painting, her effort to create is as permanent as is the desire to destroy. Although it is sometimes fair to expect an author to do what her reviewers might have done with a topic, in this case the fact that one wants so badly to contribute to the discussion is merely an indication of how much Levenback has already accomplished in her provocative and valuable book.

—Diane F. Gillespie, *Washington State University*

## Works Cited

Bradshaw, Tony. *The Bloomsbury Artists*: *Prints and Book Design.* Aldershot: Scholar Press, 1999.

Gillespie, Diane F. "Make Art, Not War: Virginia Woolf's Between the Arts." *Virginia Woolf and Her Influences: Selected Papers from the Seventh Annual Conference on Virginia Woolf*, eds. Diane F. Gillespie and Leslie K. Hankins. NY: Pace UP, 1998. 154-5.

Showalter, Elaine. *The Female Malady: Women, Madness, and English Culture, 1830-1980.* New York: Pantheon, 1985.

Spalding, Frances. *Roger Fry: Art and Life.* London: Paul Elek/Granada, 1980.

Woolf, Virginia. "Anon." Ed. Brenda Silver. *Twentieth Century Literature* 25, Nos. 3/4 (Fall/Winter 1979): 380-441.

Woolf, Virginia. *Collected Essays*. Ed. Leonard Woolf. New York:

Harcourt, Brace and World, 1967. Vol. 4: 173-77.
——. *The Diary of Virginia Woolf.* Ed. Anne Olivier Bell. 5 vols. San Diego: Harcourt Brace Jovanovich, 1977-84.
——. *The Letters of Virginia Woolf.* Ed. Nigel Nicolson and Joanne Trautmann. 6 vols. NY: Harcourt Brace Jovanovich, 1975-80.
——. *Roger Fry: A Biography.* Ed. Diane F. Gillespie. Oxford: Shakespeare Head Press/Blackwell Publishers, 1995.

*Solid Objects*
Douglas Mao (Princeton: Princeton UP, 1998), xii+308

Despite a radical omission, which I'll get to near the end, Douglas Mao's study of Woolf, Wyndham Lewis, Ezra Pound and Wallace Stevens is complex, articulate, and exciting. I use that last word for two reasons. One is the almost loving voice in which Mao presents the philosophical crises that his chosen four met through their art. While Mao's humor and passion do not preclude his negative judgments, they do encourage involvement in the well-planned but sometimes dense forests of his prose. The other reason is the relevance of *Solid Objects* to the current post-post-modern, pre-something-vaguely-awful time, when what Mao calls the central tension of modernism is taking new forms, as actual life mingles with virtual "life": "[I]f a single claim stands at heart of book," writes Mao in the introduction,

> it is that Anglo-American modernism, is centrally animated by a tension between an urgent validation of production and an admiration for an object world beyond the manipulations of consciousness—a tension that lends modernist writing its dominant note of vital hesitation or ironic idealism, and that leads modernists, as thinkers and artists, to that impasse in which all doing seems undoing, all making unmaking in the end (11).

The authors Mao studies both participated in and questioned the "urgent validation of production," especially production of art objects, as an answer to various crises of meaning, as capitalism, mass production, and science seemed to rapaciously subordinate individual things, including people, to systems and concepts. As aestheticism's emphasis on acquisition and experience seemed less and less an antidote, modernism at first emphasized the production of individual objects as a way to answer "two questions of the existential dilemma—that of how meaning can inhere in Being, and that of how human lives can be lived meaningfully" (20).

The questions were not new, but, according to Mao, took on a new character around the turn of the century. He begins the Introduction with a telling note from Freud to H.D., in which Freud makes a little joke conflating "goods" with "gods," referring to a few ancient statues of gods he owned. When, more than ever before, goods were becoming gods, the desire to preserve objects as fragments of Being beyond the reach of commodification or ideology signalled "one of modernism's defining passages, from an older tradition in which the object appears principally as a signifier of something else or a component of scenic plenitude to a newer order in which its value depends neither on metaphoricity nor marginality" (13).

One of Mao's aims is "to restore a sense of the significance of this passage" (13). He does so by bringing "stories of the object" under modernism together with "stories of production," which, he says, current methodologies tend to separate. He also works to bridge the gap between philosophical readings of modernism and socioeconomic ones by taking into account "how this interdependence functioned in many modernists' imaginations" (11-12).

After a 22 page Introduction that cites Freud, H.D., Rilke, Benjamin, Foucault and Adorno in the first five pages alone, the absorbing and lengthy chapter on Woolf begins with a leisurely explication of Woolf's "Solid Objects," a short story published in the *Athenaeum* in 1920. In the story, a man named John gives up a promising political career for collecting broken bits of glass and other scraps, orts and fragments, not for their cachet or exchange value, but as if he were possessed by the desire to surround himself with solid chunks of existence. Mao anchors his study on Woolf because her fiction brings out "with peculiar clarity the stakes of the modernist encounter with the object" due in part to her "especially naked exploration of what has come to be called existential crisis" (17). In Woolf's work, the discrete object crystallized non-human Being at a time when "the utter contingency of everything (and every thing) became a major preoccupation of imaginative writing" (17). Mao also cites the tension between modernist reaction against mass production and Woolf's "fascination with the delightful and harrowing processes of consumption" (17), which counters the traditional view that modernists despised consumerism in all its forms.

Woolf was among the modernists who first turned to production—"the making of" rather than "the acquiring of"—as a test of meaning. Initially, the "emphasis on making" diminished art's "potentially guilty associations with leisured consumption" (39). Combining a bit of aestheticism with some denatured Victorian morality, modernists could claim the work of art as "fruit of inspired labor and realization of human aspiration," a product that testified to the greatness of human capacity (38). But, like the others Mao addresses, Woolf "in the end tested production itself and found it wanting" (21).

As Woolf was aware early on, making art, like making anything else, entails an element of domination over the object world that she and others also sought to preserve as a "realm beyond the reach of ideology" (9). Like Adorno, says Mao, Woolf found in the production of art both redemptive qualities and a troubling "exercise of a will to power over that which is radically other to the subject," different substantially from violence and imperialism, but "related to them structurally and often intertwined with them in practice" (76).

Mao points to *Mrs. Dalloway* as the last novel in which "making" (the party) is not significantly counterbalanced by a sense that emphasizing production raises too many disturbing questions, especially about the workings of imperialism and patriarchy. Doubt gathers in *To the Lighthouse*, grows in *The Waves*, and shifts in "Anon," *The Years* and *Between the Acts* from "the process of making itself to the traces of human production in a world grown old" (78).

In *To the Lighthouse*, for instance, "the language of violence in which Woolf couches Lily's struggle testifies to a certain recognition that the production of a work of art will always involve a subordination or annexing of that which is most radically other to the producing subject" (66). In "Anon," according to Mao, Woolf locates the break when modern consciousness began, with the invention of printing, by "[p]ositing . . . not that the subject's drive to inscribe itself gave birth to printing but that printing gave birth to the [authorial] subject" (77). The split between consciousness and everything else is due to historical events, not to transhistorical conditions, giving birth to art as we know it, as well as to "'the past' as a phenomenon of consciousness." In the process, the prelapsarian past "whose perfection (or purity) would be defined, precisely, by the absence of art as we know it," became unreachable (78).

This brief summary of one thread in Mao's argument emphasizes Woolf's doubts, but as we know, making art occupied her life, and my summary does not begin to address the chapter on Woolf, not to mention the rest of the book, throughout which Mao's intensity, humor and attention to intricacies are sustained. As Mao reads most of Woolf's novels and several of her essays in the light of the problems he lays out in the Introduction, he makes an interesting case for Woolf's influence on Sartre, demonstrates how Woolf's work provides a bridge between Continental and Anglo-American philosophy, and traces the ways "Woolf's career reflects the modern passage . . . from the young century's faith in new making (or making new) to the suspicion of all expansion that may be the defining characteristic of the present time, Ourselves" (89).

*Solid Objects* points in many useful directions, not only for studies of modernism and Woolf, but for contending with current crises of meaning. To put it less blandly, my mind popped with possibilities, associations, and questions—all activities that an important book should generate. I discovered as I read, however, that one of my small questions (what Mao would make of the shoals of "pullulating" babies in drafts of *The Waves*) led to the discovery of an omission that seems almost inexplicable—Woolf's sense of herself, other women, and sometimes other others not only as objects, but as the objects charged with producing the excess value of pleasure as well as new human beings. In some of the most deliciously disgusting images Woolf ever created, Draft I of *The Waves* describes the hideous spawn of millions of anonymous mothers as, atop the waves themselves, the women toss millions of "little, bald, naked purplish balls," that, "worm like, eel like" commit "violent actions" upon the sand, "pullulating, bubbling, walking everywhere" (62).

This reference to *The Waves* is obscure and on the negative side, but I use it not only because it leapt into my mind while reading Mao's book, but because it is an extreme example of a consciousness that pervades Woolf's work—the connections she continually makes among her and other women's experiences as objects/producers, her art, art in general, and survival (of herself and, less grandiosely than the word implies, of civilized humanity). Mao does concede in the Introduction that he left many important problems about race, gender and sexuality unresolved. However, this aspect of Woolf's work is too central to treat obliquely, especially since the period of his study was a time when anxieties about mass-production were often displaced onto female bodies. It is not necessary to elide modernist responses to "the challenges of the feminine and of the natural," (10) as Mao says some scholars unwisely do, to address Woolf's awareness that the social and psychic experiences of real and fictional women—the objects that reproduce—are tied to the status of "the object" and "production," the two aspects of modernist thought Mao sets out to connect.

This absence led to a few accounts that were complex and engaging but strangely unbalanced. In his discussion of *A Room of One's Own*, for instance, Mao teases out Woolf's use of the monuments of literary tradition, stating that she "discreetly naturalizes the premise that a store of monuments *is* indisputably an end in itself" (38), while noting that "simple justice" for women is a major reason she dwells on the object status of great works. What I didn't see is one of Woolf's central points, one logically connected to Mao's argument: her many-layered exhortation to the women who will produce new monuments to see themselves and their characters as subjects, who, with "no arm to cling to," must go alone in relation "to the world of reality, and not only to the world of men and women" (*AROO* 118).

I'm not asking that Mao hear woman roar, since I'm sure he does. However, to twist his own words, Woolf was the only author of the four in this book who wrote so openly about the passage from an older tradition in which woman as object and reproducer appears principally as a signifier of something else or a component of scenic plenitude to a newer order (still yet to be) in which her value would depend neither on metaphoricity nor marginality. Woolf's awareness as a refugee from the object world animates not only *A Room of One's Own*, but many of those passages, such as "Time Passes," upon which Mao dwells.

Still, *Solid Objects* is a wonderful book that, among weightier things, can provide the ironic pleasure of dwelling on the sheer achievement of it as the fruit of inspired labor.

—Elizabeth Lambert, *Massachusetts College of Liberal Arts*

*The Hours: A Novel*
Michael Cunningham (NY: Farrar, Straus and Giroux, 1998), 230 pp.
*Mr. Dalloway: A Novella*
Robin Lippincott (Louisville, KY: Sarabande Books, 1999), 215 pp.
*Mitz: The Marmoset of Bloomsbury*
Sigrid Nunez (NY: HarperCollins, 1998), 116 pp.
*Virginia Woolf's "Jacob's Room": The Holograph Draft*
Transcribed and edited by Edward L. Bishop
(NY: Pace UP, 1998), xxix + 293 pp.
*Virginia Woolf "The Hours": The British Museum Manuscript of Mrs. Dalloway*
Transcribed and edited by Helen M. Wussow
(NY: Pace UP, 1996), xxx + 491 pp.

---

It used to be unthinkable to deconstruct Virginia Woolf, much less see her in a postmodern context; like biography itself, in this old-fashioned view, Woolf seemed "immune" from such interrogation.[1] She had long been considered apart from any large-scale intertextual construction, although, as Jane Marcus, Mark Hussey, and Pamela Caughie, among others, progressively altered our vantage,[2] we examined more closely how Woolf herself abandoned genre and other barriers, often finding categories—particularly "the novel" and "biography"—too confining.

It would nevertheless surprise her, I should think, to know that three contemporary novelists, Michael Cunningham (*The Hours*), Robin Lippincott (*Mr. Dalloway*), and Sigrid Nunez (*Mitz*), had found their art deriving its *raison d'être* not only from her own, but from constructions of her life and work, engaging, in fact, in an extension of what Catherine Peters calls "biographical ventriloquism" (45-47)—breaching barriers not only between self and subject,

---

[1] See John Batchelor's "Introduction" to *The Art of Literary Biography*: 2-3.

[2] Pamela Caughie's *Virginia Woolf and Postmodernism: Literature in Quest and Question of Itself* was published in 1991, the same year that Virginia Woolf Society-sponsored sessions at the MLA considered "'Who is This Woman Called Woolf?' Critical and Biographical Constructions of Virginia Woolf" and "Virginia Woolf's *Between the Acts*: A Postmodern Text?"

but between fiction and biography, sequel and parody, and (to risk sounding old-fashioned) imitation and copy. What is surprising to me, given the wealth of primary materials currently available, is that even as these three contemporary novelists blur genre distinctions, including in their "responses" to Woolf, acknowledgements and lists of sources consulted, they have neglected to examine either Edward Bishop's impressive transcription/edition of the *Jacob's Room* holograph (or, Bishop's studies antedating it), or Helen Wussow's essential transcription/edition of *Virginia Woolf "The Hours": The British Museum Manuscript of* Mrs. Dalloway, the first completed version of *Mrs. Dalloway*.

While there is reference to primary sources in the selected reading lists (and Lippincott alone fails to provide one), the novelists seem to rely on the constructions of others, though only Lippincott claims to write a *"creative response"* (emphasis added) to Woolf's work and life (Lippincott, "Author's note," np [220]) and Nunez bases her "unauthorized biography" of the marmoset on "published fact," although her model, *Flush*, Woolf's own "unauthorized biography" of Elizabeth Barrett Browning's spaniel, is not included in her Acknowledgements (Nunez 115-16). Notwithstanding Peters' proviso that the novelist (unlike the biographer) "leaves the reader free to believe or disbelieve at will" (46) or Woolf's own hope for an amalgam of "dream and reality" ("New Biography" 235), without considering these vital clues to Woolf, her life, her form, and their constructions, novelists who owe the greatest debt to Virginia Woolf may miss out on making important contributions not only to literature, but to literary discourse, and may finally only toe the line of popular commodification.[3]

I thought it appropriate to appropriate biographical discourse here not only because a biographical thread links the first two books (both of which owe their existence to *Mrs. Dalloway*) with the third (which admittedly owes much to Leonard Woolf's memoirs and Virginia Woolf's diaries and letters—and certainly to *Flush*), but because, as Jürgen Schlaeger points out, unlike memoirs, diaries, and letters, biography is about "the other" (59). And recognition of Virginia Woolf as "the other," it seems to me, is an aspect that each author both suggests and integrates differently. It may be, in fact, Cunningham's claim to skillful integration and nuanced narrative that accounts for the attention and acclaim his work has received,[4] notwithstanding the narrow prism provided by his selected biographical and other sources. There is no denying that he creates a most intricate reworking of *Mrs. Dalloway* in *The Hours*, which shares its title with Woolf's working title and which is identified as "a novel" on the dust jacket, as an "impressionistic response" by Mel Gussow (2). Yet, without

---

[3] See Silver, "What's Woolf Got to Do with It? or, The Perils of Popularity." Cf. Bayles, "Imus, Oprah and the Literary Elite."

[4] *The Hours*, by Michael Cunningham, received the PEN/Faulkner Award on 8 April 1999, and, five days later, the Pulitzer Prize in fiction.

scaring off potential readers with evocations of intertextuality, Cunningham blurs the lines between the actual and the fictional: "While Virginia Woolf [et al.] who actually lived appear in this book as fictional characters, I have tried to render as accurately as possible the outward particulars of their lives as they *would have been on a day I've invented for them in 1923*" (emphasis added, "A Note on Sources," *The Hours*, 229).

Describing his work in an early public reading as "three novellas" and "spin offs from *Mrs. Dalloway*,"[5] Cunningham involves three characters, situated on three single days at three distinct times and in three places: Mrs. Woolf (the author), in a "suburb of London. It is 1923" (29); "Mrs. Dalloway" (née Clarissa Vaughan), in New York City at "the end of the twentieth century" (9); and, Mrs. Brown, who lives in Los Angeles and who reads *Mrs. Dalloway*: "It is 1949" (37). By prefacing the work and thereby framing it with a seemingly authentic narrative of Woolf's suicide (including one of the suicide notes as it is reprinted in manuscript form in Hermione Lee's biography [744]), Cunningham may intend to undercut further his own author-ity, leaving the reader "to believe or disbelieve at will." Yet, belying disbelief "A Note on Sources," ending the book, includes Cunningham's "debt" to the editors of Woolf's letters and diaries, two of Leonard Woolf's memoirs (but not the last one, the one that begins with World War II and his wife's death), and a selection of secondary sources, including, in addition to Lee, biographies by Quentin Bell, Phyllis Rose, and James King (but not by Roger Poole); introductions by Maureen Howard, Elaine Showalter, and Claire Tomalin (but not Morris Beja) to editions of *Mrs. Dalloway*; and other "essential" texts, including Janet Malcolm's "A House of One's Own."

Clearly Cunningham has his reasons for including some incidents, settings, and characters and excluding or reinventing others and juxtaposing parts of one novella with parts of the others, and whatever the patterning (which sometimes seems to me brilliant, sometimes derivative and manipulative), he endows *The Hours* with a number of fundamental conditions and strategies found in *Mrs. Dalloway*. Yet, the novel's political affect is subtle; the only war veteran is Mrs. Brown's husband—who has returned from fighting in World War II; and, Septimus Smith is creatively recreated as Richard, a gay poet afflicted with AIDS, for whom Clarissa, a gay woman, prepares a party. In interspersing his novellas (seven episodes + eight episodes in New York), Cunningham seeks to highlight the relation and contrasts among the three characters (and to echo a pattern of *Mrs. Dalloway*) until, as one critic coyly, if hyperbolically remarks, "their final intersection is a thing of such beauty and surprise that I can't reveal it here" (Wood, 2). Yet, what may appear "rich and subtle and offbeat" to Wood, may seem manipulative and obvious and distort

---

[5] *Michael Cunningham Reads From "The Hours."* A Different Light Bookstore, NYC, 24 Nov 1998.

ing to others, a judgment that may be based, among other things on whether one is able to separate (or reconcile) what one "knows" of Virginia Woolf from (with) the fictional character Cunningham creates.[6] (Cunningham himself admits, there is "something in [*The Hours*] to offend nearly everybody."[7])

In all events, in resonantly telling each character's story ("*Life, London, this moment of June*" [75]), in some ways, Cunningham is being as experimental in his time, as Woolf was in her own, and, he says, he wants the novel "to work both ways," appealing to readers who "know" Woolf and to those who do not.[8] In fact, some knowing readers may find that there are repetitions and cadences that echo too emphatically; that the breaking up of the novellas into alternating chapters seems a gimmicky device; and, that biographical motifs running through the work are arguable and jarring. Yet, there is a depth of conviction and a layering that is unique and interesting, and the characters are, as Forster might say, rounded and capable of surprise—and, we might add, open both to postmodernist interrogation and popular appeal.

What makes Cunningham's response strong and resonant, alas, suggests the failings of Robin Lippincott's, which while identified as "a novella" on the cover, and identified as a first novel by Kirkus, seems to beg the question of how it is to be read. While *Mr. Dalloway* has almost as many pages as *The Hours* and also involves breaking gender barriers, it does not realize them with comparable skill, energy, or conviction. Though with a lighter touch Lippincott's fiction might have become a comic evocation or a parodic comedy of manners, in self-consciously aspiring to greater heights it calls attention to its own weaknesses: limited range, inadequate technique, and an unrealized vision. Set on a day four years after the Dalloways' party of June 1923 and divided into two parts ("28 June, 1927" [sic] and "The Party"), it focuses on the eponymous Richard Dalloway (Clarissa's husband), who has been carrying on an affair with Robbie Davis (a Bosie wannabe, as repeated references to Wilde suggest—and, presumably, a Septimus stand-in), and seeing a psychiatrist ("'Blitzer-not-Bradshaw'" [6]). The novella is about Richard Dalloway as

---

[6] Are the motifs of suicide and sanity, as applied to both Virginia Woolf and to Virginia Woolf planning *Mrs. Dalloway* really plausible? Not according to Daniel Ferrer, who says that there is no evidence that the version upon which Cunningham's treatment is based ever existed (9). Certainly it is not part of the manuscript of Virginia Woolf's "The Hours," the first full-length draft of *Mrs. Dalloway* (see Wussow, ix), although both Septimus and Peter Walsh are. In answer to a question about Empire at A Different Light Bookstore, Cunningham responded that this element is excluded from his novel and Peter Walsh is "demoted to a minor character: a walk on."

[7] *Michael Cunningham Reads From "The Hours."*

[8] *Michael Cunningham Reads From "The Hours."*

he prepares for and gives an avant-garde "celebration" ("9.30 P.M./Entrance to King's Court Station" the engraved invitations read [74]) to celebrate the Dalloways' 30th wedding anniversary ("Mr. Dalloway said he would buy the flowers himself" [3]), on 28 June 1927, which, as it turns out, is the historic day of the first solar eclipse to be visible in England for a century.

One reviewer kindly suggests that it was "bad timing" for his novella to be published so soon after Cunningham's more "expert retelling" (Allen). Yet, aside from obliquely punning on the issues of time that are so important to *Mrs. Dalloway*, as well as the responses to it, there is little in either Allen's short review or in *Mr. Dalloway* itself to explain what would have changed (other than prospective sales) had it been released earlier—or later than the solar eclipse of 11 August 1999 ("Someone in the crowd announced that after this it would be over until 1999 [and Richard Dalloway thought to himself that 1999 was a year so far away, so remote-seeming, that he couldn't even imagine it]" [212]). While a rush to publication may explain the sloppy proofreading and typographical anomalies, it doesn't provide a reason for the frequent repetitions and the overzealous imitation of Woolf—including the unending and gratuitous and distracting use of parentheses.

Yet, while Robin Lippincott's response to Woolf may not stand the test of time, he has provided the first evocation of the last total solar eclipse to be seen in England in our lifetimes (the next won't be until 2090)—and, by implication, refers us back to Virginia Woolf's own evocation of the 1927 eclipse (see *D3* 142-44), and the novel that was published that year, *To the Lighthouse*, which Mr. Dalloway buys for his wife.

Sigrid Nunez, the "biographer"/novelist responsible for *Mitz, the Marmoset of Bloomsbury*, is not seeking to pass the test of time so much as to exploit it, both investing the Bloomsbury cachet with value it may not possess in context and, like her colleagues, taking advantage of Pamela Caughie's characterization of postmodern art as "effac[ing] the boundaries between high culture and popular culture" (144). Caughie made this remark in relation to Virginia Woolf's *Flush: A Biography* (1933), a work that was published a year before Mitz joined the Woolf household, which, one might suppose is why she chose to exclude this seminal text from her acknowledgments (115-16) and afford it (along with *Orlando*, Woolf's other "Biography") little more than a passing glance in the text (Nunez 28-29).

*Mitz* is the story of the life and death of Leonard Woolf's pet marmoset, who lived with the Woolfs from 1934 until the eve of World War II. That said, *Mitz*, like *Mr. Dalloway* and *The Hours*, makes an appeal to a large and largely undifferentiated audience; yet as in Cunningham's response, the acknowledged sources have a clear bias, and not unlike Lippincott's novella, this "unauthorized biography" might have integrated documented material with apocryphal dialogue and details more effectively. Yet, the vignette involving the Woolfs, Mitz, and Nazis in Germany suggests Nunez's sensitivity to the times and strikes just the right note, and references to deaths, to the rise of fascism, and to the publication of *Three Guineas* point to the Second World War and propel the largely chronological movement. Yet, like a "story" out of Forster's *Aspects of Fiction*, this fictive biography (unlike *Flush*) does not challenge contemporary values and definitions; there are no "Notes" and ironical comments about "historians," or genre, for that matter. It is hard not to like *Mitz*, but, notwithstanding reader comments on the dust jacket and the internet, my impression is that it provides a simplistic (rather than an "instructive") picture of Bloomsbury, and one that effectively perpetuates its mythology in popular culture.

The narrator is a story-teller—and little more. There are nice touches culled from the sources: "Virginia Woolf, hitching up her skirts and lolloping down the road in pursuit of the father [tortoise]" (80), and the Strasbourg pie sent by Vita after Mitz had died: "It was Christmas Day, the last year of peace" (114), but, as Nunez admits in her Acknowledgements, at the end of the book, much of the "biographical detail" has had "to be imagined" (115). As a fictive biography, there is a charm to *Mitz* (it is nicely written and has a pleasant flow and rhythm), but the narrative (with its simple telling and constant syntax) lacks nuance and Nunez has written a tribute to the marmoset and especially to Leonard Woolf, her savior (as might be expected, given her sources). For the squeamish or the lachrymose, the unpleasant details of the marmoset's capture and maltreatment is not included in the narrative until we are nearing the end, before the marmoset dies. It may be that *Mitz*, unlike *Flush*, is too fragile to withstand postmodernist interrogation but finally, like *Flush* and like *Orlando*, *Mitz* may pass as "a biography."

However we classify the first three works, they would undoubtedly have been different texts had their authors included the next two as sources. We can only guess how the important work of Edward Bishop and Helen Wussow might have helped the novelists inform their postmodern responses to Woolf, and/or impacted the creative/allusive/biographical processes that preceded their composition. Certainly all of us who use holographic sources and typescripts owe Bishop and Wussow a debt of gratitude, not only for the insights they offer into Woolf's first two experimental novels, but into the intertextuality that informs them and that informs their transcriptions.

Of the two, *Virginia Woolf's "Jacob's Room": The Holograph Draft* may be the more problematic, based on the holograph manuscript in the Berg Collection, and adding the special challenge of Woolf's sometimes difficult handwriting to the mix. As Edward Bishop explains, interspersed in three bound notebooks (which he calls "volumes," dated 15 April 1920-12 March 1922) are short sketches, fragments, and other material, some of which become short stories; some of which are integrated into the novel; some of which will be included in *Mrs. Dalloway*, for example, an early outline, dated Oct. 6th 1922 (xxvi and n3). Yet Bishop transcribes only the sketches Woolf wrote in volume 2, because he is concerned with the holograph as a text *in process*, and "because of their implications for the composition of *Jacob's Room* (a novel which owes far more to her sketches than her previous novel, *Night and Day*)" (xxiii). For example, he finds only 22 pages of text for *Jacob's Room* included in volume 3, "Book of scraps of J's R. & first version of The Hours." Intertextual material (e.g., reviews and portions of *Mrs. Dalloway*) excluded from Bishop's transcription, is included in an appendix to Helen Wussow's *Virginia Woolf "The Hours": The British Museum Manuscript of* Mrs. Dalloway, which is nearly 200 pages longer.

The complementary, intertextual nature of these two volumes might be expected, not only because they are formally similar and are both published by Pace UP, but because each uses and follows similar models: Bishop, with his interest in process, relies on J.W. Graham's mammoth one-volume transcription of "two holograph drafts" of *The Waves* (1976) and Susan Dick's important transcription of the "original holograph draft" of *To the Lighthouse* (1982). Wussow's formal model is S.P. Rosenbaum's transcription of the manuscript version of *A Room of One's Own*, called *Women & Fiction* (1992), which, Wussow explains, "simplif[ies] [the] earlier transcription practices" of Graham and Dick (xxvii).[9] Both Bishop and Wussow explain methodology and include chronologies, but Wussow refers to three "notebooks."

In emphasizing process, Bishop also makes note of name changes, and their implications, and how a character in *Jacob's Room* was at first intended to take opium, a dubious distinction she would eventually bestow on a character in *To the Lighthouse*. What Bishop finds more interesting are the conceptual changes and what they suggest: importantly, that the novel was neither self-consciously seen as an experiment from the outset nor intended as an anti-war polemic nor as being about Thoby Stephen nor the generation of 1914. As Bishop says, "one finds in the manuscript a gradual, and often very tentative, process of discovery as both the subject matter and the form evolve together" (xii). This does not preclude, however, "radical revisions" (xviii) to her earliest plans for the novel; her earliest plan, to use rooms to index several characters, was altered during a "post-draft revision" that allowed Woolf to sharpen her focus (x, xiv). An interesting change is made to the narrator's comments: from collusion with the reader to love for Jacob (xix), and questions of spatial form are answered with the kind of cinematic technique that Holtby noted in 1932. In coming to terms with Virginia Woolf as the other, appearing in all three texts differently, the novelists might have found her writing practice useful in developing her "character," much more so, I should think, than the suicide/sanity motif used by Cunningham to frame his "character" of Virginia Woolf.

---

[9] See Rosenbaum, "Explanation of the Transcription," *Virginia Woolf "Women & Fiction": The Manuscript Versions of "A Room of One's Own"*: xliii-xliv.

The writing practice explored by Wussow in her transcription provides a "palimpsest" which, in Silver's terms, "refers to a text, the boundaries of whose versions blur and thereby create another work, one that is no longer single, but rather 'multiple, intertextual'" (Wussow ix).[10] As such, her transcription would clearly have been valuable to novelists responding to *Mrs. Dalloway*, especially as it relates to Woolf and her experience of the Great War (something all but ignored by the three novelists) and as it includes clues to Woolf, her life, and her methodology. For example, Wussow includes in the appendices an outline of the novel from October 1922; holograph notes, folio pages, and the like, scattered among different notebooks and files in the Berg Collection; and drafts of essays and reviews from the reversed pages of notebook 3 of "The Hours." Certainly, these are valuable to us not only for the background to the evolution of this first completed draft (including the actual writing of the novel, which is so central to Cunningham's response), but Wussow's understanding of the intertextual relation of "The Hours" and *The Common Reader*: "Side by side in her mind, in her diary and notebooks, 'The Hours' and *The Common Reader* complement and expand one another" (xvi). Through her work Wussow also suggests to us both how "'The Hours' embodies change within repetition, difference within similarity" (xxiv)—and how Woolf's vision and accomplishment can be deconstructed and imitated, but never duplicated or equaled.

—Karen L. Levenback, *George Washington University*

## Works Cited

Allen, Bruce. Rev. of *Mr. Dalloway*, by Robin Lippincott. *NY Times*, "Book Reviews" 1 Aug 1999: 14.

Batchelor, John. "Introduction." *The Art of Literary Biography*. Ed. John Batchelor. Oxford, England: Clarendon P, 1995: 1-11.

Bayles, Martha. "Imus, Oprah and the Literary Elite." *NYTimes*, "Book Reviews" 29 Aug 1999: 35.

Caughie, Pamela. *Virginia Woolf & Postmodernism: Literature in Quest & Question of Itself*. Urbana: U of Illinois P, 1991.

Cunningham, Michael. *Michael Cunningham Reads From "The Hours."* A Different Light Bookstore, NYC. 24 Nov. 1998 <http://www.nytimes.com/books/98/12/06/daily/cunningham.html>.

Dick, Susan, ed. *Virginia Woolf "To the lighthouse": The original Holograph Draft*. Toronto: University of Toronto Press, 1982

---

[10] Wussow refers to Brenda Silver, "Textual Criticism as Feminist Practice: Or, Who's Afraid of Virginia Woolf, Part II," and to Donald Reiman's explanation of "Versioning" in *Romantic Texts and Contexts*.

Ferrer, Daniel. *Virginia Woolf and the Madness of Language*. Trans. Geoffrey Bennington and Rachel Bowlby. London: Routledge, 1990.

Forster, E. M. *Aspects of the Novel*. 1927. NY: Harcourt Brace & World, 1954.

Graham, J.W.,ed. *Virginia Woolf "The Waves":The Two Holograph Drafts*. Toronto: U of Toronto P, 1976

Gussow, Mel. "A Writer Haunted by Virginia Woolf." *New York Times on the Web* 20 April 1999. <http://www.nytimes.com/library/books/042099cunningham-interview.html>.

Kirkus Associates. *Kirkus Reviews*. Rev. of *Mr. Dalloway*, by Robin Lippincott:1-2 <http://www.amazon.com/exec/obidos/ASIN/188933-299/qid=9305932.../002-2371761-723941>.

Lee, Hermione. *Virginia Woolf*. NY: Alfred Knopf, 1997.

Malcolm, Janet. "A House of One's Own." *New Yorker*. 5 June 1995: 58-79.

Peters, Catherine. "Secondary Lives: Biography in Context." *The Art of Literary Biography*. Ed. John Batchelor. Oxford, England: Clarendon P, 1995: 43-56.

Reiman, Donald. *Romantic Texts and Contexts*. Colombia: U of Missouri P, 1987.

Rosenbaum, S.P., ed. *Virginia Woolf Women & Fiction: The Manuscript Versions of "A Room of One's Own."* Oxford, England: Oxford UP, 1992.

Schlaeger, Jürgen. "Biography: Cult as Culture." *The Art of Literary Biography*. Ed. John Batchelor. Oxford, England: Clarendon Press, 1995: 57-71.

Silver, Brenda. "Textual Criticism as Feminist Practice: Or, Who's Afraid of Virginia Woolf, Part II." *Representing Modernist Texts: Editing as Interpretation*. Ed. George Bornstein. Ann Arbor: U of Michigan P, 1991: 193-222.

———. "What's Woolf Got to Do with It? or, The Perils of Popularity." *Modern Fiction Studies*. Spring 1992: 21-60.

Wood, Michael. "Parallel Lives: A Novel that echoes 'Mrs. Dalloway' features Virginia Woolf as a character." Rev. of *The Hours* by Michael Cunningham. *NY Times*, 10 Dec. 1998 <http://www.nytimes.com/books/98/12/06/daily/cunningham.html>.

Woolf, Virginia. *The Diary of Virginia Woolf*, vol 3. Ed. Anne Olivier Bell. NY: HBJ, 1980.

———. "The New Biography." *Collected Essays*, vol. 4. Ed. Leonard Woolf. NY: Harcourt, Brace & World, 1967: 229-35.

*Virginia Woolf: Feminism, Creativity, and the Unconscious*
John R. Maze (Westport, CT: Greenwood P, 1997), 220 pp.

John R. Maze's interpretation of Virginia Woolf's crafting of her unconscious states in the production of novels and essays is occasionally original and often well-researched. The study reveals Maze's interest in the historical and literary sources which permeate Woolf's *The Voyage Out, Night and Day, Jacob's Room, Mrs. Dalloway, To the Lighthouse, The Waves, The Years,* and *Between the Acts.* Less impressive is the sometimes naive stamp of causality which colors his psychoanalytic reading of her novels.

In Professor Maze's Introduction, he claims that Woolf's "search for self-understanding was an intense and enduring one, and it informs her literary work from beginning to end. Above all, it is the stages of her struggle with the internal image of her mother that link the novels together." Maze insists that Woolf's ambivalence toward her mother is apparent in every novel. However, she resolves this ambivalence differently in each one. In *The Voyage Out*, for example, Maze claims that the Helen/Vanessa figure embodies the complicated maternal/seducer whom Rachel/Virginia both adores and fears. Rachel tries to destroy Helen before she, as phallic "mother," destroys her. In one of his most perceptive realizations, Maze contends that:

> If, after having been born into the world and come to know our own mother as a separate person, we wish to get back inside her to a self-contained existence in which we did not know her and so could not feel need of her, then paradoxically we are incorporating her into our own being, and in fantasy, destroying her as a separate entity. This desire for reunion is not love, but a hostility that would annihilate its object, and such a wish must bring with it a fear of retaliation—perhaps the fear that the great genital will devour or drown one, just as it violently expelled one from bliss into the terrors of the world. (20)

Maze proposes that the individual's need for reunion with his/her mother (or mother substitute), after separation has made them two rather than one, is a hostile wish rather than a loving one. This is certainly astute. However, his allusion to some gargantuan genital which may, at any moment, retaliate against the poor person who is hostile toward his/her first authority figure, borders on the absurd. If Maze were using this body part as a metaphor, that would be another matter. But, in this instance, he simply expresses a Freudian cliche.

I do want to insist, nonetheless, that many of his ideas are useful ones. Here, as in other chapters, Maze's attention to Woolf's repressed incestuous attractions to certain family members, is convincing. For example, he says that Thoby Stephen's death was far more devastating to her than were the deaths of either Woolf's mother or father. This was true because, he claims, she was attracted to Thoby, yet resented his academic advantages: his access to Cambridge, for example. But when Maze goes on to observe that Woolf felt guilt over her unacknowledged animosity and lust for Thoby, and moreover that she thought she caused his death, he fails to document these assertions. Instead, he turns to the novel for proof. He claims that both Rachel and Thoby die at 24, and that Rachel's death represents Woolf's atonement for Thoby's death. But an unevenness prevails in Maze's process of going from novel to life. It's probably more than coincidental that both Rachel and Thoby die at 24. However, to say that Rachel/Virginia died as a sacrifice to Thoby is highly doubtful when one realizes that the entire weight of the novel points toward Rachel's inability to sanction marriage. In fact, her capitulation to illness/suicide becomes a way of evading masculinist domination and cultural mediocrity.

I like what Maze has to say about Woolf's agnosticism, which he feels only slightly diminishes as she ages and begins looking for cultural and personal panaceas. In *Mrs. Dalloway*, the narrator associates the specter of religion with other systems of belief which derive their power from force. Maze detects Woolf's agnosticism in scenes like the one where Clarissa Dalloway leaves a flower shop just in time to see a mysterious entity (was it the Prime Minister?) Riding past her in the street. ". . . mystery had brushed them with her wing; they had heard the voice of authority; the spirit of religion was abroad with her eyes bandaged tight and her lips gaping wide" (*MD* 17). Professor Maze concludes that Woolf depicts religion as a "rapacious bigoted harpy" (64). He notes that in future novels, she organizes all these states of rapaciousness under the category "Conversion." Unhappily, he fails to see that in *Mrs. Dalloway* she includes therapy within these categories of force; and that the fictionalized psychologists she so bitingly satirizes are more steeped in the ways of Conversion than are their brother-priests. Maze's understanding of Woolf's struggle to record the sanity inherent in Septimus Warren Smith's insanity is profoundly perceptive. When he derives significance from the name "Septimus" by saying that Virginia was the seventh child in the combined families of her mother and father, Maze is both original and correct.

If the author's interest in psychoanalysis leads him to focus on Woolf's struggle with her mother's image, then the reader's attention will inevitably be riveted to her *To the Lighthouse*. Here, as in earlier chapters, however, his observations are uneven. He says, for example, that "Truth-telling is Mr. Ramsay's purported trade as a philosopher. . . . While Mr. Ramsay, seeing life as the enemy, tries to deny its horrors and preserve people's hopes of something better" (*TTL* 13). He adds that despite these differences, husband and wife are alike in that they share a "love of authority and the sexism it promotes" (90). Certainly, his analysis of the Ramsays' similarities is a sharp one. But when he reverts to the reductive reading of the lighthouse as phallic symbol, coupled with his complaint that Woolf "denied that it symbolized anything" (90), he has simply failed to do his homework. What Woolf said is that the lighthouse provided a symbol, to which each reader could attach his or her own meaning.

*Virginia Woolf: Feminism, Creativity, and the Unconscious* reads well, though conceptually it is sometimes weak. Nonetheless, it gives both scholars and general readers new ways to focus on the psychoanalytic premises which permeate all of Woolf's novels.

—Madeline Moore, *UC Santa Cruz*

*The Nightmare of History:*
*The Fictions of Virginia Woolf and D. H. Lawrence*
Helen Wussow. (Bethlehem: Lehigh U P, 1998), 204 pp.

Helen Wussow's *The Nightmare of History: The Fictions of Virginia Woolf and D. H. Lawrence* takes its title from Joyce's *Ulysses*, suggestive of the bondage to the wheel of time embodied in that work. In her conclusion, Wussow records a conversation with a colleague about her work-in-progress on Woolf and Lawrence which encapsulates the problem at the heart of her project. Her colleague's comment—"strange bedfellows!" (177)—suggests what many of us might feel at the yoking of these two. Wussow succeeds, however, in offering convincing evidence that the fictional discourses of Woolf and Lawrence reveal the presence of conflict which metaphorically replicates the historical processes of war at work in the contemporary context of their writing.

War, Wussow argues, is a basic structure of human existence, and it is especially the presence of World War I in Woolf and Lawrence which interests her. Woolf and Lawrence held opinions which may be considered as foils to one another, uncovering their differing attitudes. Each creates a discursive site which reflects the violence in their world but also provides itself a new site of conflict. For both, war possessed "a dialectical structure similar to the Hegelian struggle for self-definition between the subject 'I,' and the other" (15). Both, in that struggle, saw themselves as "excluded from the language of the subject" (15); however, Woolf focuses on masculine aggression and Lawrence blames women for the continuation of the war. Both regard strife in sexual relationships as parallel to armed conflict—thus war is heightened to the level of gender war. War and language, and the attitudes toward both by Woolf and Lawrence, are explored by Wussow within the context of Bakhtinian "interdependence between social milieu and discourse" (16).

Wussow's book divides into five chapters, each examining a differing segment of the works of Woolf and Lawrence which have special reference to the Great War. In the first chapter, "Our Sad Eventful History: Woolf, Lawrence, and the Great War," Wussow begins by inquiring into Bloomsbury's pacifism, but points out that, unlike the rest of Bloomsbury, Woolf believed the war to be a completely masculine preoccupation. Lawrence's experiences with spy alarms left him feeling victimized at the hands of the authorities—Frieda, we remember, was German. In contrast to the disillusion found in Woolf's wartime letters and diaries, Lawrence collapses the war into a "'fight to the death'" (46) with Frieda, which itself succumbs to resurrection, the theme of Lawrence's wartime letters. Indeed, Lawrence's entire worldview during the war, Wussow suggests, was affected by the domestic violence in which he lived with Frieda. Thus both writers, Wussow concludes in this chapter, perceive war "as an event occurring between individuals as well as countries" (49).

In her second chapter, "The Battle Between Them: Sexual Conflict in the Early Fictions," Wussow reads Woolf's *The Voyage Out* and Lawrence's *The White Peacock, The Trespasser*, and "Once!—" in the context of war and warlike sexual strife between individuals. Though completed before the outbreak of war, Wussow contends that *The Voyage Out* clearly indicates an interest in conflict that would dominate Woolf's later fiction. The novel seems fashioned around threats and predictions of danger: Helen and Ridley Ambrose are at odds early in the novel, Rachel Vinrace is assaulted with the unwanted kiss from Richard Dalloway, and warships and empire are invoked throughout. The struggle here appears to be one to protect the self against destruction "through extreme intimacy with another human being" (57). Woolf illustrates, Wussow concludes in her discussion of the novel, that "war plays 'a considerable part in determining the structure of the world'" (58-59). For Lawrence, too, the Great War and "'the *real* tragedy'" is the "'great war'" of domestic life, and his focus extends to a theme prominient in the later writing, "the cruelty inherent in human relationships" (59).

"The Prisonhouse of Language: Writings of the War Years," Wussow's third chapter, reiterates again, with substantiation from Paul Fussell's *The Great War and Modern Memory*, that "the First World War revealed the incapacity of language to relate the horror of battle" (69). Taking as her cue in her title Fredric Jameson's well-known attack on structuralist and Russian formalist conceptions of language,*The Prison-House of Language*, Wussow wants to invoke the "emphasis placed upon the role of language by those who remained at home during the war" (69). Implied in that concept is the role that government might play in controlling the language of those at home—specifically those married to Germans like Lawrence. Lawrence's letters, for example, may have been tampered with, and Woolf was well aware of the power of "jingoistic" sentiments in the press. In fact, Lawrence had reason to be concerned about the perceived impropriety of his upcoming publication *The Rainbow* in the light of the Defense of the Realm Act. Michael Holroyd has suggested that *The Rainbow*'s prosecution occurred "'ostensibly on the grounds of obscenity but actually because of its denunciation of war'" (70). The suppression of *The Rainbow* briefly became a "cause célèbre" for Bloomsbury; but Woolf's concern lay primarily with the propagandistic power of the press, a concern which Lawrence obviously shared. Both writers, Wussow reminds us again, "portray language as simply another area of conflict in which the self does battle with the threatening other" (75). Wussow goes on to read a number of Lawrence's short stories and Woolf's *Night and Day* as fictions which exemplify this theme.

In *Night and Day*, for example, Wussow suggests that Woolf appears to purposefully ignore war when in reality Woolf depicts a disintegrating world. The novel exemplifies, in Wussow's view, the "Bakhtinian vocabulary of verbal conflict," where there is a "'constant struggle between the centripetal forces that seek to close the world in system and the centrifugal forces that battle completedness in order to keep the world open to becoming'" (101). Using Bakhtin's *Marxism and the Philosophy of Language*, Wussow argues that the antipathies of dialogue in *Night and Day* "have their social correlative in the First World War" (101).

The last two chapters, "The Senseless Boxing of Schoolboys: The Sport and Comradeship of War" and "The Silver Globe of Time: War and History in the Postwar Fictions," continue Wussow's theme of the parallel levels of discourse and historical conflict in these two authors by taking examples from Woolf's *Jacob's Room, Mrs. Dalloway, Orlando, To the Lighthouse*, and *The Waves* along with Lawrence's *Women in Love, Lady Chatterley's Lover,* and *Movements in European History*. These chapters repeat what Wussow has already made abundantly clear, that conflict in the fiction mirrors the writer's perception of conflict in the outer world. Wussow adds in the fourth chapter discussion of Woolf's imagery of war as child's play and in the fifth chapter, she revisits Lawrence's fictional clashes between death in resurrection and Woolf's interest in cyclical historical patterns.

Wussow's great strength here is her extensive use of historical background within which to frame discussion of each writer's discourse, and her conclusion underscores her belief that, rather than having little in common, Woolf and Lawrence—in their response to the Great War—"complement and reveal one another" (177). Her weakness is that as she repeats her theme for yoking Woolf and Lawrence together, its novelty wears thin and it becomes easier to be less convinced that there is a compelling reason for continuing to read them in tandem. Her closing statement, though, is one I applaud—that through continuing to read Woolf, Lawrence, and their contemporaries, Wussow hopes, "we can come to better understand the nature and scope of conflict in their and our postwar worlds" (178).

—Merry Pawlowski, *California State University, Bakersfield*

### Mappings: Feminism and the Cultural Geographies of Encounter
Susan Stanford Friedman,(Princeton: Princeton U P, 1998), 416pp

At first glance, Friedman's *Mappings: Feminism and the Cultural Geographies of Encounter* might seem to rehash what has already been stated in more detail elsewhere. Yes, feminism needs to go beyond its culture wars and negotiate a peacetime settlement. Yes, that settlement needs to address the needs of all genders, resolving the many differences of identity politics that have hindered the formation of any united feminist movement. Yes, feminism needs to remember what it has learned from cultural border skirmishes and geopolitical engagements and incorporate that knowledge into whatever feminism evolves in the future. However, by the time I finished *Mappings*, I became convinced Friedman has indeed accomplished more than a restatement of the work of others. She has provided a useful "map" for any future practice of global feminism, outlining strategies I have already applied effectively in my literature and women's studies classrooms. If one is willing to wade through Friedman's often dense prose, novices and experts alike will be able to forge a more constructive global feminism without apology and without aggression.

In perhaps more detail than anyone well-read in cultural and postcolonial theories might need, Friedman's "Introduction: Locational Feminism" maps a solution for the impasses identity politics have created. However, if one is not yet familiar with issues delineated and debated by such diverse theorists as Bakhtin, Anzaldua, Spivak, Saïd, and Bhabha, the introduction serves as an excellent primer uniting ideas about dialogism, borders, the subaltern, Orientalism and hybridity, and how such ideas have come to impact current debates in feminism. What is unique about "locational feminism" is Friedman's attempt to "embrace" the "contradiction, dislocation, and change" identity politics has brought to academic feminism (4). She argues for the power of academics to influence the material play of identity politics beyond the institution; we are not neutral (7). Friedman points out that we can enact changes in feminism and identity politics if we are willing to rethink feminism "beyond fundamentalist identity politics and absolutist poststructuralist theories as they pose essentialist notions of identity on the one hand and refuse all cultural traffic with identity on the other" (4). Her diction re-enforces the assertion that this new united locational feminism is going to be most attractive to academics.

How is such a global feminism to be accomplished? Friedman is quite clear on this point, outlining specific aspects of feminist practice that should inform individual and public acts of locational feminism. First, a locational feminist recognizes and practices feminism based on assumptions of changing geographies and historical "specificities" that "produce different feminist theories, agendas, and political practices" (5). Locational feminists must be aware of the spectrum of shifting geographical and historical instances, incorporating those differences into practice. But awareness is not enough. A locational feminist "acknowledges the travels and travails of feminism as it migrates across multiple borders adapting itself to new conditions." She recognizes and gives credit to "the way in which the local is always informed by the global and the global by the local." Feminism itself needs to be understood in its "global context, both historicized and geopoliticized to take into account its different formations and their interrelationships everywhere."

If, at this point, worries arise about the dangers of "chi chi" academics fetishizing the lives of people beyond their own ethnic, cultural, national, political, geographical, class, and historical borders, fear not. Friedman's approach addresses this possibility directly, arguing for a locational feminism that would gaze first and longest at its own locations and positions without assuming these apply beyond their own locational frontiers (6). As an enactor of situational feminism, I can avoid "the imposition of one set of cultural conditions on another" if I assume "the production of local agencies and conceptualizations" and if I "remain attentive to the way these differences are continually in the process of modification through interaction with a global system of diverse, multidirectional exchanges" (7). Certainly, this has already long been a recommended practice, but Friedman reminds me to do my homework and not expect women from different "locations" than my own to carry the double burden of informing me and of correcting my mistakes. Relying heavily on Anzaldua's metaphor of the border as a place where the "deconstructive free play of signifiers" can occur, Friedman argues against the binarism that plagues most feminist theories in current academic practice (4).

Friedman's work can be read as a progressive meditation. She examines possible feminist constructions and applications of the emerging discourses of cultural geographies of encounter. However, each chapter can—and does—stand alone. Three chapters of particular note for theorists interested in understanding Friedman's approach and its particular applications either to Woolf or multicultural and postcolonial studies are "'Beyond' Gender: The New Geography of Identity and the Future of Feminist Criticism," "'Beyond' Difference: Migratory Feminism in the Borderlands," and "Geopolitical Literacy: Internationalizing Feminism at 'Home'—the case of Virginia Woolf." In these chapters, Friedman defines the problems identity politics have created and then demonstrates how to move beyond their limitations and stalemates using locational feminism.

"Beyond Gender" charts six discourses in the "geographies of identity" that have arisen during the past twenty years: multiple oppression, multiple subject positions, contradictory subject positions, relationality, situationality, and hybridity (20). As Friedman argues, these discourses "do not represent stages of feminist discourse" developed through time. She works, after all, to move feminism beyond the linear logics of Showalter's gynocriticism and beyond Jardine's concept of gynesis—beyond but not without these two frames for American feminism (18). Friedman asks us to incorporate the ideas of gynocriticism and gynesis into the widening circle of global feminism: "The new geography of identity insists that we think about women writers in relation to a fluid matrix instead of a fixed binary of male / female or masculine / feminine" (26). At times, this new geography would make the pairing of writers for a literature course (or a women's studies course, a history course, e.g.) align male and female rather than all female or all male. Lawrence and Woolf might become, accordingly, a more logical pairing than Woolf and Rhys or Lawrence and Joyce. Characterization in such works as *Jane Eyre* and *Wide Sargasso Sea* would also be considered within a fluid matrix. We should not be able to privilege one position above another except within certain circumstances and contexts. Locational feminism should enable the examination of authors and characters within a spectrum of multi-locational identities as these identities intersect.

In her re-examination of androgyny in "Beyond Difference," Friedman relies on Bhabha's theory of hybridity—what Renato Rosaldo in the Foreword to *Hybrid Cultures* defines as "the ongoing condition of all human cultures, which contain no zones of purity because they undergo continuous processes of transculturation" (Friedman 84). She constructs a very useful diagram of hybridity, charting the "Type of Cultural Mixing," the "Function or Cultural Work of Hybridity," the "Spatial and Temporal Orientation toward Hybridity," and the "Power Relations of Hybridity." Her point centers around the question of whether or not politically savvy feminists must always "regard the liminal space in between difference as *merely* utopic, an unaffordable luxury, a lyric impossibility, a dream without realities, a myth without historical referent" (73). Friedman argues that we can use poststructural concepts of play, and postcolonial concepts of hybridity, to move feminism "beyond pure difference" discourse, a position that inevitably reinscribes the "absolute barriers between white and color" (74). In Derridean terms, Friedman emphasizes the idea that difference always already enforces the idea of sameness. If feminism would move beyond the deadlock of difference, then attention needs to be given to "the interplay of cultural markers of identity" and how this interplay "depends upon an oscillation of sameness and difference that is historically embodied within the context of complex power relations" (76).

Relying on the structures she develops in the first three chapters, Friedman's discussion of *To the Lighthouse* and *A Room of One's Own* in "Geopolitical Literacy," breaks some new ground for placing Woolf's most frequently taught works into a larger, global context. However, her intention is not simply to reveal Woolf's common "(inter)nationalizing of the domestic with allusions to the global" (126). She recognizes instead the cultural "ghost in the machine" that "must be brought to visibility." Juxtapositioning and re-placing *To The Lighthouse* in the historical context of the Crimean War allows Friedman to demonstrate how "Woolf's representation of the domestic carries within an invocation of the international and geopolitical so that her notion of intimacy in the privacy of the family circle has a transnational valence" (125).

To understand the full scope of *A Room of One's Own*, Friedman places Woolf's woman writer in the "room" with Zora Neale Hurston who, in 1928, embarked on a journey away from the white world of Barnard College into the South on her anthropological quest for "Negro folklore" (128). Friedman's subsequent comparative discussion of Hurston and Woolf cannot be done justice in such a short space. I urge readers to place *Mappings* on their reading lists and use its ideas to construct their syllabus during the coming years. While there are, perhaps, some misalignments in her readings of different positionalities, Friedman has definitely opened up the borders of feminist approaches to literature by women and men, however we might define those two categories. In doing so, she has re-negotiated the androgynous space of which Woolf and so many other early feminists dreamed.

Maps, as theorists Saïd and McClintock remind us, more often than not delineate our own psyches rather than proffering accurate models of the world. Friedman's book offers yet another map. However, unlike so many maps, Friedman's is aware of its limitations as a map. In its self-awareness, *Mappings* becomes a useful guidebook to the concerns of contemporary feminists and for contemporary Woolf critics. While I cannot always agree with Friedman, I do admire the project she has outlined.

—Theresa Thompson, *Valdosta State University*

## Note on Contributor

**Anna Snaith** is a Lecturer in English at Anglia Polytechnic University in Cambridge, England. She is the author of *Virginia Woolf: Public and Private Negotiations* (St. Martin's Press, 2000), as well as articles on Woolf, Katherine Mansfield and Angela Carter. She is currently working on a book on postcolonial women writers living in London 1890 to 1930.

# Policy

*Woolf Studies Annual* invites articles on the work and life of Virginia Woolf and her milieu. The *Annual* intends to represent the breadth and eclecticism of critical approaches to Woolf and particularly welcomes new perspectives and contexts of inquiry. Articles discussing relations between Woolf and other writers and artists are also welcome.

Articles are sent for review anonymously to a member of the Editorial Board and at least one other reader. Manuscripts should not be under consideration elsewhere or have been previously published. Final decisions are made by the Editorial Board.

## Preparation of Copy

1. Articles should not exceed 8000 words or 30 pages, double-spaced, with at least 1½" margins.

2. A separate page should include the contribution's title, author's name, address, telephone and fax numbers and email address. The author's name and identifying references should not appear on the manuscript.

3. A photocopy of any illustrations should accompany the manuscript. (Black-and-white photographs will be required for accepted work.)

4. Manuscripts should be prepared according to most recent MLA style.

5. 3 copies of the manuscript and an abstract of up to 150 words should be sent to: Mark Hussey, English Dept., Pace University, One Pace Plaza, New York, NY 10038. Only materials accompanied by a self-addressed, stamped envelope (or international reply coupon) will be returned.

6. Authors of accepted manuscripts will be asked to submit two hard copies and a disk version. Authors are responsible for all necessary permissions fees.

**Please address inquiries to**: Mark Hussey, English Dept., Pace University, One Pace Plaza, New York NY 10038. mhussey@pace.edu Fax: (212) 346-1754.

Printed in the United States
128821LV00004B/151/A